Daniel Metcalfe left Oxford University in 2002 with a degree in Classics. Long fascinated by Central Asia, he taught himself Persian and headed to Iran and the steppes. An energetic traveller, Metcalfe – who also speaks Russian, Swedish and Portuguese – has journeyed extensively throughout Asia, Eastern Europe and the Caucasus.

Out of Steppe is his first book and was shortlisted for the 2009 Banff Mountain Book Festival Award. He is currently exploring the legacy of the Portuguese in Africa.

Praise for OUT OF STEPPE

'*Out of Steppe* is enterprising and finely written . . .
Mr Metcalfe, a polyglot Oxford classicist, strikes an exotic figure in what used to be called Turkestan. He can justly be compared with British adventurers such as Robert Byron, the interwar traveller who wrote the *Road to Oxiana*' *The Economist*

'Fresh, witty and full of quirky detail . . . the book is also a serious, sometimes moving account of environmental degradation, political repression and social isolation'
Financial Times

'Metcalfe writes with sensitivity and great flair. Following him across this little-known region, I was totally absorbed in his world of emirs, shamans and cynical apparatchiks'
Paddy Ashdown

'This is a book of great warmth and immense scholarship, in the best tradition of travel writing. It opens up a region about which most of us are vague. It is fascinating reading'
The Irish Times

'This book's idea is timely: a quest for six ethnic communities that, after surviving the depredations of Sovietism, are now, as Central Asia modernises, disappearing . . . [Metcalfe's] book has many virtues, the greatest of which are courage and a keen eye for detail, plus an ability to convey the essence of a place through the briefest of anecdotes' *The Independent*

'This is an important book: a first-hand account from an adventurous traveller who has dared to explore the fulcrum of Asian geopolitics. Read this and you will understand why we need to care about Central Asia. Metcalfe has reminded us of why travel-writing matters' Nicholas Crane, author of *Clear Waters Rising*

'Metcalfe recounts . . . always with a noble heart, his search for the forgotten peoples of Central Asia ' *The Times*

'This is a fascinating document of how the political turmoil of the past century is threatening far more people than many of us realise. Metcalfe's journey is a worthy addition to the canon of books capturing these moments at the crossroads of history' *Wanderlust*

'In *Out of Steppe* Daniel Metcalfe goes in search of what he calls the "lost peoples of central Asia". . . an area suffering from a profound identity crisis . . . steeped in myth and history, from Genghis Khan to the famous Silk Road . . . Metcalfe is entertaining company as he meets the many tribal people caught up in the turbulence of post-Soviet politics; plus he has a seasoned attitude towards the absurd levels of bureaucracy that can make travelling in the area a nightmare' *Metro*

'Daniel Metcalfe journeys through the five 'stans, as well as Pakistan and Afghanistan, and brings to life the human tapestry they comprise' *Sunday Tribune*

OUT OF STEPPE

DANIEL METCALFE

arrow books

Published by Arrow Books 2010

2 4 6 8 10 9 7 5 3 1

First published in Great Britain in 2009 by
Hutchinson
Random House, 20 Vauxhall Bridge Road,
London SW1V 2SA

www.rbooks.co.uk

Addresses for companies within The Random House Group Limited can be found at:
www.randomhouse.co.uk/offices.htm

The Random House Group Limited Reg. No. 954009

A CIP catalogue record for this book
is available from the British Library

ISBN 9780099524991

The Random House Group Limited supports The Forest Stewardship Council (FSC), the leading international forest certification organisation. All our titles that are printed on Greenpeace approved FSC certified paper carry the FSC logo. Our paper procurement policy can be found at:
www.rbooks.co.uk/environment

Printed and bound in Great Britain by
CPI Bookmarque, Croydon, CR0- 4TD

To my parents

Contents

Acknowledgements

I am indebted to a great many people for their help, kindness and inspiration, not only in 2003–4, but also in the four years it has taken to put this book together. Not everyone has been named, and some people's identities have been obscured.

In Iran I'd particularly like to thank Fariba and Farid Hessami for being my second family, Samer Srouji, Navid, Chari Muhammadmoradov, Karim in Gonbad-e Qabus, Anahita Rezvani-Rad, and Leila and Lala Massoudzadegan; in Uzbekistan, Bohodir and his mother Inobat, Meus Meyer, Andre Mann, Farhod Fathullin, Katie Vang, Shavkat Boltaev, Yosef, Zinnat and Ari, Bahtior Javharov and Jalol Nasirov; in Kazakhstan: Gennady Khonin, Alexander Dederer, Irma Janssen, Ella Ilyenkova, Yuri Timofeevich, Peter and Moira Kettner, Corinna Kühn, Zhenya Zieb, the whole Wiedergeburt network, and Alix Chambris for her wonderful companionship; in Kyrgyzstan: Edmund and Flora Hayes, Beyshebay Sidykov, Kimsan Maqsutova, their daughters Tattigul Sidykova, Aymuchuq Beyshebay Qizi and their son Qumbat Bek Beyshebay Ulu, for taking Ed and me into their yurt; in Tajikistan, Abdullo Murodov, Bruno Paulet, Alisher at TajikIntourService, Sadriddin Yarov, Anne, Niyoz and his family, and Rakhmatkhan; in Afghanistan: Jack, Nur Shah Shahkar, Ali Heidar, Mohammad Reidi, Ehsan and his father,

Ismail; in Pakistan: Akram Hussain Kalash, Kazi Khoshnavaz, Kazi Mas, Maureen Lines, Maqsood ul Mulk, Major Geoffrey Langlands.

I seemed to have been unable to write the book in one place. My writing getaways have led me to America (twice), Sweden, Georgia, Belgium, Afghanistan, and around England. I must thank my sister Luisa in New York, the Doxi family in Skåne (Berit, Michel and Robina) for their boundless hospitality; Nick Conway who offered me his Kabul flat within hours of meeting me; Alix Chambris in Brussels; Natasha Shengalaia in Tbilisi; and the Coleridge family in Pershore, Worcestershire. For their friendship and forbearance, I owe a debt to Daniel Levitsky, Adam Croucher, Annabel Pinker, Nicholas Jackson, and Helen Qubain. For their invaluable comments on the manuscript: Thomas Welsford, Bijan Omrani, Nicholas Jubber, Zarrina Muhammadieva, and Jemma Wayne. I would also like to thank Nicholas Crane; Norman Cameron at the Royal Society for Asian Affairs; Mark Richards, who introduced me to my agent, Hannah Westland, at Rogers, Coleridge and White whom I rediscovered with delight after 17 years, and who has been a consistent support; my publisher Paul Sidey at Hutchinson's for his solid guidance; and Amelia Power for a beautiful map.

Most importantly, thanks to my parents, George and Lillian Metcalfe for their unwavering moral support, and my sisters, Luisa Metcalfe, Rebecca Metcalfe, and Georgia Coleridge for being there.

London, December 2008

OUT OF STEPPE

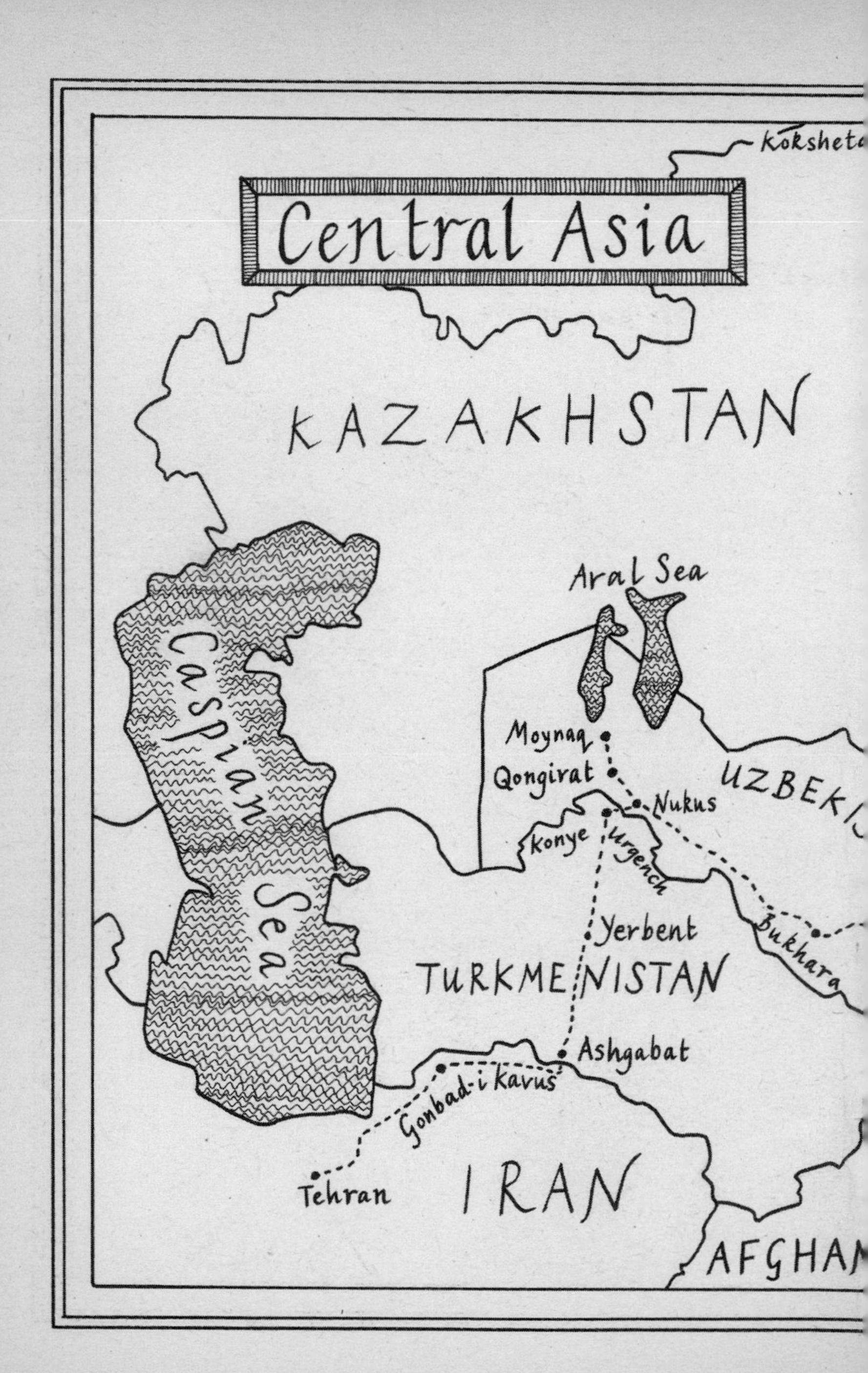
Central Asia
KAZAKHSTAN
Caspian Sea
Aral Sea
Moynaq
Qongirat
Nukus
Konye Urgench
Yerbent
TURKMENISTAN
Bukhara
Ashgabat
Gonbad-i Kavus
Tehran
IRAN

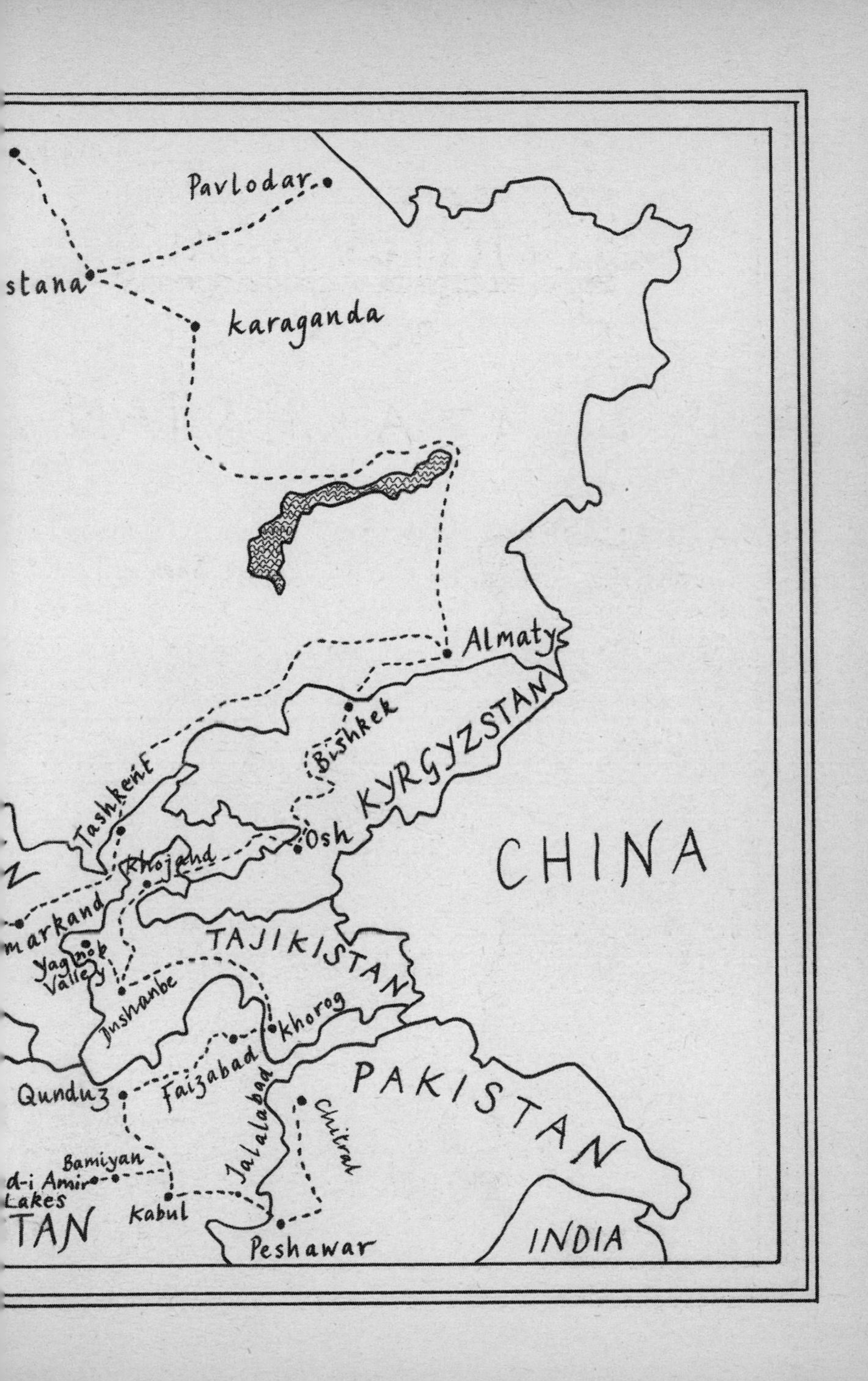

Pavlodar
stana
karaganda
Almaty
Bishkek
KYRGYZSTAN
Tashkent
Osh
Khojand
CHINA
N
markand
TAJIKISTAN
Yagnob
Valley
Dushanbe
Khorog
Qunduz
Faizabad
PAKISTAN
Jalalabad
Chitral
Bamiyan
d-i Amir
Lakes
Kabul
TAN
Peshawar
INDIA

Prologue

The Kazakh Embassy, Tehran, 22 June 2004

I'm fighting my way through a brawling queue. My chest has been jabbed raw and sweat is streaming. I've already witnessed one fight and abuse is never far away. With just six minutes to go, none of the petty traders is going to be outdone by a foreigner. But I fight my way to the consul before his hatch snaps shut.

'What is the purpose of your trip?' he says, as my head cranes to the low aperture.

'I want to find the Volga Germans, they live in the north of the . . .'

'There is a country in Europe,' he remarks coolly. 'It's full of Germans and it's called Germany.' He shuts himself in for the day. There is a collective groan, as the tired queuers amble home. I'm despondent, but not defeated.

Getting the visas for Central Asia was hard. Finding the embassies could be harder. One woman at Tehrani Directory Inquiries had never heard of Kyrgyzstan, but put me through to a greengrocer in Niavaran who pretended he was the consul and insisted that he could help me for a fee. Vaccinations weren't much fun either. The lack of stock in Tehran's clinics was cleverly disguised with nonchalance: 'We don't have hepatitis A in Iran,' they assured me.

These were my final days in Tehran, where I'd spent a year learning Persian and preparing for a journey that would take me to the far corners of Central Asia. The plan was to set off from Iran and journey round the neighbouring 'stans – five republics sandwiched between Iran and China – to find some of the world's most unsung peoples in the most unlikely places. I wanted to go now, to put myself to the test, but for the moment I'd have to wait. There was a mass of red tape to get through. My visas had stalled, the cost of my British Embassy 'letters of recommendation' was mounting, and Central Asian embassies had a habit of closing the moment you arrived.

I spent my last weeks trawling through the cobwebby collection of the British Council Library on Shar'iati Street. There seemed to be no limit to the literature on Central Asia, and I lost whole days among its periodicals and travellers' accounts, flicking through the sorting cards in the half-light. The woman who sat filing her nails at the counter, immaculate in her hijab and glossy lipstick, would fetch my books from the stack until, when she knew no one was watching, she let me hop over the counter to roam the bookshelves myself.

There I immersed myself in the literature on the region. I re-read books on Tamerlane and Genghis Khan, on the Turkmen slave traders, on spies in Samarkand, and sequestered Tajik tribes, said to be the distant cousins of Europeans. I found new customs, new peoples and, more than anything, new questions. I wanted to know about the Daoodis, apparently a nineteenth-century Jewish splinter sect that believed in the divinity of King David; or the Mountain Tajiks, a people who long ago had converted to Islam, but were said to be still worshipping fire at the beginning of the nineteenth century; or the Luli gypsies, who struck fear into Central Asians with the threat of the evil eye; or the Kuchis, some of the last nomads of Afghanistan; or the Germans who had somehow found their way to Kazakhstan. I'd long felt a powerful urge to track down some of these peoples myself. I knew their ways of life were slowly dying out and I wanted a mental snapshot of their communities before that happened.

Since childhood I've felt drawn to obscure and little-known parts of the globe. My interest in this region was kick-started at 14 when my parents sent me to Moscow for two weeks. I'd already learnt a little Russian from a grammar book I'd been lent. Now Vladimir, one of my hosts, a rangy fellow with a laconic turn of phrase, caught me gazing at the glass-fronted map of the former USSR. He got up to show me Birobidjan, the capital of the Jewish Autonomous Oblast, the far-eastern Siberian province Stalin hoped would be the new Jewish homeland. He showed me where Chukchi herders followed their reindeer over the tundra, and Svaneti, where north Georgian clans kidnapped wayfarers. He showed me that Russians were just one of hundreds of ethnic groups in the region, and how his vast country had only been settled by ethnic Russians in the last few centuries. Vladimir had opened my eyes.

Now, in 2004, I was on a quest of my own, to the Asian underbelly of the former USSR, to answer some of the questions I had asked myself as an adolescent in that summer of 1993.

Yet none of my researches had ever given me a clear definition of Central Asia. What was it exactly, except for a convenient geographical term? Central Asia defies definition. More than 15 years after the republics of Turkmenistan, Uzbekistan, Kazakhstan, Tajikistan and Kyrgyzstan found themselves suddenly independent in late 1991, the issue remains so uncertain that London's Asia House held a debate in March 2007 to try to solve Central Asia's 'identity problem'. In the *Encyclopaedia of the Literature of Travel and Exploration*, the English travel writer Charles Foster puts it this way: '[Central Asia] has a distinctive smell about it, but using that smell to draw clear boundaries is impossible.'

It's an apt evasion, because a smell is what it does have. Geographically, Central Asia is a no-man's land between Iran and the Caspian Sea in the west, Mongolia and China in the east, Siberia in the north, and Afghanistan, Pakistan and the Indian subcontinent in the south and south-east. It's a place where continents collide, steppes sprawl, cordilleras knot and ideologies clash. But if you ask for an exact definition, few people concur. Can anyone define a land mass that is home to more than a hundred ethnic groups; where there are deserts so severe that one of them – the Taklamakan, which sprawls thousands of salty miles across western China – is translated as 'you won't come out if you go in'; where mountains are so tall that their snowmelt waters more than a thousand miles of farmland; or where there are cultures so diverse that you can actually find yurts in concrete, Soviet-era back gardens and burka-clad women (as I once witnessed in Kazakhstan), selling home-made vodka from mobile kiosks?

But Foster is right. As soon as you think of wide Turkic faces, endless steppe-lands, Bactrian camels and greybeards in green quilted coats, then there is a very distinctive sense of Central Asia. Its strongest and most evocative association must be the Silk Road.

Central Asia was not just the crucible of this legendary trade network, but rather it sat in the middle of it. Coined by the geographer and traveller Ferdinand von Richthofen (1833–1905) as the *Seidenstraße*, the Silk Road was in fact a series of trade routes between Europe and China active from *c.* 200 BCE (Before Common Era) up until *c.* 1500 CE (Common Era).

Westbound caravans brought armour, lacquerware mirrors and silk bales over a nexus of routes, one via southern Russia and the Baltic, another across Persia, the Caucasus and the Levant. Eastbound, the routes followed the Gansu Corridor to Chang'an, or skirted the Taklamakan Desert to Kashgar and Dunhuang, bringing corn, wine, oil, gold, woollen goods and glass. Its southern route was the source of Afghanistan's medieval wealth, running through Bamiyan, Kabul and the Khyber Pass to India. Yet the land astride the traffic, the muddle of empires and city states we call Central Asia, has somehow taken this mythic sobriquet all for itself.

Whatever it was that travellers came to trade – gunpowder or cobalt, 'mare's teat' grapes or Ferghana's 'heavenly horses', it was always silk that held the popular imagination.

The discovery of the silkworm, which produced a thread so

fine to the touch, yet more tensile than steel, would be the mainstay of long-distance trade. A single cocoon containing up to a mile's worth of silk thread could be used to make cloth, bowstrings, fishing equipment, currency or military banners. According to legend, the Romans first encountered silk at Carrhae (today's Harran in south-east Turkey) in 53 BC. Blinded by the shimmering light from the Parthians' silk standards, the Romans lost 20,000 men to the Parthian sword, and their leader, Marcus Crassus, had molten gold poured down his throat. Subsequently, 10,000 Romans were sent as prisoners to guard Parthia's eastern borders, where they first made contact with the Chinese, whom they called Seres or 'silk people'. It was an inauspicious beginning to a lasting passion.

Gradually the caravanserais, or modern-day truck stops, where travellers rested and changed their horses, grew larger and more sophisticated. They acquired protective walls and became city states in their own right, through which the world's traffic passed. Chinese merchants, Iranian farmers, Soghdian scribes, Buddhist pilgrims all came to Central Asia for trade or diplomacy, to tour pilgrimage sites or to worship in the churches, monasteries, and fire-temples of every oasis town.

Round about the fifteenth century, overland trade started to sputter. There were many reasons for this. The xenophobic Chinese Ming Dynasty sealed off its borders, the Portuguese discovered a sea route to India, rendering the land route obsolete, and Byzantium fell to the Ottomans. For three hundred years, inland Asia became a dangerous backwater, and overland trade, on which the entire prosperity of Central Asia hung, simply ceased. The region was taken over by warring despots, and all the cosmopolitanism of former centuries was lost to ignorance and religious fanaticism.

For many people the phrase Silk Road conjures up romantic images of caravans loaded with silk and spices. But few think of the Russians, who conquered much of the region in the nineteenth century, and heavily Russianised their new colonies. For anyone who has travelled in Russia, the tastes and smells are immediately familiar: the liberal use of dill, the sour black bread, fat-spitting shashliks, and the daunting range of alcohol on offer. From the 1920s, the Bolsheviks, the successors of Imperial Russia, would drag Turkestan – as much of Central Asia was then called – violently into the modern age. Each republic was given electricity, housing, employment in factories or collective farms, literacy, a dubious national heritage, and of course, Communism. 'Charming' Central Asia – the crumbling, pre-modern society hunted by tourists and travel-writers – was in many cases replaced by belching factories, faceless apartment blocks and the ubiquitous murals familiar to many of us from photographs.

Amid this subcontinent were the peoples I'd come to find. It was fascinating to think that each conqueror, settler or deportee in the last three millennia must have left some kind of footprint – whether in the beaten gold earrings of a museum display case or in the existence of a living community. Despite centuries of near constant warfare, religious dogmatism and Soviet levelling, more than a hundred ethnic groups still survive. Many have abandoned the ways of their ancestors, but even today an incredible range of customs and languages can still be found.

I'd decided to visit six groups of people that particularly fired my curiosity, peoples spanning five faiths and sects: Shia, Sunni, Jewish, Christian and 'pagan'. It was a spectrum that would take me from the borders of the Caspian to the Himalayan foothills, from the south Siberian steppes to the central plateau of Afghanistan. My feeling was that if I didn't talk to some of these people soon, in a few years their culture may be indistinguishable from their neighbours', and the human tapestry of Central Asia, hitherto so vibrant and diverse, would begin to fade.

Tehran: One year before

When I arrived in Iran's capital, my Persian was in a very poor state. In preparation I'd faithfully worked through the exercises in a meaty, old-fashioned tome called *Persian Grammar*, which, for a self-tutor, was almost unimaginably forbidding. The grammar sections lasted for eighteen pages before the exercises began, and hardly any of its vocabulary was recognised in modern Iran. Still, in the year or so it took me to save up for the trip in London, I went everywhere with the book. I never managed to secure a grant or scholarship for my journey, despite receiving a number of encouraging letters, so I took on as many jobs as I could. I waitered, I leafletted, I taught Classics whenever I found a child who wanted to learn ancient Greek, I worked as a 'Russian' in an undercover promotion for a vodka brand, I distributed a Middle Eastern glossy magazine. All the while, *Persian Grammar* was never far away. I read it in my lunch breaks, I transferred it onto flashcards and chanted the words as I cycled from job to job. I ended up with a supple, but antiquated knowledge of Persian, which I found was almost useless.

And when, in September 2003, I arrived at the dormitory of the University of Tehran, the vast campus in north central Tehran, I said to the dorm guards in their box, '*Hazrat-e āghā, lotfan befarmā'id otāgh-e bandeh-dādeh kojāst?*' (literally: 'Excellent Sir, please command where the room of son of a slave is.') the guards, normally bored, unhelpful people, whose jobs consisted of tea-drinking and obstructing others, collapsed into fits of giggles. Delighted at this comic English curiosity, they were helpful to a fault.

But it wasn't going to be that easy. The yearly anti-government riots made the university dormitory a hotbed of intrigue and dissent. Built by the US military in the Forties, the dorm was a mass of residential blocks in a guarded enclosure. Thousands of students from all over the country were cooped up in chicken-hutch dorms. There was no privacy and complete separation from female company. My fellow students would spend hours on the phone ringing girls whose numbers they'd been slipped discreetly in the street. They'd work off their frustration in the gym or in the sweaty computer room surfing illegal sites, and a vague sense of despair hung over the corridors. I was put in the foreigners' block with Pakistanis, Yemenis, Syrians and Moroccans, who had spent decades on their doctorates. It felt distinctly like a prison, and my bed was little more than a plank of wood with a sheet. The Iranian dorms, however, were even worse, often squalid and overcrowded with six students to a room.

My room-mate, Navid, who maintained a firm grip on his sanity, was an astute Pakistani studying for his Master's in engineering. On my first day he showed me the canteen where I handed my coupon to a rosy-cheeked cook doling soup out of a huge cauldron. Wary of the unidentified slop, I opted for the solids, which were contained in a small polystyrene box. I opened the lid to a cocktail of carbohydrates: cubes of potato and pasta swirls on a bed of rice, sprinkled with chips, and a large fold of flat-bread. I looked doubtfully at Navid, who smiled and took me off for a home-made curry. From then on, every meal involved curry, because Navid and I cooked together in protest, and we ate cross-legged on the floor, watching Iranian soap operas on TV.

'Down there,' he explained on my first day, pointing to the end of the corridor, 'are the *hezbollais*. They're political and you'd better steer clear of them. And up there lives Arash, you might want to avoid him too.'

Arash was a grey-haired student in his late forties, who had the air of a permanent resident. He never seemed to study – though he was rumoured to have an Aeronautics degree from Texas University – and he talked to himself. He kept a kitten, which he would beat, and every day would leave a thimble-sized coffee pot on the stove until it boiled dry. He was avoided by everyone and there was talk that he was a spy, passing information about the students to the Government.

'Be very careful what you say,' Navid advised me. 'Many of these students are hired to watch and listen.' It had only been a few years since the dorm riots when the police had stormed the foreigners' block, smashing the rooms with batons and dragging students away. Arash was eventually kicked out for not paying his dorm fees, but he returned to his room one day by breaking in through the rear window. There was relief all round when he was seen from the balcony being forcibly removed by the guards.

Three days a week, I attended language classes at the university. But my real language practice came from long journeys in shared taxis, which shunted for hours through Tehran's congested streets. Most people travel this way. They flag down a Paykan – an old British-built Hillman Hunter – which crosses the city in fixed routes. There are usually three passengers to the front and three to the back, which means that if you are sitting next to the driver, you have a gear stick thrust into your groin and a sweat patch on your right shoulder from your neighbour's outstretched arm. The traffic is hellish and there is always time for a lengthy debate, which was a great opportunity to absorb the living language. As long as no mullah was within earshot, commuters were strikingly outspoken, carping at the clerical government, reminiscing about life under the Shah, and howling about the price of petrol. It was fascinating to compare these moments with the images of Iran that I'd grown up with.

As a child, all I can remember from BBC news reports is young, bearded men burning American flags, and later, ayatollahs fulminating against Western imperialism. It is true that since the election of President Ahmadinejad in August 2005, and the heightened tensions prompted by Iran's uranium enrichment programme, the Iranian media have taken a much harder anti-Western line. Yet only a year earlier, under President 'dialogue of civilisations' Khatami, Iran's anti-Western propaganda had seemed tired, as if the Government were jumping through hoops to satisfy the hardliners.

Outside these official channels I found a Tehran where anti-Western feeling was rarely expressed. There was a vibrant youth scene, which was incredibly easy to join, whether sitting in tea-houses or partying illegally with smuggled bottles of Absolut. It was where both men and women displayed their post-op nose-plasters, and the girls stretched the Islamic dress codes with ingenious insouciance. I discovered to my surprise that Tehran is one of the biggest retailers in lingerie, and that it is the nose-job capital of the world.

Another important discovery was the aspect of Iranian culture called *ta'ārof*. Very roughly, *ta'ārof* means 'etiquette', but it's a quintessentially Iranian institution that the English translation fails to capture. *Ta'ārof* is all pervasive, not just in the 'pleases' and 'thank yous' of polite conversation, but also in 'don't be tired', 'may your hand not hurt' and 'I am your sacrifice.' Every form of social contact will involve its own bewildering sequence of *ta'ārof.* To the uninitiated, a simple transaction in a shop could take forever. You choose the object and offer the money. The seller says: '*Qābeli nadāre*' ('It is not worthy of you') i.e., 'How could I possibly let you pay for that?' You reply with '*Khāhesh mikonam*' (something like 'You're welcome' or 'please') and offer the money again. The seller will refuse the money, say '*Qābeli nadāre*' again, you offer the money again, and it carries merrily on.

Ta'ārof is also used as a powerful form of obfuscation, protecting the user's true feelings under layers of formality. This often leads to two parallel conversations: the external world of *ta'ārof,* with its formalised system of etiquette; and non-*ta'ārof,* the real, unspoken interchange running alongside it, too pragmatic, brash or commercial to be allowed its own airtime. Many Iranians insist they hardly use *ta'ārof,* but everyone would agree that if you don't understand it, you are lost. It was invaluable training. In Afghanistan, which has its own similar system, a knowledge of *ta'ārof* would help me through almost all social encounters, from negotiating and asking directions to arguing and getting out of trouble.

After a few weeks of life at the dorm, I approached the *Tehran Times.* I wanted to see the inside of a hard-line, state-run newspaper and meet the kinds of people that worked there. They were keen for more native English speakers, of which they only had one. They gave me a short Persian language test, which I found I could work through with a dictionary and, within minutes, I was shown a desk and computer.

'Well? Can you start now?' asked the Editor-in-Chief.

'Sure,' I said, taking stock of my surroundings, as the *ābdārchi* (or tea-man) handed me a tiny glass of tea. I spent the next few months working away at translations and editing Iranian English. Most of the journalists were genuinely frustrated by the anti-Western rhetoric they were expected to write. Some were intellectuals who thought they deserved better than a post on the state's mouthpiece. The rest were a bit odd.

Much of my time was spent avoiding Mr Hamadani, a creepy, oleaginous character, whose status on the newspaper was uncertain. He would saunter round the office, greeting everyone with a slightly moist handshake. Without fail he would come over to my desk, smearing me with *ta'ārof* and a gaze that lingered just a little too long. Sometimes I caught him watching me work from the other side of the office. I assumed he was a spy for the newspaper's government sponsors, whoever they were.

But I grew fond of Zubin, an Iranian-American hippie, who had a penchant for heavy metal and fundamentalist Islam, having spent years as an anarchist in Washington. After the Islamic Revolution of 1979–80, Zubin had moved back to Iran to work as a journalist. He was unusual to look at, with jutting teeth, wiry, unwashed hair and his trademark Dead Kennedys T-shirt. He had a small, booth-like office where he would vent his spleen in political opinion pieces. Regularly he would burst out of his office, ranting about the latest crisis to beset Iran, and how nobody took any issues seriously any more. He frequently blamed the regime for not being fundamentalist enough.

The Editor-in-Chief, a forbearing man, would hear him out for a while, nodding sympathetically, and then say, 'All right, Zubin,' before politely manhandling him back to his office as if he were a patient, not a staffer.

I suspect Zubin was the only one to take the paper seriously. When in 2003 Shirin Ebadi, a renowned critic of the regime, won the Nobel Peace Prize, Zubin sat in his office, almost floored by the news. I knocked on his office window to see if he was all right, at which he shrieked, 'She was a judge under the Shah! She was one of them! She's a typical, lying, Western imperialist trying to undo the work of the Islamic republic!'

Zubin really was born in the wrong time. He would have been much happier in the turbulent Eighties. Few believed in the revolution now, certainly not the staff of the *Tehran Times*. Most Iranians wanted an open dialogue with the West – something they'd been denied since the revolution – and were sick to death of their turgid, corrupt regime.

When Ramadan came, the pace of the office slowed right down. According to Koranic – and national law – nobody ate, drank or smoked from dawn until the breaking of the fast at sunset, at which Zubin would emerge into the courtyard, ashen from nicotine withdrawal. It was generally the least productive time. Without the usual eight cups of tea virtually everyone spent the afternoon slumped over their desks. I even caught Mr Hamadani asleep once. But Zubin, with his neurotic energy, kept a scrupulous fast. I asked once if he ever found it difficult.

'Man, this is nothing,' he said. 'You ever tried to keep the fast in East Berlin, in winter, when your clothes have been stolen and you haven't eaten in days, and there's a bitter wind behind you? That, my friend, is hard.'

As the weeks drew to a close, my passport grew slowly in width, thickened by curious visas in modified Cyrillic, blackened by the thumbs of embassy staff, and pleasingly stamped. I boarded the bus heading east and, as I watched the forests of Mazandaran melt into the plains of Khorassan, I knew I was speeding to the border of my first 'stan.

It was time to start weaning myself off Persian for a while. The status of Persian as Central Asia's *lingua franca* – the language of diplomacy and bureaucracy – had largely been usurped by Russian now. Apart from Tajikistan, Afghanistan and the two Uzbek cities of Bukhara and Samarkand, Russian would be of vastly greater use than Persian. With *Ogonyok* in hand (a Russian news magazine), ploughing through an article on eighteenth-century duelling, I felt as if I'd hopped from a smooth intercity train to a shunting Pullman. My Russian needed an oiling. But practice wasn't far away now.

In the late afternoon the bus stopped somewhere in the eastern Iranian steppe and a group of gold-toothed men shuffled on board, stacking their watermelons in the luggage rack. They huddled together in their leather jackets, jumping between Russian and Turkmen. Their faces were wide and as lined as walnuts, their eyes were wide and thin. 'The eyes of the steppe,' I murmured to myself. I knew I'd already arrived.

1

'The haunt of the owl and the kite': Turkmenistan

'Let the life of every Turkmen be as beautiful as our melons.'
President Saparmurat Niyazov (1940–2006)

There was something terribly wrong with Konye Urgench. Like sloughed-off skin, a salty scurf covered everything in sight, the awnings and fruit stalls, the street signs, a deserted children's climbing frame. I knew I wasn't far from the wasteland of the Aral Sea. Whenever I approached a stranger, as I trudged my way around town, they would turn and fade from view.

Turkmenistan is mostly flat, sandy scrub. Its people, the one-time nomadic Turkmens, were, until the late nineteenth century, the curse of the Silk Road. Renowned for their lightning raids or *alamans*, they would enslave whole caravan parties to sell at the bazaars at Khiva and Bukhara. But these days Turkmens are meek and law-abiding, their hold on the desert broken by a bloodthirsty Russian invasion in 1883, which was, in the words of Lord Curzon, 'not a defeat, but an extirpation'. Lately they've been the victims of a Turkmen strongman called Saparmurat Niyazov, who'd retained power at independence in 1991, and started calling himself Turkmenbashi, or 'Father of the Turkmens'.

Every year a few thousand holidaymakers visit Turkmenistan. Basing themselves in the capital, Ashgabat, they shuttle from one gaudy post-Soviet eccentricity to another. Few make it to Konye Urgench, with its rich assembly of medieval mausolea. Rained on by sands from the dying Aral Sea, the city was on the wrong side of the desert.

The portrait of Turkmenbashi in the lobby of my sorry hotel should have warned me that haggling was off.

'Foreigners pay the foreigners' price,' said the wizened administrator with tired resolution.

'There's no running water,' I protested. But Turkmenbashi was watching us both, his hairpiece as hard as the rock on his finger. My eyes flickered to the picture, then back at the weary-eyed administrator. Patience, I quickly gathered, wouldn't work. In Konye Urgench, rules were rules.

She showed me my room, banging on the door until it bounced open and hit the wall with a crack of plaster. Quite bare, except for a bed and a frazzled plughole, my room contrasted starkly with the one next door, the well-swept, electrically lit Ruhnama Reading Room, whose walls swooned with images of the leader: Turkmenbashi smells wheat in a sunset backdrop; Turkmenbashi lays an anointing hand on model Turkmen boy's head; Turkmenbashi rests his chin on his heavily bejewelled hand.

I went in to have a look. The Ruhnama Reading Room was the perfect place to reflect on the wisdom of the great leader, and to read his book, the *Ruhnama* (*Book of the Soul*), an appalling ramble of pseudo-philosophy, which promised within its 400 pages a complete solution to all of life's malaises. The *Ruhnama* was ubiquitous. It formed a major part of the school curriculum, was invoked during state driving tests, and mullahs were enjoined to place a copy outside every place of worship, or else risk demolition.

It would be another two years – in December 2006 – before Turkmenbashi died of heart failure, leaving the country with an uncertain future. When I visited, Turkmenbashi's grip on power was as strong as ever. At independence he retained his position as Communist Party boss since 1985, only he renamed it the Democratic Party of Turkmenistan, before outlawing all other parties and appointing himself president for life. Siphoning billions of dollars into private bank accounts he left more than half of the six million-strong population living below the poverty line. Recently he'd closed down every hospital outside Ashgabat and replaced the doctors with poorly trained army conscripts. He'd bulldozed residential districts to make way for his ghostly modern capital, full of statues of himself and empty trade emporia.

However, he did provide foreign journalists with almost inexhaustible comic potential. Obsessed with his own personality cult, Turkmenbashi had turned his quiet desert republic into a fantasy world where Turkmen heritage was emphasised in a variety of original ways. According to newspaper reports, Turkmenbashi had proscribed opera and ballet (because it was 'not necessary . . . not part of Turkmen culture'), he'd banned men from growing beards (the opposite of the Taliban next door, who'd punished clean-shaven men with imprisonment), forced female newsreaders to wear lipstick (because otherwise he couldn't tell the sexes apart) and made 10 July National Melon Day. He fiddled with the Turkmen language too, replacing the Turkmen word for bread with his mother's name, 'Burbansoltan Edzhe'. He also renamed the month of January after himself. He was even rumoured to be planning an ice palace in the Kara Kum desert (where the temperature can hit 40°C), but made do with an ice rink through lack of funds.

Turkmenbashi's presence was almost palpable, from the product labels 'Turkmenbashi tea' and 'Turkmenbashi vodka' to the endless street posters, neon-sized *Ruhnama* quotes and grand monuments in his honour.

But there was a pre-Turkmenbashi Turkmenistan that I wanted to see before the light faded, and it was in Konye Urgench that I would find it. The curious thing about this dusty province was that it was home to much of the country's glittering bygone splendour. Gurganj, as the old city was once called, is one of the country's only historic complexes still standing.

Blinded by the glare of the setting sun I could barely make out the mausolea. And then I saw them all at once, huddled on the horizon like petrified giants. These were the majestic, disintegrating records of the old town, a small reminder of when the Khorezmshahs ruled Asia from the Persian border to the edges of India in the thirteenth century. The odd flash of turquoise tiling or a band of Kufic script was all that remained of its days of greatness. All around was the mess and dust of an unkempt necropolis.

I approached the hulk of the Soltan Tekesh mausoleum, a huge brick structure with a battered turquoise roof which looked like an upended ice-cream cone. It had seen better days, but it was the finest thing I'd encountered in Turkmenistan so far. An old janitor with a toothless, lopsided mouth rummaged around for his key. He opened the great wooden doors of the mausoleum, and a flock of pigeons flapped out all at once. 'Not so many visitors,' he said.

Inside, I tried to conjure up scenes of medieval Gurganj. I followed the line of the cupola, examining its rich decorations and stalactite plasterwork, the tomb of Soltan Tekesh, Khorezm's greatest king, anointed by centuries of pigeon droppings.

This region, known in past days as Khorezm, was an odd part of the world. It was a vast land of scrub and desert, relieved by the humid wetlands of the Amu Darya Delta and the Aral Sea to the north. Perhaps a millennium BCE, this region was settled by Iranians following the Aryan migration from the north. Khorezm was rarely its own master. It was the wild eastern satrapy of the Persian empire or the wild western province of the Ghaznavid empire. But when Khorezm achieved greatness for itself, for a few decades, it was very great indeed.

Soltan Tekesh had managed to shake off his Seljuk Turkish overlords at the end of the twelfth century, and together with his son, Ala ad-Din Muhammad II (1200–20), made Gurganj the capital of the most powerful Islamic empire of the day, stretching from Iraq and Azerbaijan to eastern Afghanistan. Enriched by the spoils of Central Asia, and enjoying a rare moment of peace and security, one short-term resident, the medieval traveller Yakut, who lived here from 1219 to 1220, described Gurganj as one of the most extensive and richest of all the towns he'd ever seen. Caravan routes were revived, coming in the west from Kievan Rus and Khazaria on the Volga, carrying amber, furs and slaves across the wastes of Ust-Urt to the markets of Gurganj, then on towards Bukhara and Samarkand. A ring of protective forts were built, guarding the Khorezmian heartland from marauding Turkic nomads. Yakut writes of undisturbed peace, overflowing bazaars, metropolitan grandeur and scholarship. The word 'algorithm' is traced here, through the ancestors of the eighth century Arab mathematician Al-Khorezmi, who is accredited – among other things – with the invention of the zero.

But Khorezm was no match for the Mongols. Genghis Khan had sent a diplomatic mission to king Muhammed II. Making a grave tactical error, the king dismissed the ambassadors, had all of them shorn of their beards and one beheaded. He was blithely planning an invasion of Iraq when news of Mongol revenge arrived. Samarkand, Bukhara and Otrar had fallen (the governor of the latter was killed by having molten silver poured into his ears and eyes). Genghis Khan sent a detachment of his army, led by his two sons, Jochi and Chagatay, to besiege Khorezm. For months the Mongols surrounded the city. They destroyed it house by house, killing its inhabitants as they went. But the Mongols at least had an eye for craftsmanship. Once Khorezm was obliterated, they separated out the city's 10,000 artisans, and sent them off for service in the new Mongol empire.

The rest were not so lucky. Women and children were driven into slavery, while the surviving men were separated among the Mongol soldiers, whose orders were to execute twenty-four each. The smoking, bloodied shell of Gurganj, emptied of its inhabitants, suffered a further assault when the Mongols destroyed the Amu Darya dam. The torrid waters of the great river surged over the ruins of the city and the damage was complete. 'Khorezm,' wrote Juvayni, a contemporary Persian historian, 'became the abode of the jackal and the haunt of the owl and the kite.'

Khorezm's rich pastures fell to scrub and the outposts were left to rot. Even today the right bank of the Amu Darya is strewn with the fortified remnants of the Mongol assault, Kavat-Kala, Guldursun, Toprak-Kala where they lie cracked and sun-blanched. Within a hundred years Gurganj had staggered back to its feet again, only to be knocked down by another conqueror, Tamerlane, who wreaked untold destruction on this beleaguered city. This time Gurganj hadn't the strength to rise again, and the site stayed deserted ever after.

I sat for some time listening to the stillness of the tomb until I felt my neck bristle at the presence of the janitor. He was clinking his keys and wanted me out. I set off again across the sands to the other side of the necropolis, where a mass of graves and conical shrines sat shattered on earth mounds or amid dry green brush. The sun ducked behind the horizon and the orange-bathed earth turned again to russet brown. A flock of swifts flitting overhead suddenly swooped around the Fakhr ud-din Razi mausoleum, following the line of its frieze. They seemed to caw urgently.

I stumbled on a dip in the ground and fell. Brushing off the earth I realised I'd stepped into an open grave, a shallow hole about two feet deep, in which lay two decapitated skulls, yellow and cracked. One lay next to the other, both jaws missing, and next to them, as casual as a clod of earth, lay an entire human femur. I wanted to leave Gurganj now.

I jogged back through the city's dilapidated streets, the roads emptied of all but some scrawny cats scrapping around in the rubbish. Hungry, I headed off in search of a late dinner. Even in Konye Urgench, it never occurred to me that I was being watched.

Next morning there came a knock at my door. Opening it, I saw a holster, peaked cap and rice-gut. It was a policeman. Grabbing my passport, I followed him into the Ruhnama Reading Room. The administrator watched my shake-down from across the hall.

'What are you doing here?' said the policeman, tapping a box of *polyot* until a thick, filterless cigarette fell out. According to Turkmen law, smoking was only permitted indoors.

'I'm on a transit to Uzbekistan.'

'I know you're going to Uzbekistan,' he said, as a tar-filled cloud momentarily obscured his face, 'but I'm asking you why you didn't fly there. Why did you come to Turkmenistan at all?'

'I prefer to travel by land.'

He grunted. 'And the cemetery? What were you doing there?'

'I'm a tourist.'

'You see,' he took another long drag, 'we have a ten o'clock curfew here. You were out until 10.40 p.m.'

'I was?'

'Konye Urgench is a very . . .' – he searched for the right word – '. . . beautiful city.'

I nodded agreement.

'And we want to keep it that way. Understand?'

'Of course,' I said, failing to see the connection between the town's questionable beauty and a ten o'clock curfew. He stared at me for some seconds.

'I think you'd better go now,' he said, finally. He handed me my passport, adding, ominously, 'No more trouble.'

If trouble meant looking for food at 10.40 p.m. in a nothing town in a neutral country, I regretted having to leave. There was so much more to experience. As I returned to my room, the administrator looked up from her mop with mild superiority, as if to say I should have known better than to go sight-seeing. Little did she know, my next stop was the antithesis of tourist attractions.

2

'You can't eat cotton': The Karakalpaks

'In Aral Sea, too, the people have their far-reaching dream. They are deeply enthusiastic about a scheme bearing on the future of their blue sea. Let us see what it is . . .'

Viktor Vitkovich, *A Tour of Soviet Uzbekistan* (1944)

Karakalpakstan means little to most Westerners. This is the region where a healthy inland sea was shrunk catastrophically by hare-brained Soviet agricultural policies. It is both the home of the Karakalpaks and an environmental disaster.

Karakalpakstan was in many ways a museum of a Central Asia that had elsewhere long disappeared: Karakalpaks have a vigorous oral culture, they still keep camels and drink tea with milk – more in common with Mongolians and Tibetans than their settled neighbours – and it was worth a visit with or without the sea.

I'm ashamed to say it, but I was one of a long line of travellers who wanted to see with their own eyes the horror of a land that has the highest mortality rate of the former USSR. I wanted to feel the cracked sea-bed under my feet, to prove that news features weren't simply playing up to a prurient audience.

Karakalpakstan is a very large, flat piece of land tacked onto the western edge of Uzbekistan, roughly a third of the country. A lesser known Central Asian minority, Karakalpaks are overshadowed by the Uzbeks to the east and Kazakhs to the north, and are descendants of Turkic and Mongol tribes (Nogay, Mangit, Kipchak) that appeared as if out of nowhere in the sixteenth century, roaming the banks of the lower Syr Darya and Aral region until the 1920s, when they were forcibly settled by the Soviets.

The 'autonomous' Republic of Karakalpakstan is a sham. It has its own flag, president and theoretical right to secede from Uzbekistan, but Karakalpaks, who make up only half of their republic (the rest being mostly Uzbeks, Kazakhs and Turkmens), know that independence will never be granted. Most of the land is steppe and desert, part of the Ust-Urt plateau and the huge Kyzyl Kum desert that extends as far west as the oasis of Samarkand.

There was nothing much going on here, except that Karakalpakstan possessed a jewel that set it apart from anywhere else in Central Asia: the Aral Sea, a huge, freshwater inland sea, once the fourth largest in the world and a magnet for holidaymakers, boaters and fishermen. Blue, clear and brimming with fish, it tempered the harsh continental climate and gave Karakalpakstan all the character its countryside lacked – until Moscow shrank it.

So obsessed was the USSR with the cotton crop and the foreign currency it could earn, they robbed the Aral Sea of its water in order to irrigate the 'white gold', as it was called, spraying millions of litres of fertilisers and pesticides over the fields of Uzbekistan until the environment was wrecked. From the Sixties onwards the sea began to shrink, taking the livelihoods of its inhabitants with it. Now, having lost half its surface-area since 1960, the sea is utterly depleted and there is no money to turn back the clock.

The life the Karakalpaks once had is gone. The viscous pond that the Aral Sea has become is so polluted that few fish survive, though once it provided a tenth of the entire Soviet catch. The soil around it has disintegrated. Salt crusts everything, grits engines and flavours the tea. Nothing much grows. The good climate, previously humid and temperate, is now dry and searingly hot. Half the native animals have died off and the desert is creeping closer. Drinking water is heavy with metals, chemical run-offs and bacteria.

Yet the people carry on without a murmur, because they have to. I discovered – to my eternal astonishment – that Karakalpaks simply didn't make a fuss. They only said meekly that they wanted the old days back. Didn't they know, as A. A. Gill wrote in the *Sunday Times Magazine* of July 2000, that this was the 'worst place in the world'?

Nukus

Nukus, the capital of the Karakalpak republic, was not a good introduction. The name alone recalled nasal effluent and the arms race, but the look of it made you want put your head under a pillow. My first vision on arrival was of grey apartment blocks, gunge-spewing Ladas and apathetic street amblers.

Nukus was built in 1932 to house the nomads, freshly collectivised and sent to work in the cotton and chemical-refining industries, whose indiscriminate dumpings have been leaking steadily into the drinking water ever since. As with so many Soviet industrial cities, charm was not a priority, but the place functioned perfectly well until the environment turned. Then the factories stopped running, the soil rebelled and the sea groaned. Almost everything was dropped and left quietly alone.

I approached my hotel with trepidation. Naively I'd opted for the hotel Tashkent, a gargantuan block in the style of the Moscow suburbs, which, I later discovered, was avoided by those in the know. I entered a large and empty atrium. Doors that would have led to the 'bar' or the 'laundry' were locked. I surveyed the hall for signs of life. Tiny behind her desk sat the administrator, scratching at a crossword. '*Dokumenty*,' she droned, hardly looking up.

She gave me the key and I took a shuddering lift to the seventh floor. I emerged on to a concrete-and-carpet interior, with concave ceilings like the inside of a space ship. This was once the best hotel Karakalpakstan had to offer, beloved of party members, agronomists and engineers. But when the land stopped giving, the experts stopped coming.

I threw down my things. The washbasin hadn't seen water in so long it was encrusted in a yellow metallic deposit. Next to it stood a pail of brackish water. No piped water, not even in the capital. I went over to the window and drew apart the netting. The city below was a blur of heat and exhaust fumes, little blocks of grey housing strung together with wires.

I took out all the papers I'd packed in my bag. For each of the peoples I was going to visit I'd prepared a small research file consisting mostly of articles I'd found on the Internet and some newspaper clippings. For Nukus I'd photocopied sections of a Soviet travel book called *A Tour of Soviet Uzbekistan* (1944) by a Viktor Vitkovich, published in the Stalin era to promote the glories of the republic for foreigners. Pure, unabashed propaganda, its photos depicted crinkle-skinned nomads driving tractors and women bent cheerfully over cotton plants. The smelly wood-pulp pages celebrated the wonders of the region: reeds, willow and tamarisk, wild boar, cormorants, the shovel-headed sturgeon. The Aral Delta was apparently once a life-giving wetland. It was, to quote Vitkovich, 'exceedingly pure . . . as bright as Badakhshan azurite, and as translucent as sapphire'.

When Stalin's agronomists discovered that Uzbekistan could be turned into a huge cotton monoculture, Moscow couldn't contain itself. They ripped up paddy fields, wheat fields and orchards to plant it, and from the Thirties onwards rice-growing was banned. But cotton was a particularly thirsty crop. It needed more water than the rains could provide. So the experts took the two rivers, the Amu Darya and Syr Darya, which emptied into the Aral Sea from their sources more than 2,000 kilometres away, and stole the water.

Between 1940 and 1980 cotton production rose from 2.24 to 9.10 million tons. But even these yields were not enough. The Soviets wanted to outstrip US output, they wanted to bathe in white gold, turn the red desert white. Still more water was diverted, the quotas fixed yet higher, until finally locals started to object. 'You can't eat cotton,' complained Faizullah Khojaev, one of the pioneers of Uzbek Communism. He was shot.

Virtually all the water from the two rivers was used for irrigation. The tributary rivers: Zeravshan, Kashkadarya, Murgab and Tejen no longer flowed into the Amu Darya, and little of the latter reached the Aral Sea at all. Bled of its water, the Aral Sea began to shrink. But Moscow was addicted to cotton wealth and no attempt was made to change its policy.

By the Eighties, the Uzbek Supreme Soviet had no option but to falsify their yields. On paper the output soared. Meanwhile cash was diverted away from the cotton industry. The ruse – nicknamed 'The Great Cotton Swindle' – was as practical as it was dishonest: people felt they were drowning in the stuff. But when Soviet satellite pictures revealed undeveloped cotton fields and more than a billion roubles missing, a massive KGB inquiry led to a huge shake-up within the Uzbek bureaucracy. The minister for cotton production was executed and 2,600 employees sacked. Even more damaging, when it was discovered that this 'national resistance' consisted entirely of the Uzbek top brass siphoning millions of dollars into their own coffers, Uzbekistan became a byword for corruption. It was never really trusted again.

By the twenty-first century, the ecosystem was wrecked. By 2008, the sea was down to less than 10 per cent of its original size. Everything once green and good and life-giving had disappeared, and a strange new desert was left in its place. To the south was the Kara Kum (Black Sand), to the west the Kyzyl Kum (Red Sand). Now the seabed was a salty moonscape nicknamed Ok Kum (White Sand).

Without the tempering effect of the Aral Sea, there were terrible wind storms, spreading the polluted earth and salt over all the crops. The fertilisers, pesticides and insecticides used to boost the yield had depleted the soil and spread widespread disease, even among neighbouring republics. All the nitrates, benzenes, phenols, dioxins and DDT dumped onto the crop were seeping into the groundwater. People developed jaundice, TB, enteric typhoid, viral hepatitis and almost everyone had anaemia. Young Karakalpak conscripts were so unfit for the army that they were sent to join labour battalions instead.

When the Soviet era drew to a close in 1991, Karakalpakstan had become a poor, useless province in the thrall of its overlord, Uzbekistan, which had neither the money nor the inclination to help its dying citizens. Cotton is still the country's main crop, albeit a much reduced one. Karakalpakstan struggles on like a dead limb. Finally the world is beginning to take notice. Only Uzbekistan looks away.

I had to psyche myself up for my morning excursion. I was going to the Museum of Karakalpakstan. I walked the sweltering, gridded streets at a good pace, but was soon slowed to a shuffle. I noticed that in Nukus people didn't really walk. Old men lounged on shaded steps, child cigarette-sellers sat listlessly by their cartons. None of the air-conditioners that jutted from the tenements gave the slightest noise.

Having located the museum, I climbed some steps into an empty looking interior, dark and refreshingly cool. A woman handed me a ticket from a new roll. I asked if I was the first visitor that day. She nodded.

From the gloom, a guide materialised. She was young and bespectacled with long, lilac-painted fingernails.

'Hello, are you American?' she asked, smiling, which filled me with a sudden, unexpected cheer.

'English,' I said.

'I am Zinnat, your guide. Please follow.' The tour, it appeared, was compulsory.

She showed me maps, paintings and stuffed animals of the great Republic of Karakalpakstan, from the days when there actually were animals here. Glass cabinets reeking of wood polish were crowded with life: herons, owls, snapping reptiles and prancing gazelles, all with second-rate painted backdrops, as if the money had run out once the taxidermists had been paid.

'Here you see rich wildlife of Aral region,' she embarked. 'Karakalpakstan is 165,000 square kilometres with population of 1.2 million inhabitants.' She rattled on for a while, wincing whenever I threatened to ask a question.

'We have many animals in region,' she said. 'Salmon, pike, sturgeon, carp. In total 170 species of animal life.'

'Are you saying,' I asked, 'that all these species are still flourishing despite the great changes in the environment?'

'You know something of Karakalpakstan?' she said, pursing her lips.

'Yes, a bit,' I said. 'I have read that the Aral region used to be very different.'

'You are right,' she conceded, looking uncomfortable. 'It is worse now.'

'Worse? In what way?'

'It is just worse.'

'Well, how many species of animal life are left now?'

She looked around her, and said, with lowered gaze, 'Not more than forty. Probably less.'

'I see.' I waited for more, but she didn't go on. She flipped back into her former, well-worn patter, listing the Egyptian ibis, coot, cormorant and grebe. I'd engaged her for a tantalising moment, and then I'd lost her. I looked at the exhibits: marble-eyed pheasants and hen-harriers, all the wealth of a lost paradise. Here was a handsome-looking tiger, a native of the region, stalking through a mock-up jungle, its back arched, claws flexed like the Rousseau painting.

'What sort of tiger is that?' I enquired.

'That,' she sighed, 'is Turanian tiger.'

'Ah. It was climate change that did it,' I surmised. 'Its natural prey was gone, and it had nothing to eat. Or the forests were chopped down for cotton farms, and the DDT seeped into its genes and weakened its offspring? Was that it?'

'No,' she said, affronted, 'authorities shoot last one in 1972.'

She led me on to the chamber of Karakalpak history, an array of glass-boxed historical figures and costumed mannequins, some gorgeously clad. Warriors in statuesque poses stood with scabbards on their belts and sheepskin hats pulled over their eyebrows. Fairy-tale brides wore magnificent headdresses,

Amazon-like, from which their long black tresses tumbled to the end of their camisoles. Everything jingled with tiny bells of beaten silver. In spite of their blank faces, in my imagination I saw the wonder of the steppe, the romance that so captured Western travellers.

There is a long tradition of writers who have romanticised the lives of nomads, conveniently forgetting the harshness of the steppe, the rigid formality of social interaction and the violent skirmishes with neighbouring tribes. But there was one European whose fancies I can forgive, for her sincere and open-minded attitude. The Aral region is so remote, with so little to attract visitors that hardly anything has been written about it in the West. But one woman, a lone 29-year-old Swiss adventuress called Ella Maillart, was lucky enough to witness Karakalpak society in the very throes of change. It was in the winter of 1932, the final days of nomadic feudalism – or freedom, as she would put it.

After a tour of a region starving in the wake of collectivisation, Maillart found herself on a boat on the Amu Darya, sailing towards the Aral Sea and on towards the Russian settlement of Kazalinsk on the sea's north coast. As she huddled together with the other passengers to try to keep warm, the vessel made slow progress. With a snapped tow rope, the boat eventually ran aground, leaving the passengers shivering to the howls of jackals on the reed bank. They stole paraffin from the boat's tanks to keep warm and plundered the decking for firewood, and finally, frozen but alive, she arrived at the village of Takhtakopir, in the eastern Amu Darya Delta. There she found a camel train heading north – the largest animal, she writes, 'had tears of ice hanging from its long eyelashes' – and she was soon wending her way across the steppe.

Travelling by night to avoid bandits, and with little for comfort but a block of ice for tea and some frozen camel meat, she slept in the open like the rest of the party, listening to the dry brushwood snapping like glass in the fire. Day after day she spent 'in somnolent stupefaction', her mind emptied by the movement and the unending flatness of the land, where the saxaul gave way to dunes as 'smooth as suede'.

Born a furrier's daughter in Geneva in 1903, Ella Maillart was desperate to escape. Jaded by Western consumerism and the anarchy following the Great War, she longed for a simpler, more meaningful life, and balked at her father's advice. 'Security, situation, consideration meant little to me,' she wrote. 'I was going to do something else.' Her early years were filled with sporting adventures. She was the first to create a Swiss female hockey team and came ninth in the women's single-handed sailing category in the Paris Olympics of 1924.

But it was a trip to Russia in her late twenties that changed her life. In 1930 Maillart arrived in Moscow with a plan to write a short book on Bolshevik film. Invited to the first theatrical Olympiad, she became suddenly aware of the remarkable ethnic diversity of the USSR, performing theatre and dance to an uncomprehending audience: 'The Bashkirs of the Urals, the Jewish artistes of White Russia, the unforgettable Georgians of the Caucasus, or the Uzbegs [*sic*] of Tashkent with their brightly coloured kaftans. Muscovites, no less than myself had to follow the action by guesswork.' Reading her description of this event in her autobiography *Cruises and Caravans* (1950), I thought of my own Damascene moment in Moscow 1993, when my teacher, Vladimir, opened my eyes to this universe of unfamiliar cultures, kept so successfully from the world's consciousness.

'Books on Central Asia made me long for Turkestan and its nomadic tribes,' Maillart later wrote, 'to join them, live life on the steppe and become a child of nature in their midst and be good . . . yes, the wild was calling.'

The trip she had in mind was longer and much more ambitious, one that would produce *Turkestan Solo* (1932), the account of her journey across Siberia, Kyrgyzstan, Uzbekistan and the deserts and steppes around the Aral Sea. The year 1932 was an unlikely year to travel in this region, one of the worst in the whole history of the USSR. Up until then Central Asia had been nearly self-sufficient. Its economy had relied on a symbiosis between town-based farmers and pastoral nomads. This was now being replaced with a completely alien Soviet system.

The pastures, where horsemen had roamed for millennia,

were being turned into *kolkhozes* or state-run collective farms, where quotas were fixed absurdly high and workers often received their wages in kind. Self-sufficiency was broken and people were made completely dependent on the state. By 1930 Stalin was well into his first five-year plan and collectivisation – which had been brutal in its implementation – began to spell starvation and despair for millions. Nomads were herded off the steppes, pushed into factories or *kolkhozes*, given homes and urban conveniences, and told to abandon their God or gods for Socialism.

When Maillart travelled along the east bank of the Aral Sea she witnessed first-hand some of the last Karakalpak nomads. She describes whole families emerging from the distance, crying babies, and asses carrying samovars and yurts. All were going south to Nukus where the food was cheaper, the weather warmer. Many had no idea of the distances they would need to cover. One man, she described, without food, money or papers had left *kolkhoz* 6 at Aktyubinsk, and was heading south for work. 'He would rather eat sorghum all his life and never see meat or sugar than have a master over him,' she wrote.

When she arrived at the Russianised town of Kazalinsk, with its rows of poplars and western ways, she felt profound dismay: 'There is little chance of anything unexpected happening now. The real journey is over.'

There is no question that Maillart was a romantic, but she knew that nomadism was not the only way to live. Nevertheless, she understood what nomads could teach us: the value of a simpler lifestyle and the ability to sustain life on the land, rather than wrench it from the soil as the Soviets did, and as we do today. 'Only by returning to their way of life,' she wrote, 'can we ever hope to find a way out of the bogs in which we vainly stumble.'

Zinnat jogged me from my reverie.

'Why do you shake your head?' she asked.

'Well, look,' I said, worked up now. 'You've lost so much. No one dresses like this any more. It's been destroyed by the Soviets.' Modern Karakalpak dress sense wasn't great. Women went about in velveteen maternity dresses with curtain-like flower patterns, and men's fashion consisted of Western-style jeans or fake leather jackets.

'But this is old times,' Zinnat protested. 'We are a modern people. Soviets make us modern. They give us education. In last times we were feudal. Now we are modern.'

'But what does "modern" mean when they destroyed everything Karakalpaks had? Aren't you angry?'

'Stalin make many mistakes.' I noticed her hands were clenched.

And then I saw it at once. This wasn't denial – it was resignation. Truth and transparency are the privileges of the hopeful, and what did she possibly have to hope for?

I left the museum and stepped into a blast of heat. Ahead was a large building, one wall painted with the image of a 1920s movie camera. The front door was open and bedraggled workers were rushing out, clutching briefcases, as if escaping a fire. I stopped one hurrying past. 'Air-conditioner broken,' she said. 'Power cut.' In this heat it was as good as a fire. Perversely, I decided to go in, hopping up the stairs. This, I discovered, was the Karakalpak State Studios.

Walking along a stifling corridor, the windows all jammed shut, I found a little office where two workers were holding the fort. One was the director, Alisher, a round, grey-haired man with a football-shaped head; and the other was his wiry, unassuming assistant, Bohodir. I introduced myself and asked if they could spare ten minutes for a chat.

'Normally, of course,' said the director, examining me carefully, 'but . . .' He waved his arm towards piles of paper and a powerless computer. We stood in silence. 'OK, come,' he sighed, defeated.

He led me into a spartan office, which was devoid of anything to do with film-making. But it did exert an executive power. There was a large, leather-topped desk, a pair of pen holders like hollow cigars, and oil portraits of former studio directors on either side of his throne. His assistant followed us to help, if needed, with translation. Alisher dabbed his forehead with a sodden handkerchief.

I told them of my project, and began with the Aral Sea. This elicited an almost inaudible sigh. Clearly, it was a well-worn topic. It was only when I asked him about post-Soviet Karakalpakstan, the regime of President Karimov and the bitter independence years, that he started to become fidgety.

'Some have talked about human rights abuses in Uzbekistan,' I began. 'What has been the experience of Karakalpakstan?'

'Who are you?' he breathed, sweat dripping down his forehead.

'I'm sorry,' I said, taken aback by his reaction, 'I just wanted to build a picture of Karakalpak life.'

'Talk to Bohodir here,' he said. 'He's a lawyer. He can tell you what you want to know. Now if you'll excuse me . . .' He disappeared more nimbly than I thought possible for a man of his bulk and left an apprehensive Bohodir in his place.

Turkmenistan may get the worst international press of the Central Asian republics, but Uzbekistan is not much better. Its corruption is well-documented, but Uzbekistan has been busy ratcheting up a list of quiet but horrifying crimes, noticed only, it sometimes seems, by non-governmental bodies. Strategically situated north of Afghanistan, and thought to be an ally in the 'war on terror,' the Uzbek regime has been heavily supported by the United States, and condoned by Britain. The truth is that Uzbekistan – along with its dead limb, Karakalpakstan – was voted by the US-based NGO Freedom House as among the world's most repressive societies of 2006, sharing the prize with Turkmenistan, Burma, Cuba, Libya, North Korea, Sudan and Syria. Political resistance of any kind is heavily punished and any religious activity, violent or peaceful, operating outside tightly controlled 'state Islam' is persecuted. Not only Muslim activists, but also journalists, human-rights lawyers and writers, have been imprisoned. 'Torture [in Uzbekistan],' said the UN in 2002, 'is institutionalised, systematic and rampant.'

Slave labour is still the major means of production. Every summer, pupils and university students all over the country are obliged to 'help out' with the cotton harvest. Unbelievably, given the state of the soil, cotton is still Uzbekistan's biggest export. Citizens work for months without pay. Permanent labourers are only marginally better off, earning often a mere $2 a month.

Craig Murray, the British ambassador to Uzbekistan from 2002–2004, found he couldn't hold his peace. In 2002, after photos of a suspected member of Hizb ut-Tahrir, a radical Islamic group, landed on his desk, Murray turned to the University of Dundee to have them examined. The report concluded that the man had had his fingernails removed, before being boiled to death. Murray's public comments were not well-received. Britain's Foreign & Commonwealth Office, embarrassed by Murray's indiscretion (and, indeed, by his flamboyant lifestyle) subjected him to a disciplinary investigation, before recalling him for good in October 2004.

But Murray's attacks on the 'kleptocratic regime' may have borne fruit. In July of the same year the US State Department declared that the Uzbek human rights record had rendered it no longer fit to receive aid.

President Karimov, meanwhile, continues as normal. He caused international outrage in May 2005 when his security forces shot 700 anti-government demonstrators in Andijan in cold blood, using the threat of Islamic extremism as cover. Completely unrepentant, his rhetoric is that of a medieval khan. 'I'm prepared to rip off the heads of 200 people to sacrifice their lives in order to save peace and calm in the republic,' he told Agence France Presse in reaction to anti-government violence in 1999. 'If my child chose such a path, I myself would rip off his head.'

So I could see why Alisher had been reluctant to talk to me. 'I don't know if I can answer all your questions,' Bohodir said. 'I'm only a trainee lawyer.'

Somehow, I managed to calm his fears. Whatever I was going to write, I assured him, I'd hide his real identity, which I have.

Bohodir was a 23-year-old law student working in his grandfather's private firm, and he occasionally helped out in the studios. His loose tie and shirt concealed a painfully thin frame, and he walked with a stoop. He didn't look happy, but he was extremely earnest, which was endearing. Young, skinny, naïve, he was a world away from Alisher. And his English was uncannily good for someone who was self-taught.

We settled on plastic chairs in an outdoor café, where a drunken Russian was droning karaoke in the corner. A Korean waitress brought us *shorbo*, a clear broth with a knot of gristle at the bottom of the bowl.

'I apologise for him,' said Bohodir. 'This is the way it is here. We have so much fear. I'm just waiting to get out.' He slurped his soup. 'This is why I must get my law scholarship to America. If I don't get it, there's no hope.'

'No hope?' There it was again.

'Look around you.' He pointed to the dirt-streaked tenements on the other side of the road.

'Appearances aren't everything,' I said, weakly.

'Nothing works . . .' He rolled his eyes up to the ceiling. 'Karakalpakstan is no place to live. There are no jobs, no careers, nothing.'

I asked him how he became a trainee lawyer. His eyes darkened.

'My grandfather.'

I looked up.

'He hates me,' he added.

Apparently, Bohodir's father had left his wife for another woman, but his grandfather blamed his daughter-in-law for the breakdown. According to him, she'd brought shame on the family for failing to keep her husband. Now the old man was bitter and lonely. His only son had left to join his new wife in Kazakhstan and he spent his days carping at Bohodir, his only other relative.

'This is Karakalpak culture,' said Bohodir. 'He is angry that his son has gone and always he insults me, forces me to work for him in his law firm. I tell him I can't stay here forever, I'm going to America. But he just laughs. He says, "You can't go to America. You don't have that sort of money." But he doesn't understand that in America they don't take bribes from students.'

The karaoke was becoming unbearable and I wanted to ask a favour.

'Listen, Bohodir,' I said. 'You know the countryside. Would you come with me to the Aral Sea for a few days?'

'My grandfather will never allow it.'

I promised to match his wage. He took an uncertain sip of cherry *kompot.*

'Just a few days?'

'Yes, two or three.'

He didn't give me an answer, but when we reached my hotel he shook my hand formally.

'I will come. My mother lives in Qongirat, on the road to Aral. This is a good chance to visit her, as she is not well. I will see you at nine o'clock tomorrow right here.'

I skipped into the hotel atrium and resolved to celebrate with a beer. The lobby doubled as a bar now and the administrator had managed to tear herself away from her crossword. She was doling out beer bottles with all the enthusiasm of a child-weary dinner lady. A drunken Kazakh was slumped over one side of a table, his spectacles half-crushed in his fist. On the other side were two Uzbek army officers playing cards – not people to mess with. On the high stools sat a grotesquely fat man next to a Russian girl with a pair of painted arcs for eyebrows and a skirt so short I wondered why she bothered to wear it at all. I assumed she was for hire, but then, looking at some of the girls on a night out round here, you never could tell.

The emptiness, the silence, the faded glory of the morning now seemed almost poetic compared to this. The moment I took a beer from the administrator I thought better of it. But it was too late. I was a welcome distraction for the officers. I felt a blow to my stomach as one of them grabbed a fistful of my shirt, pulling me towards the table and knocking over empty beer bottles like ninepins.

'*Ty otkuda*?' he slurred. 'Where are you from?'

'*Anglia,*' I sighed. This could be a long one.

'*Anglia*, ah?' he slopped in my ear. 'What are you doing here?'

'Please, let me go,' I murmured.

Suddenly the lift door opened and a breathless man with a towel round his middle walked panting up to the desk.

'Where is the water?' he said angrily, his face beaded with sweat. 'I need to flush. I am ill.' I couldn't work out his accent, but he was a foreigner like me.

Even the sleeping Kazakh woke up, blinking. The administrator looked at the man blankly.

'Well?' he tried again.

'*Nyetu.*' The creature spoke. *Nyetu* is the most common word in the former USSR. It means 'no' or 'there is none'. Reasons are rarely appended.

'What do you mean "no"?' The man, whose Russian was poor, looked worried.

'*Nye-tu,*' she said louder, enunciating each syllable. The poor foreigner gave up and padded away. With a hearty laugh, the officer released his grip and let me retire, at last, to bed.

The next morning I felt awful. It was a mixture of the beer, dehydration, the mosquitoes and, worst of all, the stench from my open-sewer lavatory. I staggered down to meet Bohodir, who was waiting patiently, a leather bag under his arm. He flashed a smile and looked at his watch. It was the dot of nine.

We found a shared taxi and left for Qongirat, a few hours' drive north of Nukus. For miles the countryside was flat. The only landmarks were telephone poles and undulating wires. This was not a clean flatness like the Argentine pampas or a Midwestern prairie. This was a dirty beige nothingness, where sky met land in an underwhelming blur. Occasionally we drove past a bleak town – breeze-block constructions and concrete reinforced with rusted webs of iron.

For a Swiss mountaineer like Ella Maillart, who was also an Olympic skier, the Karakalpak steppe was a shock. 'Who sang the flaming colours of the East?' she wrote, as she peered from her train carriage. 'Far from being intensely bright, the landscape on the contrary is dust-coloured, grey, monotonous; and the broken horizon is circular as at sea . . .' The flatness also inspired one of her amusingly dubious theories:

> Now I understand why nomads have such narrow eyes. Dazzled, only the narrowest slit is permitted to remain open between eyelids so clenched that they form a parallel line. There is nothing around them on which to rest their gaze, but the horizontal infinities of sand that tremble in the heat; flat sea, unending steppe and disappearing rails . . . nowhere the vertical line of a building or a tree.

When she saw Nukus for the first time it was not the burnt-out metropolis I found. Her Nukus was little more than a tea-house and telegraph office, the plot ear-marked for a great industrial city. Workers were flooding in from all directions, hurrying to build the city with wood scaffolding from the Urals. Viewing the desolation around Takhtakopir, she announced, 'I have an astonishing impression of having come to the ends of the earth.'

There *was* something ends-of-the-earth about the landscape, as if its Creator had suddenly run out of ideas. The further we went, little patches of white started to appear, frosty glazes clinging to the ground. As we drove further, the patches coalesced until acres of land were taken up by this mysterious white acne. This, I finally realised, was salt. What no one seemed to understand when the Soviets irrigated the region for cotton, was that under the soil lay an enormous amount of natural salt, just waiting to be released. Eventually the shrinking sea would uncover millions of tons of not only salt but toxic residues. And once the cork was out of the bottle, the particles flew about everywhere in great corrosive mistrals. Salt got into machinery, corroded buildings, and dried skin. Babies in Moynaq were said to refuse their mothers' milk. But worst of all it covered the crops, which would have to be washed with yet more precious water. The crop-washing or 'leaching' took away the salt, but would eventually release yet more from the soil. Irrigation began to resemble a coin-hungry launderette where the wash never ended.

'We're not there yet,' said Bohodir, dryly.

Qongirat, a middle-sized town halfway to the Aral Sea, had the feel of a blasted weather station. We arrived in the middle of a dust storm. Sand swirled around the wheels and streaked the roads ahead. Mini-dunes by the road disappeared into people's eyes as they fought home, their shopping bags in front of their faces. Loose metal clacked with the wind. The salt here was virulent, just as Bohodir warned. It pocked the cityscape, the pavements and the forecourts of the massive square tenements we passed – block after block of soul-crushing uniformity. One 'message' from President Karimov on a roadside placard read, with humiliating irony, 'We will pay to create the best conditions of life for our people.'

The winds were still high when we got out.

'Hurry,' called Bohodir, 'too many policemen. This way.' He led me up a side alley to a small bungalow with a large covered balcony. Out of the wind we were met by a worn figure at the door wearing the standard velveteen-curtain dress.

'Meet my mother, Inobat,' he said, as a beautiful but wan woman extended a skeletal hand. Her eyes sloped with disappointment like Bohodir's.

'And that,' he said, pointing to a figure in the far corner rocking to and fro, 'is Great Uncle Timur.' He was a toothless pensioner, smacking his lips and muttering. He was counting stacks of Uzbek som, worthless banknotes, which he leafed and sorted, oblivious to our arrival.

Inobat ushered us in for lunch. 'Plov,' she said, the Central Asian dish of mutton and rice. She beckoned me to wash my hands and I followed her to an outdoor basin. The tap water had eaten through the enamel into the tin underneath, where it had deposited a bright orange crystalline growth that bubbled in fungal flakes.

'Don't worry,' said Bohodir, 'as long as you don't drink it . . .'

We ate cross-legged on cushions on the floor. Inobat left us alone, as was the custom, and we talked. Bohodir showed me a flowerpot hanging from the window containing a single dead geranium, its soil white and crusted.

'You know, that was the only flower my mother cared for,' said Bohodir. 'She watered it every day – nearly drowned it, but you see . . .' he cast an eye to the backyard behind, 'Nothing makes any difference any more.' Peering over into the garden I saw a near-white gravel square patched with salt, great crystalline circles like the lichen that grows on Hebridean boulders.

He told me of his family. Great Uncle Timur, Bohodir explained, was ill. He'd worked as a cotton labourer all his life and his health was broken. He was senile and had intestinal infections. But then, he remarked, so did everyone.

'And you?' I asked, tentatively.

'Of course,' he shrugged. 'Not only that. I have many things wrong with me. All of us do. My best friend died of hepatitis. I have gastro-enteritis and my spleen is inflamed. I have a stomach ulcer. And I have . . . other things.'

'I'm so sorry.'

'I also have insomnia. How do you think I learned English so well? I was up all night reading,' he laughed. 'But I am worried now for my family. My little sister has a goitre. My little brother is fine now. He's seven, but there is so much food he won't eat. I worry for him.'

We drifted onto the porch and sat with Inobat in the dim light of a lantern. It was a cool evening. The town was deathly quiet now, but for the chirruping of cicadas. No human noises. There was no entertainment in Qongirat, not even for the dog that was sniffing around the locked cinema.

'What do young people do here?' I asked.

'Nothing. No sports. Nothing,' said Inobat, smoothing her dress. 'Drugs mostly. But,' she changed the subject, 'Bohodir is going to America.' She stroked the back of his head with her palm.

Inobat described her life as a teacher. First, half the class was regularly absent through illness. Anaemia was one of the worst complaints, followed by viral hepatitis. The soil's iodine-depletion had led to goitre. The rest of the pupils, she explained, were too apathetic to concentrate. State education, as everyone knew, wouldn't make a blind bit of difference to their lives. None of them had the connections, or the cash, to get them into university. Moreover, Inobat didn't get paid. She hadn't received a som in two years. But she soldiered on in the hope that one day the corrupt government would distribute enough funds for teachers' salaries. As her blood rose, she switched to Karakalpak. Bohodir translated.

Two years earlier, school salaries in Qongirat simply stopped. No reason was given. The teachers got together and petitioned to the local council, the *mahalla*, which promised to look into it. Nothing happened. So they went a step higher. Marching to Nukus, the republic's capital, they approached the state authorities. Still nothing. Finally, the desperate teachers gathered hundreds of names and sent a petition to President Karimov himself in Tashkent, the Uzbek capital. An inquiry was promised. They returned to Qongirat, relieved that their initiative had paid off. And it did pay off – for a while. After a rebate of five months' unpaid salary, their pay cheques from that day on came in the form of coupons from the state shop: sugar, tea, tin cans, flour.

'You can't pay bills with *produkty*!' she said, throwing up her hands.

Then even the coupons dried up. The Qongirat *mahalla* was humiliated that the teachers had gone over their heads and now the teachers were left with nothing. They were back to square one – and now, much worse, they had a vengeful *mahalla* on their hands. In local matters they were completely vulnerable.

I was amazed Inobat had the energy and will to continue.

'Maybe one day someone will pay me,' she said. 'Most of the other teachers have left. Perhaps I should too, but then there would be no one for the children.'

They made me a bed that night in the backyard. I wrapped my mosquito net round the bedposts until it was insect-tight and lay down, staring at the moon. A strange assortment of sounds sent me to sleep: the howls of stray dogs, and the shuffling of Great-

Uncle Timur to the privy – the trickle of his pinched urethra and his trudge back to bed.

As night wore on, the sounds of insects grew. They were on the march. Louder came the scraping and scratches of hooks as they tried to get inside the tight lattice of my net. Their wings hummed as loudly as dragonflies and they seemed to call to each other, vying for the prize of human blood.

Karakalpakstan may have resembled a death camp for living things, but now it had become, literally, alive with bugs. Pollution and climate change had killed off most of the birds – the insects' natural predators – and now the Turkestan termite, which thrives especially in arid conditions, was breeding wildly out of control. In the village of Tausha alone, they'd chomped through more than a hundred houses, creeping into the roofs and turning them slowly to dust. Desperate villagers, terrified of being crushed to death by their collapsing houses, try to flush them out with oil and water.

I couldn't sleep. I was stunned that here, in 'the worst place in the world', a place of hopelessness and resignation, existed a kind of normality. And more than that – there was a humanity here that I'd rarely encountered: how Inobat welcomed me without question; how she worked at the school for nothing; how a couple of dollars from my money belt would be a week's food, but I knew she'd never ask for help. I was amazed, too, that Bohodir hadn't succumbed to the apathy that was a curse on the Karakalpaks. He saw a way out, even if he couldn't feel it.

Moynaq: 'Former Seaside Town'

There can't be many places worthy of the epithet 'former seaside town', but Moynaq, which was now miles from any water, hadn't moved an inch. The shoreline had simply receded by 40 km. Along with Aralsk, Kazalinsk, Uchsai and Bugun, the only reminder of the sea was in the ubiquitous remains of the good old days: the beached boats, the rotting tackle and the eerie placards hailing the goodness of water and the importance of fishing to the Soviet economy.

Once Moynaq was more than just economically prosperous.

It had been a famous holiday resort, the Crimea of Central Asia. In summer, several flights a day brought Soviet citizens to the beach. What was it Viktor Vitkovich had said? The Aral Sea 'is exceedingly pure, as deep and delicate as aquamarine, but without the touch of green, as intense and bright as Badakhshan azurite, and as translucent as sapphire'. The entire town lived and worked with the sea and its related industries, packing and canning. Without it, the town was as good as dead, and I did wonder how a town with no means of livelihood and almost 100 per cent unemployment could be anything other than that. The only vague hope for Moynaq was tourism, but even that wasn't exactly the healthy kind.

Bohodir and I found a yellow Moskvich at the Qongirat taxi rank. The engine growled, then died. A sigh, a clatter of instruments, and soon we were gliding through cotton flats and scrub.

'May I ask,' enquired the driver, 'what are you doing in Moynaq?'

'Business,' said Bohodir.

'Oh,' he said, knowing full well there was no business in Moynaq.

As we drove along the cotton petered out and the farmed flats turned to wasteland. The salt patches weren't so prevalent here. These were cotton plantations, desperately watered, leached and watered again and the air was humid with evaporation. On the approach to Moynaq we spotted some artificial lakes, great dug-out bowls that had been filled with imported water and fish to give the fishermen something to do. It was a stab at rescuing Moynaq, but it wasn't enough.

At last the sign came: ARAL KHOSH KELDINIZ (WELCOME TO ARAL). This was the part I'd been waiting for. We'd scarcely glanced at the town before the taxi driver had skidded off with a spray of sand. There were no customers in Moynaq. Bohodir and I stood together in the main street. As we hoisted up our bags, we noticed the deathly quiet. There was just no one around, no cars, no sound. It was like a Sunday afternoon in mid-summer, when everyone should be away – but holidays were a luxury no one could afford. Everyone was still here. So where were they? The wind swirled the sand and the odd bit of metal clacked, increasing the silence. But there was no birdsong. The road ran straight ahead between two rows of run-down housing, the tarmac obscured by drifts of sand that crept silently.

Bohodir and I started the trudge to the hotel, passing one or two bent-backed women with babies.

'Where are the men?' I asked him.

'In Kazakhstan, mostly,' he said. 'They send money home. Keeps Moynaq alive. Same in Qongirat.'

The population of (supposedly) 9,000 had been whittled down to a few mothers and children. The only men I could see were a crowd of puffy-faced drinkers at the taxi-rank.

It felt like walking through a film set: a broken tractor on its side, a train carriage rotting on the street, miles from its track, bleached skiffs parked on the pavement, their wood split and tackle rotten. I recalled that Morrissey lyric, 'This is the coastal town. That they forgot to close down . . . Come, Armageddon! Come!'

Most astonishing were the placards. These were a fixture of Central Asia, it seemed. All of Karakalpakstan was hung with signs, messages from Karimov, pearls of wisdom on nationhood, happiness and unity, as if only the father of the nation knew the answer. This was an enduring legacy of the Soviet era, and it was patriarchal and patronising at the best of times. But here, in the context of what had happened, it was unbelievable. Every few metres hung another placard. Bohodir translated as we passed: 'WATER IS THE SOURCE OF LIFE', 'LABOUR LEADS TO JOY', 'MOTHER'S HAPPINESS IS PEOPLE'S HAPPINESS', 'FISH OUR WEALTH'. Why no one had torn them down I never understood.

Finally, we passed the canning factory, the city's pride and one-time mainstay of the economy. We poked our noses through the chicken wire and saw inside a mess of rusted machinery and broken glass. The security guards shooed us away in sharp bursts of Karakalpak. But what were they protecting? The last native Aral fish had died in 1986, drowned by the noxious waves.

By 1986, 50 years of the Mengele school of ecology had taken their toll. New fish were shuttled in, but they too died. Moscow panicked. They had to keep the canners canning, whatever the cost. Fish caught in the Caspian and Baltic were hauled thousands of miles to remote Karakalpakstan just to keep the factory open. This was clearly unsustainable. Wild schemes were hatched to replenish the sea. One idea, the Sibaral Project, was as mad as it was expensive. The plan was to take the Ob and Irtysh, two massive Siberian rivers that flowed north into the Arctic, then dam, reverse and direct them south into the Aral Sea. If this were successful, cotton wealth could be enjoyed in perpetuity.

Orpheus was said to have piped so beautifully that he could change the direction of the River Styx. But by now the USSR could barely feed itself, let alone turn back nature. Even in the Forties, Viktor Vitkovich refers to the idea in his book. 'If the plan goes ahead,' he writes, 'Central Asia would then have so much water that it could wipe the desert off the map for good.' Thankfully, Siberia was spared this assault by massive popular criticism and lack of funds, so nothing was done. The canning factory closed, the fishermen hauled in their boats and the Aral Sea was sententiously proclaimed to be 'Nature's error'. When the damage was deemed irreversible the authorities cried, 'Let it die a beautiful death.'

At last we arrived at the hotel. On the edge of the town, where the low buildings seemed to disappear into the scrub, stood a small, white-washed building decked in lush, trellised verdure. A tubby man in a string vest and flip-flops was splashing the greenery liberally with a hose. Heaven only knew where the water was coming from. He greeted us with a smile and led us through the lobby – walls stencilled with rowing boats and fish. Bohodir and I, both uncomfortable at this wanton display of plenty, walked up to the desk, where a pair of German travellers were waiting. They were in their mid-thirties, urban types with stylish haircuts and hemp bags. Anywhere else in the world we might have struck up a rapport, formed a temporary friendship built around our experiences. But not here. There was something each of us recognised in the other: a morbid curiosity in the disaster that was taking place. We confined ourselves to a nod.

As Bohodir and I were led upstairs, we peered from the staircase window to see a scrap-metal dump, a horizon of creeping scrub, and barefoot children making mud pies among the mess. The hotelier beckoned me to follow, loping around in his boxer shorts and vest. He was probably the richest man in Moynaq. Two or three guests a week and he was probably tied over until winter, when the place turned into a gulag.

Bohodir knocked at my door at eight.

'You will need sunglasses, sunblock and a hat,' he said.

I noticed he had none of the above, as we set off to the beach. The sun screamed down now and steppe winds were blowing sand in all directions.

'Cover your eyes,' called Bohodir, 'don't get the dust in your eyes.' He was right. The yellowy soil wasn't natural. It was infested with DDT and anthrax. We marched against the wind for a while, pushing against a flat and scrubby horizon. We weren't far now. The sky was scraped an awesome blue by the scouring winds. A jogger panted past, with sweatbands and a visor. We stopped him, half to check if he was real, half to ask where the 'ships' graveyard' was. The ships' graveyard was the lodestar of Karakalpakstan, the point of visiting Moynaq: an eerie assemblage of beached boats on the dry seabed.

'No more ships,' he said, jogging on the spot. 'They've taken them away. Don't bother,' and jogged off. I also wanted to ask him what he was doing exercising by a toxic seabed. It was like going to Chernobyl to 'take the waters', but he'd already vanished.

Soon, on the right, a finger of concrete appeared, an obelisk to the Karakalpak contribution to the Great Patriotic War.

And there in all its horrific majesty was the great Ok Kum, the White Sand Desert formerly known as the Aral Sea, a clumpy seabed that seemed to stretch forever. There were thickets and tough bushes that could probably survive in a post-nuclear world. Here and there were scattered the detritus of a huge maritime industry, engine cast-offs, bolts and rowing boats like bath toys on the horizon.

We scrambled down the scree onto the dry bed to feel it under our feet. It felt hard and brown, pitching in small troughs, and disconcertingly moist underneath. Bohodir shoved a twig into a hard, glazed hummock. A gelatinous ooze slithered out like crème caramel.

It seemed the jogger was right, the tugs and trawlers really had been taken away. From where I stood, there were only the indentations of their hulls on the mud, as if some warm, full-bellied beasts had sloped off to die. I felt cheated of my prize. I stood on a bluff and looked into the distance. A shepherd was towing a line of cattle across the seabed. Their coats were matted and their udders deeply sagged. This toxic soil served as their daily pasture. I began to feel sick.

Far out of view, in the middle of the sea, was the island of Vozrozhdenie, or Resurrection. Karakalpaks had always been wary of it, and folklore claimed that an enchanted castle stood there, surrounded by flaming quicksand. They were half-right. The castle was a major Soviet bio-weapons plant called Aralsk 7, built in 1954 to study the dissemination patterns of biological weapons. Unluckily, the prevailing winds blew south to Karakalpakstan, carrying a cloud of toxins: anthrax, tularemia, brucellosis, plague, typhus and smallpox. The plant was abandoned in 1991, leaving the live anthrax spores to fester until in 2002, when the US Pentagon, fearing the use of this anthrax-laden soil by terrorists, sent the Threat Reduction Agency to decontaminate the anthrax dumps. Which they did, leaving the rest of the site untouched. Today any visit without full body protection would be tantamount to suicide.

As Bohodir and I eased out of Moynaq that afternoon, we spotted a man by the road. He had tattoos on his thin white arms. We offered him a lift as far as Qongirat. His name was Roger and he was an American Peace Corps worker. On the ride back he told us that he'd illegally put a group together to work with schoolchildren over the summer. President Karimov wanted NGOs as far away from Moynaq as possible, said Roger. He didn't want foreigners to see how little was being done.

'See,' he told us in his deep Virginia drawl, 'the official population here is nine thousand. But the real population is more like two. A lot of people think that Karimov is just watching and waiting for the last of the Karakalpaks to die off or disappear into Kazakhstan so it can then be repopulated by "ethnic" Uzbeks who will then make use of the mineral wealth lying under the ground. This is the rumour. But it doesn't matter whether you believe it or not, because they're already drilling for oil on the seabed. That wealth is not for Karakalpaks.'

Roger, a doctor by training, despite his unhealthy pallor, was a passionate activist. But there was something hard in his voice, a protective shell he'd developed after staying too long out here.

'I don't believe the republic will survive in the long run,' he continued. 'Perhaps another twenty, thirty years. They're going already. They'll go even quicker if HIV takes off. It's a known fact that areas of high emigration, drugs, alcoholism and hepatitis like this are just waiting for an AIDS explosion. That should just about kill off whoever's left.'

Roger got off at Qongirat without much of a goodbye and we carried on to Nukus. I tried to think what I'd gained by seeing all this. My desire to witness a dying society had been fulfilled. I'd observed the drawn-out suffering of a people without the resources to change their fate. Bohodir, who'd understood every word Roger had told us, sat watching the horizon without expression.

The midday heat had passed now, leaving the salt flats rippling to the horizon. The knots of telephone wires thinned into a line that pitched and fell by the side of the road, the plains opened and I stared, blankly, into the distance.

Few Karakalpaks I met – not even Bohodir, who was educated – showed any nostalgia for their historic nomadic days. That time was gone, and its significance lost. Today they mourned the Aral disaster and the losses that came in its wake

– their livelihoods, pensions, factory jobs, farm jobs, office jobs, all of which vanished with the collapse of the Soviet Union.

But I couldn't help feeling sadness at the end of the nomadic way of life, and the loss of the deep understanding of the natural environment once possessed by the now-settled Turkic peoples. There was a wealth of ancestral knowledge that the steppe-dwelling peoples could have taught the USSR, but they were never given the chance. 'Only by turning to their way of living can we make our way out of the bogs in which we vainly stumble,' said Ella Maillart. But it was already too late. Today's Karakalpaks watched the steppe as uncomprehendingly as I did.

3

'The ones that know the way': The Jews of Bukhara

'The Turkmen believes the Jew to be a magician, and holds him in the deepest dread; he does not molest him, as he cannot sell him, for the children of Israel are so despised on the other side of the desert that they cannot even be disposed of as commercial articles.'

Arminius Vambéry, *Scenes from the East: Through the Eyes of a European Traveller in the 1860s* (1876)

Bukhara, a few hours east of Nukus, sits comfortably in the Zeravshan Valley, a rich agricultural oasis surrounded by scrub and desert. Founded by the legendary Persian prince Siyavush, and famed for the storks that nested on every tower, Bukhara is a pillar of Persian civilisation. Its architectural treasures celebrate centuries of Persian influence, and its mixed residents are a pocket of Persian-speakers in Turkic Uzbekistan. Bukhara is also Central Asia's most ancient and holy city. In its long lifetime it has drawn not only Muslims but peoples of all faiths and nationalities – Uzbeks, Hindus, Tajiks, Armenians and Arabs – to its once bustling bazaars.

Of all the peoples that still inhabit Bukhara's winding streets, one of the most ancient is the Jews – their religion the only one to survive the coming of Islam.

Thought by some to be descendants of the Israelite tribes of

Issachar and Naphtali, many put the arrival of the first Bukharan Jews in the second half of the first millennium BCE. The Bukharan Jewish rite is perplexing, belonging neither to the Sephardic or Ashkenazi tradition, and often simply called Mizrahi or 'Eastern'. Their language, Judaeo-Tajik – a mixture of Hebrew, Russian and Tajik – is not spoken anywhere else and, most extraordinary of all, Central Asian Jews were until recently – like their Muslim neighbours – polygamous.

But centuries of anti-Semitism and state repression has made the Bukharan Jewish community suspicious of outsiders. Decimated by recent emigrations, the dwindling few are often shy and non-committal, sometimes defensive. I encountered something of this at a Bukharan Jewish synagogue in Queens, New York, when I was attempting to track down some of these émigrés a year after my journey, in 2005. Entering the synagogue in search of the rabbi, I was stopped suddenly at the door by a young woman with a small child.

'What are you doing?' she asked, as if I'd been rumbled trying to crack a safe. I explained my Central Asia project and told her I'd come to further my research.

'Uh-huh,' she said, arms crossed, chewing her lip. 'Well, I consider your project offensive.' She told me it was not up to an outsider like me to write about the Jewish community, but up to the community members themselves. Who did I think I was?

I told her I didn't mean to cause offence. Few in my own country knew anything about Central Asia at all. I suggested that a travel account is a way of giving these peoples a voice, whether they are Jewish, Muslim, Christian or Zoroastrian.

The woman relented slightly, though still blocked my entry. She did, however, promise to give my phone number to the rabbi.

'By the way,' she asked, 'do you have any ID?'

Not wanting to seem secretive I showed her my passport, forgetting my visas to Iran and Afghanistan.

'Afghanistan?' she spluttered, reading the entry stamp in green ink. 'Are you serious?'

I'd blown it now. She grabbed her daughter and banged the gate behind her.

In Bukhara, suspicion of outsiders was very much the norm: decades of Soviet rule had taught them to avoid strangers asking questions. But the horrors of the twentieth century were one chapter in a long story of decline. In the first half of the nineteenth century Central Asian Jewish communities had reached a very low ebb. European travellers returned from Bukhara with dire reports of their state. A Hungarian Jewish scholar called Arminius Vambéry, who visited Bukhara in 1863 disguised as a Sufi dervish, was appalled at their situation. 'There is no more surprising, and to be honest, no more tragic situation than that of the miserable Jews in the various lands of Moslem Asia,' he wrote.

These 'Central Asian' or 'Bukharan' Jews must not be confused with Ashkenazi Jews, who arrived in great numbers with the Russians in tsarist times. Ashkenazim were by comparison modern, Russified and often considered their Central Asian counterparts to be boorish and unlettered. Bukharan Jews, on the other hand, were their considerably poorer kinsmen in the cities of the emirate, with Bukhara as their unofficial capital.

After the Russian invasion in the 1860s, freed from their status as playthings of the emirs, Bukharan Jews for the first time gained rights equal to their Muslim neighbours. Of all the peoples of the Tsar's new Asian conquests, Jews (both Ashkenazi and Bukharan) were the only ones considered loyal to St Petersburg. They bought land, traded goods and some became wealthy as factory owners or merchants, trading with Moscow and the Baltic.

But Communism would plunge them back into darkness. Whereas centuries of attrition by Asian despots had had a withering affect on Jewish life, Stalin's method was swift and brutal. Having dismantled the Jewish clergy in the 1920s, and shot and imprisoned almost the entire literate elite, he hounded Jewish people, seized their valuables for hard currency, and sent their sons in disproportionate numbers to the front against Hitler – three quarters of whom would die. Even in the milder Khrushchev and Brezhnev years anti-Semitic feeling was still rife.

From the early Seventies, when exit regulations began to be relaxed, a trickle became an exodus under Gorbachev, and then a flood at independence. Central Asia's exhausted Jewish population seized the opportunity of life elsewhere, and in the last decade and a half since the end of the Soviet Union, up to 70,000 Jews have abandoned Central Asia for Europe, Israel and America, leaving an ageing 10,000 or so to carry the torch in Uzbekistan and Tajikistan.

The great tragedy is that, while recent history has seen an inexorable decline in the fortunes of the Jewish community, their stature in an earlier age couldn't be more marked. The very thing that made Central Asia great in the first place – the flow of trade along the Silk Road – is in part indebted to itinerant Jewish traders who developed the long-distance routes, bringing goods and scholarly texts to the kingdoms of Asia.

Asian Jews were the great innovators and businessmen from the very earliest days. They burst onto the scene in 559 BCE, released from Babylonian bondage by King Cyrus of Persia, and ever afterwards showed themselves to be notably versatile within the Persian Empire as businessmen, scholars, administrators – even royalty: Shushan-Dukht was the Jewish wife of the Sassanid Persian king Yazdigird I (399–420 CE).

With encouragement from the Achaemenid and Sassanid Persians, Jews settled all over the Persian Empire: from Asia Minor in the west up to the eastern satrapies of Khorezm, Gandhara, and Soghdia and Bactria (now northern Afghanistan). Some even travelled as far as Kaifeng on the Chinese Yellow River, where they took local wives and assimilated Confucianism and, incredibly, survived until the nineteenth century.

Jews found greatest renown as travelling merchants. Nicknamed Radanites or 'the ones that know the way', they knew all the best routes from the markets of Verdun to the bazaars of Chang'an, trafficking eunuchs, furs, swords and silk. As privileged intermediaries between the Islamic and Christian worlds, Jews became experts in their field. So great was Jewish influence in commerce that the Khazars – the Turkic rulers of an empire straddling vital trade routes north of the Caspian –

saw fit to convert en masse to Judaism in 750 CE. It was largely Jewish commercial activity that invigorated the bazaars of Bukhara and Samarkand under Mongol and Timurid rule in the thirteenth and fourteenth centuries. Persians talked of being 'as wide awake as a broker of Bukhara'.

The Bukharan oasis, a natural stop on the long silk routes, would become a hub not only of commercial, but also intellectual activity. With long-distance caravans came pilgrims and Islamic scholars. Bukhara's library rivalled the 'house of wisdom' in Baghdad and it was here that Abu Ali ibn Sina (980–1037) – otherwise known as Avicenna – composed his medical canon, used in Europe until the seventeenth century as a standard medical textbook.

With its estimated 360 mosques and 80 madrasahs, and 30,000 students wrestling with jurisprudence, theology, logic, music and poetry, Bukhara was at the forefront of medieval Islamic thought. Here Al-Bukhari (810–870) composed the Hadith or 'Sayings of the Prophet' – second in holiness to the Koran – and Bukhara became an important centre for Sufi mystics seeking transcendence through the repetition of the holy verses.

Contrasted with the religious fanaticism of later rulers, or the vicious atheism of Stalin, medieval Bukhara was remarkably tolerant of faiths outside Islam. Muslim rulers of eleventh-century Central Asia famously said, 'Keep agreements with *dhimmi* [non-Muslims of the Koran] and let Jews live peacefully.'

Kublai Khan, the first Mongol ruler of China, was also relaxed in matters of faith. In most cities of his empire people of all faiths mingled generally peacefully: Jews, Christians, Manicheans and Hindus. The Mongol Khan struggled to embrace even one religion, for fear of neglecting the gods of all the others. Marco Polo, who visited his Beijing court in 1275, quotes a disarmingly agnostic Kublai Khan in his *Travels*:

> There are four great prophets who are reverenced and worshipped by the different classes of mankind. The Christians regard Jesus Christ as their divinity, the Saracens

> – Muhammad, the Jews – Moses, and the idolaters – Sogomumbar-Khan, as the most pre-eminent amongst their idols. I do honour and show respect to all four, and invoke to my aid whichever amongst them is in truth supreme in heaven.

From the sixteenth to the nineteenth centuries, the fortunes of the Jewish communities started their slow but definite decline. With Europe's discovery of a sea route to India and China – causing the Eurasian land routes to dry up in the late fifteenth century – inner Asia found itself cut off from the brisk trade that had made it so cosmopolitan.

Between 1500 and 1510, Turkic-speaking Uzbek nomad warriors from Siberia captured the gleaming Timurid cities of Samarkand and Bukhara, and after less than a century were overturned by a series of successor dynasties. By 1600, Central Asia had plunged into deep obscurity. It became a xenophobic nowhereland, each ruler more ignorant than the last. By the early nineteenth century, the outline of the Timurid Empire had crumbled, replaced by three rump emirates centred on the cities of Kokand, Khiva and Bukhara, their courts dominated by intrigue and internecine strife.

In Bukhara, the Jewish community found itself subjected to a litany of daily humiliations. Forever under the watchful eye of the emir's spies, Jews were forbidden from riding horses or owning lands. They suffered unofficial pogroms from Muslim fanatics or forced conversions, and were forever plundered for the emir's private coffers.

Today the Jewish community feels no better for Uzbek independence. Dogged by poverty, jaded by the corruption of the elite, and fearful of a resurgent nationalism whose catchphrase is 'Uzbekistan for the Uzbeks', most have sought a life elsewhere. The time seemed to be up for this 2,500-year-old community.

I'd parted from Bohodir now, and I was going it alone for a while. After an interminable ride across the Kyzyl Kum desert,

I finally caught my first glimpse of a minaret from the taxi and wound down the window to feel the city on my skin. A glint of majolica, a fluted Timurid cupola, a flash of *naskhi* calligraphy. I was in Central Asia's cultural heart, a relic with every glance, a sequestered *iwan* or precariously leaning minaret. Of all the fabled Silk Road cities that have surrendered to desert or bulldozer – Balkh, Merv, Samarkand or Kokand – Bukhara still evokes the swooning metropolis it once was.

It felt good to speak Persian again. The Persian here was in fact Tajik, a local variant, which was hard to understand and I felt that my driver, nonplussed by my Iranian sing-song accent, was grateful to get rid of me. He dropped me by the *Lab-i Hāuz*, a calm pool in the shade of mulberry trees, surrounded by three sun-buffed madrasahs. Here carpet sellers flogged their wares, old men played draughts and reclined on lazy tea beds.

I'd specifically sought out the Nodirbek, a hotel in the heart of the Jewish Quarter, still Bukhara's most historic residential area. It was a handsome townhouse, uneven with adobe and battened by a sturdy iron-bossed door. It oozed romance. But as I hauled my pack inside, I noticed with horror that the young Uzbek owner, Otabek, was ripping the door apart. The interior was apparently not historic enough for tourists, he explained, and he was thoughtfully replacing it with something 'even more authentic'. My heart bled, but Otabek grinned with pride. Did I like his work? How did I hear about it? Did it look nice and old-fashioned and Jewish?

Ushered into the courtyard, Otabek showed me the cruel facelift that was underway. Original Mangit-era cornices were being hacked off, tilework ripped apart and all was disappearing under faux-Jewish regalia in a heartbreaking attempt at 'authenticity'.

'I'm going to called it Thousand and One Nights,' he said, which didn't sound very Jewish to me. 'What do you think?' His young wife placed a tray of bread and yoghurt before me.

'It could work,' I said. He beamed with delight.

'My plan is this,' he said, 'disco, air-conditioning, everything, but still traditional, to give it that *traditional* feeling.'

A white-haired westerner to my left, who'd been scribbling in his diary, raised an eyebrow. Otabek, who had noticed something on the scaffolding, rushed off to marshal his workers.

'You know,' said the traveller, who's name was Willy, 'he told me he plans to put a huge Star of David in the entrance hall, to attract tourists. I told him you don't just put a Star of David on the floor to be trampled on, but this guy . . .' He rotated his pencil next to his temple. Willy was already checking out as he spoke.

'Watch out for the sparks at the breakfast table,' he warned, buckling his bag.

I spent the day getting lost in Bukhara's backstreets, gawping at the tilework of the Nadir Divanbegi and Mir-i Arab madrasahs. I was trying to make some sense of the *girihs*, the complex vegetal knots that wheeled over their cupolas and façades, but I had a feeling one wasn't supposed to. They were designed simply to instill wonder. You watch, you marvel, you contemplate the divine. Here in the UNESCO-protected centre, majolica gleamed, cupolas shone, mosque porches were swept clean.

But in the nexus of alleys off the main drag, where tourists rarely ventured, there was serious neglect. I stumbled across a small mausoleum dedicated to an Uzbek grandee called Turki Jangi, and his scores of grandsons (his relatives were said to be stacked 30 metres deep). It was a modest and well-proportioned monument, but the plaster was cracked and flossy with cobwebs, and I wondered what exactly the curator, who sat swilling vodka with three compadres, was up to.

'No money from the state,' he burbled, shuffling between the tombs, his breath viscous with drink. 'So much better under the Soviets. We had money then. Do you know how much the som was worth in those days?' He was swaying now.

I didn't.

'Equal to the rouble!' he cried, and his cronies muttered agreement. 'You understand?'

I nodded.

He held his forefingers side by side to indicate parity.

I nodded again.

Still unsatisfied, he took out his house-key and proceeded to scratch numerals on the inside of the mausoleum wall. I placed my hand on his key, and he shot me a look of offence.

Despite this curator's singular approach to preservation, he was right about the economy. Bukhara had hit hard times. The post-Soviet collapse had knocked the country off kilter. After 70 years of Soviet intimidation, the modern Uzbek state is still just as authoritarian as it ever was, only now the orders come from President Karimov instead of Moscow. There was barely a person I'd spoken to in Uzbekistan who was optimistic about the future. It seemed that anyone who could leave, did leave.

The *mahalla-i yehūdi* – the Jewish Quarter – was built 400 years ago to separate Jews from Muslims, and it's a glorious labyrinth of narrow passages of adobe and timber houses that lead into maddening knots. There was no sense of planning. It seemed designed to beguile and frustrate the visitor, however charmingly. One time the Jewish community numbered several thousand, dressed in *joma* robes and gold embroidered caps. They were steeped in the cloth and dyeing trade, making scarves, robes, bed cushions and flower-printed silks. They were peddlers, shoemakers and pharmacists, crushing and preserving plant extracts to ward off the myriad ailments the city was famous for. Now there was barely a soul to be seen.

It was very hot that day and almost everyone was inside. Only the street children sallied forth to harry the tourists, and an old woman with black eyes sat in her doorframe, her muttony forearms resting in her lap. I tried to strike up a conversation, but she stopped me with a turn of her head.

Bukhara, despite the showy majolica and soaring minarets of the guide books, is an intensely private place. The winding streets seemed to taunt the visitor with their exquisite locked doors: great wooden slabs, etched with stars, zigzags and polygons. And in the middle were thick iron bosses, pierced with rings the size of pram wheels. Where did they lead, what chambers did they conceal?

I found the synagogue at last, one of only two in the *mahalla*.

In previous centuries rabbis could only patch up their places of worship, forbidden to build any more. I rapped on the door of the one nearest my hotel. After a few moments an elderly man creaked it open an inch, just wide enough for me to see his grey eyebrows bristling with irritation.

'What do you want?' he barked.

'Hello, I'm from England and . . .'

'Go away. I have no time.' He slammed the door and I heard his footsteps clack away across the inner courtyard.

I resolved to return later in the day. But I grew increasingly concerned. With Karakalpaks you only had to approach them and they'd speak, but Bukhariots were clearly more suspicious.

After street upon street of battened entrances, I found myself drawn towards a door that was slightly ajar, affording me a glimpse of a sumptuous interior. A woman was watering her pot plants out in front. Her name was Esmigul and she had a kindly face, lined beyond her middle-aged years. I helped her water some of the higher flowers, wondering if I'd ever get to look beyond that tantalisingly half-open door. Minutes later, with a sunny, gold-toothed smile, she invited me in for a cup of tea.

She went off to the kitchen, leaving me to marvel at this living museum. It was prime Bukharan bourgeois, a traditional nineteenth-century townhouse, probably owned by rich merchants at one time. The dining room was a showpiece of bright stencilling and stalactite plasterwork, painted Stars of David and cartouches of Hebrew characters. At the far end of the courtyard was a dais with a carved wooden column that tapered up to a delicate cornice. The walls were studded with tiny niches that had once held ceramic trinkets, and tall, recessed arches decorated with polygon patterns in blue and cream.

'I know what you mean.' I turned round. 'Excessive, isn't it?' she said, clattering a tray of black tea on the courtyard table. 'We moved here from Tashkent for work. My husband – he's a manager – wanted a nice big house, so we found this. An old Jewish couple was moving to America. I told my husband I don't like it. It's just so . . .'

'Detailed?' I suggested.

'Jewish,' she said, with the ghost of a sneer.

'I see,' I said, taken aback. 'You're not Jewish yourself?'

'Me?' She was aghast. 'I'm Uzbek. Can't you tell?'

'I'm only a visitor,' I said, quietly.

Then her laughing, gold-toothed smile disappeared.

'I don't like Jews,' she said, 'They're cunning. They say a nice thing, but they always mean something else.' The warmth left her face. 'I don't mind Russians, but Jews . . . !'

I said nothing.

'You play chess?' Esmigul asked, casually.

I told her I didn't.

'My niece plays chess.'

Where this was leading, I couldn't tell, but she handed me an article from a Russian-language newspaper. It depicted a girl in a black and white photo staring at a chessboard in a tournament in, of all places, Sheffield. Her entire family were chess champions.

When our tea turned cold, and Esmigul realised I wasn't going to play chess, it was time for me to continue my search in the *mahalla*.

'Are you sure you don't want to play?' she asked again at the door, with a hint of desperation. I smiled my thanks and left her to await her husband's return.

The sky was black and the emir's palace, the Ark, looked awesome and terrible against the stars. Outside my restaurant, where ten-year-old waiters hurried around barefoot, nothing much moved. A stray dog limped over the cobblestones and a few valueless banknotes rustled in the hands of a cigarette-seller. I'd wandered far from the *mahalla*, but Esmigul had stayed in my head all day. I should not have been surprised by her anti-Semitic comments, as prejudice is still widespread in the former Soviet Union, but I was still a bit stunned.

The Russians were partly to blame. Russian governors, who could have done much to diffuse anti-Semitism in the nineteenth century, had exacerbated the problem. But not at first. Central Asian Jews looked to the first Russian conquerors that took the Bukharan Emirate in 1868 as a welcome relief from years of the emirs' oppression. But the Soviets, the inheritors of tsarist Turkestan, would become the Jewish community's worst nightmare.

The early years of Bolshevism began well. For the first time ever Jewish life was encouraged by the state as part of Soviet policy for nationalities. Judaeo-Tajik was taught in schools and printed in newspapers and there was even a Jewish arm of the Communist Party, *Yevsektsia*.

But in 1924 Stalin, as Commissar for Nationalities, hit Soviet Jews hard, putting them to work as machine operators in factories and emptying their houses of valuables. Armed guards raided property for anything that could be turned into hard cash, and when they began to flee to Afghanistan and Persia Stalin sealed the borders. His grip was so tight that by the outbreak of the Second World War almost the entire cultural and religious Jewish elite was dead or toiling in prison camps.

Even after the war anti-Semitism was in no way discouraged. The state press would print Nazi-style Jewish satires, casting Jews as obscurantists and diversionists that sucked blood and kidnapped children. But if anyone thought anti-Semitism would fade away with the end of Communism, it would be a false hope. What surprised me was not so much what Esmigul said, but how casually she said it, as if I would simply nod in agreement.

On my way back to the hotel I felt a violent jolt in my belly, as if an incubating beast had awoken. It couldn't have been the shashlik – I knew things didn't happen that quickly. It must have been that perfectly harmless (although in retrospect evil-smelling) *laghman* soup I'd eaten in a desert kitchen on my way across the Kyzyl Kum Desert. I had to get back to my hotel – fast! I slapped down some money and set off on a brisk walk. I knew the route, no cause for alarm. Past the Kalon minaret, left a bit, right a bit, past the *lāb-i hāuz* and up the alley. But once I'd passed the Ark I was lost. I asked directions in a hoarse whisper: '*Mahalla*.' They didn't understand and I repeated it more urgently: '*Mahalla-i yehudeeee*.' They pointed – I ran. Wide-legged, I staggered up to the hotel entrance. I pounded my fist on the door. The neighbours' lights came on. Otabek's wife opened the door. I pushed past her and thumped up the stairs, rattling my key in the lock.

A rush of endorphins. My eyes glazed in a sweet, psychedelic haze as every drop of moisture was expelled from my body in that God-be-praised lavatory. Never had I been so grateful for Uzbek sanitary facilities.

I spent the day feeling very weak, lying on my bed never far from the bathroom. I forced myself to read trashy novels I'd picked up from other travellers. But all the time, half-delirious with illness, my mind returned again and again to my purpose for being here. I knew no one and there was no reason why anyone should talk to me. I began to devise all sorts of crazed plans for gaining access to the Jewish community. I'd be a visiting Israeli dignitary, a Daoodi dervish (if they ever existed), a descendant of King David.

Then I began to wonder if it would be so terrible to tell them I was a Jew. It was a lie, certainly. But was it morally dubious? I have several Jewish friends, some of whom take their ancestry seriously, others of whom have only the vaguest knowledge. Would it be so terrible to pretend to be one of the latter? In any case my mother's ancestors, who were from southern Italy, must have absorbed many peoples into the family. Every Mediterranean in history seems to have settled southern Italy: Greeks, Romans, Arabs, Normans, Phoenicians. I saw no reason to deny a stake to one of the most significant peoples in the Mediterranean and the Near East.

So by the end of the next day, as I emerged from my stuffy bedroom, I tried a new tack. From now on I was Jewish, of Italian-English descent, whose origins lay in the misty Bukharan past. All records being lost, I was back to find out more about my heritage. Feeling weak but stable, I stepped forth into the dusk.

It was Friday evening, and tonight was the service that marked the beginning of the Sabbath. I donned my mental disguise with the thrill of impending deception. Who could possibly know what I was up to? But as I walked the narrow street I began to feel an unnerving heat, as if I were being watched. Sure enough it was that same old woman, sitting as ever in her doorway. For a horrifying few seconds our gazes met, and she seemed to be reading the very clouds of my conscience. My newly found poise began to totter.

But the door to the synagogue was open. I grabbed the rags of my identity before it was too late and joined a line of tattily dressed old men shuffling in. Without a murmur or hesitation I reached for a yarmulke and followed them into the main chamber.

The synagogue was a simple structure, a courtyard and main worshipping room of pine furniture and white carved plaster-work. A single column supported the ceiling, not unlike the house of Esmigul, and there was a U-shaped table covered in red velvet. It had the unpretentious atmosphere of an after-school club.

I poured a cup of green tea, occasioning only the slightest flicker of an eyelid, a quickly averted gaze, a stifled whisper. I sat down. This congregation – a handful of balding men in late middle age and a single, mop-haired teenager with an Iron Maiden T-shirt – pretended not to see me. Just ten men were murmuring quietly as they waited for the rabbi. Was this all the synagogue could muster? Apart from the bushy eyebrowed janitor watching me from under the shadow of his panama hat, no one took any notice.

Finally the rabbi, a stately figure in black with a privet-hedge beard entered in a hurry and mounted the *bimah* like a professor late for a lecture. Not familiar with Hebrew or Aramaic, and with only the barest grasp of the Jewish liturgy, I was lost. But I stood when they stood, sat when they sat. I mumbled with them, kissed the Torah scrolls as they came by and rose periodically to shout *'Ne, ne'* in a spirited manner. Then, as the rest of the congregation coughed and mumbled and poured each other tea, I listened, uncomprehending, to the rabbi's rich, undulating Hebrew.

Until the sixteenth century Persian-speaking Jews had formed a single community from Turkey's western border right up to the Hindu Kush. Then, when the newly Shiite Safavid Persian monarchy severed Persia from Sunni Central Asia, Central Asian Jews (whose numbers were boosted by Persian Jews fleeing the Safavids) were deprived of contact with their western brethren and steadily declined. Weakened by years of oppression and forced conversions, Judaism reached its lowest point to date. By the early nineteenth century, Jews had no rabbis to lead them and, following the Muslim custom, they became polygamous. The *kashrut* or dietary laws were rarely observed, few prayed regularly and fewer could remember the Hebrew of their forefathers.

Many Jewish Bukhariots, unwilling to convert fully to Islam, took a third path and became *chala* (literally, 'incomplete'): they converted to Islam outwardly, but in the silence of night would pray and carry out Jewish rites in secret. They were a despised group and watched continuously by Jews and Muslims alike. It was a dangerous route and, if caught, whole families could be hanged or thrown from the 50-metre-high Kalon minaret.

Periodic oppression has always plagued Jewish communities in Asia, even in the generally tolerant ancient times, but the last few centuries have been especially grim. Forbidden to dwell outside the *mahalla*, which was built to be a ghetto, Jews were under constant curfew. They were forced to wear an identity patch, a black cap and a girdle of rope in place of a belt, and the *jezyah* – a tax paid by *dhimmis* – was always delivered to the tax-collector in return for a ritual slap on both cheeks. These petty, day-to-day restrictions could have been bearable had it not been for periodic outbursts of Muslim fanaticism and forced conversions that dogged Jewish life in the eighteenth and nineteenth centuries.

It was in this atmosphere of decay that a certain Moroccan rabbi arrived at the gates of the city. Rabbi Joseph ben Moses Mamon Maghrebi had travelled from Tetouan in North Africa in 1793 to raise funds for Jews in Palestine, but he was so horrified by the state of the Bukharan community that he resolved to stay and educate them. From his arrival until his death in 1823 Maghrebi revived every aspect of Jewish life. He outlawed the celebration of the ancient Persian festival of Nouruz, a vestige of Zoroastrianism, which is still a public holiday in the Islamic Republic of Iran and widely popular in Central Asia today. He established a yeshiva, or religious academy to train rabbis and *shohatim* (ritual slaughterers). He introduced the study of cabbalistic texts of mystical Judaism, in particular the Zohar, and brought many of his people to Jerusalem. Most radically he introduced the Sephardic rite, followed by the Jews of North Africa and much of the Middle East. Today the Bukharan rite is a strange and unique combination: Iranian in basis with a heavy Sephardic overlay. Scholars still argue about whether Bukharan Judaism should really be classed as Sephardic.

I wondered if these ten men were the last living repositories of more than two millennia of Jewish continuity. When the service ended, I prepared myself to approach the rabbi. I wanted to introduce myself, talk to him, request an interview. But he exited from the synagogue as breathlessly as he had arrived. The men filed out quickly. The boy with the mop of hair left sharply with his father, the bushy eyebrowed janitor, and within moments the room had emptied, everyone eager to continue the Sabbath over dinner. I kicked myself for failing to talk to a single one of them.

'I am Yosef,' said a hangdog face to my right. I turned round. It was the man who had been sitting next to me.

'Welcome to Bukhara,' he added in a slow nasal drawl that reminded me of my old Russian teacher. 'You are not from here, I think.'

'No, I'm from England. My ancestors were from here.' He examined me for a few moments, looking for Jewish traces in my English features, which he evidently didn't find.

'Welcome,' he said again, getting up to go.

I regretted lying now, and I guessed I would spend the evening by the *Lab-i Hāuz* working out what to do next.

'Where are you eating tonight?' he asked, from the door.

'I don't know.'

'Your family?' He looked concerned.

'Not any more.'

'Will you come with us to have Sabbath dinner?'

I felt thoroughly unworthy to be invited to a complete stranger's for Sabbath dinner, but I was touched by his offer. I was also intrigued.

'Thank you,' I said.

I walked with Yosef deep into the *mahalla*, threading this way and that through the dark passages. The pale moonshine flickered between the houses and danced on the ordure that trickled down the unpaved alleys. It felt like the eighteenth century again, a city under curfew, with barely a soul to be seen. Yosef's house was not far, but I could never have found it alone. Passing door after door, battened against outsiders, we finally arrived at his own. It was a wonderfully riveted oak slab, as thick as ship's salvage, etched with interlocking stars and an iron hoop that hung like a torturer's tool from its boss. The door swung heavily on its hinges, creaking open to reveal a different world inside.

Feeling the same exhilaration that I had experienced on entering Esmigul's house, I was all of a sudden in an enchanting courtyard, shaded by an almond tree, illuminated by lanterns. The balmy night air was already thick with street smells, drains, mud and humanity, but there was a keener edge within, a strong strain of shoe-polish and leather. Next to the kitchen, where Zinna, his wife, bustled, was a workshop stacked with shoes, anvils and dirty smocks. Yosef was a shoemaker and Zinna a hairdresser – the two quintessentially Jewish professions in Bukhara.

'Come in, come in,' she flapped from inside the kitchen. I sat at the courtyard table, which gradually filled with dishes: cabbage salad, stuffed vine leaves, chicken and a bottle of sweet Armenian wine. She lit a Sabbath candle. Yosef sat at the head of the table. Zinna settled her ample frame in her chair, their small son Ari on her knee, and wriggled herself into position. Yosef was now all gravitas. Yarmulke on head, hands clasped, he muttered the kiddush and broke the plaited challah bread.

'Did you follow the prayer?' he asked me, eyes hooded. I confessed I didn't.

'You don't say the kiddush in your country?'

'Yes we do, but . . . we are lapsed.'

'Why lapsed?'

And then I told him of my long-forgotten Bukharan roots, more out of a need to say something than any real necessity. My story had by now become somewhat convoluted. It was like this: In the fifteenth century a Neapolitan woman had married a Jewish merchant from Salonika, who traded silk with Persia. The family settled in Esfahan, but after the coming of the Safavids they fled to Bukhara, where they lived until the end of the eighteenth century. Then, oppressed by conditions under the emirs, they made their way back to England. Via Holland. This was my story. Would he buy it?

'You seem to know a lot about your family history,' he said, half-smiling again.

I began to feel a bit stupid.

But Yosef warmed up. He told me he spent much of the week in the synagogue studying the Talmud, and the rest of the week fixing shoes, from which he made a pitiful $15 a month, completely at odds with our sumptuous dinner. I asked him how he managed it.

'*Ekonomia*,' he said, cryptically.

To Yosef's dislike, Zinna had just taken up work as a hairdresser in the new town.

'He doesn't want me to work,' she said. 'He says I should stay at home with Ari.'

They started to gabble in Judaeo-Tajik, of which I understood nothing. He put down his bread to gesticulate and she bounced Ari too quickly on her knee until the boy started to cry.

But what they both agreed on was that they were there to stay, and neither was going to be lured abroad by better prospects.

'You could get a visa without too much trouble,' I said.

They shook their heads.

'Certainly we could go like the rest, Tel Aviv, New York,' said Yosef, 'but this is our home. There's almost no one left now.

We will not leave like so many others – like your ancestors.' He pinched me on the shoulder. Did he suspect?

'My mother went to Israel once,' said Zinna. 'Said men and women live together before marriage.' Her eyes were wide. 'Not only that, but all the women work, they leave their children in kindergartens!' She rocked Ari slowly now, but he was inconsolable.

I asked Yosef about the community, whether he thought it would survive. He didn't answer me immediately, but reverted to the expression he assumed when he broke the challah, one of gravitas and reflection.

'You were in the synagogue today. You saw how we worship. My friend, we are alive.'

'But how many of the community are left?'

'Come,' he said, wiping his hands on a napkin. He disappeared into the house and came back with a little plastic bag. 'Open it. Tell your family we are still here and they can come back some day to join us again.' It dawned on me, with a mixture of surprise and dismay, that he did buy my story.

Inside was a tightly wrapped *joma*, a robe of red velvet, embroidered with intricate patterns of gold thread, elegant stitches, sequins and Stars of David. It was magnificent, a ceremonial robe worn at special occasions. They made me parade in front of a camera as Yosef clapped and Zinna cooed. I'd never felt such a fraud.

I walked with Yosef back to the Nodir Bek, clutching my undeserved present, and we arranged to meet next day at the synagogue.

One of the strangest characters to come to Bukhara and survive was a Victorian missionary called Reverend Joseph Wolff. Travelling with a suitcase full of bibles and a shovel-hat, he called himself the Grand Dervish of England, Scotland, Ireland and the whole of Europe and America, and his mission was to convert everyone he met in the deeply conservative Islamic societies he visited, to Christianity. By turns he was enslaved, tied to the tail of a horse, flung into a dungeon, bastinadoed and, so he claimed, forced to walk 600 miles across Afghanistan naked. But Wolff was nothing if not dogged.

Born a rabbi's son in 1795 in Weilersbach, Bavaria, Wolff converted to Christianity in 1812, but he was expelled from the Colleggio di Propaganda, the Catholic Missionary Training School in Rome, when he questioned the doctrine of papal infallibility – an early sign of his contrary nature. He went to London to join the Anglican Church and study theology and oriental languages at Cambridge. It was in England that he managed to attract the attention of Lady Georgiana Walpole, sixth daughter of Horatio Walpole, Earl of Orford, whom he married in 1827. The union was as canny as it was unlikely. She funded three more of his daredevil missions to the east, which kept him travelling until the end of her life.

In 1828 Wolff set out with his wife and child on an expedition to locate the Ten Lost Tribes of Israel (with a mission to convert them to Christianity). It was a tall order, and he failed. But his journeys were never without adventure. He'd barely crossed the Mediterranean before his ship was fired on by the Turks at Navarino and he was forced to seek land. In Jerusalem he managed to offend everyone. He alienated Jews by heralding 1847 as the end of the world, and angered Muslims by distributing a printed manifesto calling on the 'Mahometan grandees to repent and return to Christ'. After spending close to a year recovering from poisoned coffee (a foiled assassination attempt), Wolff was asked politely by the British consul to leave.

At Alexandria his wife and child returned home. But Wolff, ever eager, managed to find a Greek scholar in Malta to lend him some money to go on to Bukhara, Afghanistan and India. At Tehran the British mission begged him to turn back. Two adventurers, William Moorcroft and George Trebeck, had recently disappeared and the mission's hopes for Wolff's survival were not high.

But Wolff was undaunted. He was guided across eastern Persia by an Afghan, whom Wolff discovered was suffering from leprosy and therefore was forced to sack. Later, he was himself enslaved by bandits in Khorassan and valued (he says) at two pounds, eight shillings. Wolff managed to escape with the help of an invitation letter from a local potentate, but at Torbat-e Heydariyeh, only a little way further, his gospel-preaching ways got him imprisoned again. The local ruler, Muhammad Ishak (who had killed his own father, mother, brother, sister and son-in-law, and had sold 60,000 slaves to Bukhara's slave market) only spared his prisoner because a letter had arrived from the governor of Khorassan demanding the missionary's release. Once more, Wolff managed to escape with his life. He then travelled by caravan via Mashhad to Bukhara.

Wolff's notes about the Bukharan Jewish community are one of the chief sources for historians, particularly his estimates of population numbers and descriptions of the *chalas*. His observations also paint a vivid picture of Bukhara in the 1830s, a little known chapter of Jewish life. Wolff writes that before Maghrebi's arrival this people had 'forgotten their laws, rites and customs', and that they 'ate the meat of the Muslims' and were no longer able to distinguish the 'clean from the unclean'. Despite his erudition, however, Wolff's notes must be taken with a pinch of salt. He claimed to have converted 20 Jews to Christianity (including the chief rabbi), and he concluded that the Jews of Khorassan, Bukhara, Samarkand and Balkh, as well as the Muslim Turkic population, were all remnants of the Ten Lost Tribes of Israel. However, the truly fantastic part of his travels was his survival, and that he managed to leave this poisonous city three months later completely unharmed.

Bukhara in the 1830s was dangerous and unsanitary. The city's pools and marshes had attracted numerous waterborne diseases, and Bukhara was legendary for its resident parasite: the Guinea worm. 'Every fifth person suffers from it,' wrote Lord Curzon coolly, having examined the nematode himself. 'One man had 120 in his body. When extracted it is sometimes almost a metre long, with the consistency of vermicelli. Each one contains half a million to a million embryo worms. One of the commonest causes of reproduction is the shocking carelessness of the barbers, who are the professional extractors of the worm, and who throw down the living parasite, which crawls away and multiplies in pools or puddles.'

Bukhara was also depraved. The Mangit Dynasty, which had seized power in 1754, was cruel and decadent. Forever at war with their neighbours, the emirs taxed the population to destitution and were renowned for their xenophobia. Gone were the days of the Silk Road, when merchants, goods and ideas passed through the markets of Bukhara. Now ignorance and fanaticism ruled, and slaves were the most valuable commodity.

Alongside Khiva, Bukhara was the busiest slave emporium in Central Asia, regularly restocked by Turkmen nomads that seized caravans and fishermen wherever they strayed from safety. Young Persian women fetched the best price, followed by Russian males, then Persians and Kurds. Jews, however, were not kidnapped at all. They simply didn't sell at market, which was perhaps the sole advantage of being born Jewish in this period. Now the emir saw unmanacled foreigners as thoroughly suspect, particularly Christians of Jewish birth like Wolff – whose heritage was to the emir an absolute novelty.

Emir Nasrullah Khan was the most hated man in Central Asia, having seized power in 1826 by beheading three brothers and 28 relatives. One of his favourite pastimes was watching prisoners being hurled from the Kalon minaret or the public beheadings in the Registan from his viewing spot on the royal Ark.

The Ark is an impregnable structure on a base of ashlar blocks, lined with a row of battlements. As a natural vantage point it had been occupied by Bukhara's rulers since before Islam. Today it is only inhabited by the odd tour guide and souvenir seller, but it still exerts an eerie power.

Below the Ark was an infamous pit, 22 feet deep and infested with every kind of vermin, including purpose-bred reptiles and huge sheep ticks. It was the private dungeon of the emir himself, and there he had consigned one Briton, Lieutenant-Colonel Charles Stoddart, who had the misfortune to be its long-term resident from Christmas 1838.

Stoddart had been sent that year by the British East India

Company to Central Asia to find out what the Russians were planning. The Russian advance at that moment seemed unstoppable. First they had taken the Caucasus and the lands beyond the Caspian Sea. Then, unsatisfied with the whole of Siberia, the Tsar's armies were inching south to the lands of Central Asia with an eye on British India. Stoddart's mission was to persuade the Emir of Bukhara that Britain had no military intentions towards him, and to forge some kind of anti-Russian alliance.

Unfortunately, Stoddart was no diplomat. From his arrival on 17 December 1838 his every step was jinxed. Parading in full regimental gear in front of the emir, he failed to dismount – a grave error of protocol. He might have got away with it had he not struck down the court usher who was encouraging him to perform a symbolic act of submission. As he strode, unannounced, into the royal inner sanctum, the emir was stunned at the man's audacity and had him flung into the dungeon below the Ark. There Stoddart remained for two and a half years alongside a pair of thieves, a murderer and a thriving community of vermin.

Attempts were made by the khans of Khiva and Kokand to save him, but to no avail. In November 1841 another Briton named Captain Arthur Conolly arrived at Bukhara's gates. He was a more sophisticated diplomat than his predecessor but entertained wild ambitions. His plan was to unite the khanates of Khiva, Bukhara and Kokand under British protection and turn them into a buffer state against Russia. He also wanted to abolish slavery, convert all Bukharans to Christianity, open the market for British goods and – while he was at it – save Stoddart.

At first Conolly was received well and kept for months in congenial apartments at the emir's expense. But when Nasrullah Khan gained intelligence that the khan of Kokand was raising a force against him, he flung Conolly into the dungeon too.

The British government had warned both Stoddart and Conolly of the dangers of their missions. Having suffered a humiliating defeat in Afghanistan and newly embroiled in the Opium Wars in the Far East, Britain was not in a position to rescue the prisoners. The emir, piqued at his still-unacknowledged letter to Queen Victoria, decided they were a pair of spies, and in June 1842 brought the two men blinking into the sunlight.

Meanwhile, Reverend Wolff was chafing for another adventure. He set off for his last journey to Bukhara on 14 October 1843, specifically to hunt for news of Stoddart and Conolly. His succinctly titled travel account, *Narrative of a Mission to Bokhara, in the Years 1843–1845, to Ascertain the Fate of Colonel Stoddart and Captain Conolly* (1845) would gallop through seven editions, but Wolff was too late to see the men alive, let alone intervene.

Wolff packed for the trip as only he knew how. His luggage contained two dozen Hebrew bibles to distribute on the way, some silver watches as gifts for important hosts, and three dozen copies of *Robinson Crusoe* translated into Arabic. But Wolff was adamant that 'the Ameer [*sic*] shall not get one single thing,' he said, 'in case he was the cause of the death of Stoddart and Conolly.'

Wolff knew how lucky he was to still be alive. His previous trip had gone seriously awry when he had tried to pass himself off as a hajji, a Muslim who has been to Mecca as a pilgrim. Forced by Afghan bandits to say the Kalima, the Muslim statement of faith ('There is no God but Allah, Muhammad is Allah's Messenger'), Wolff dutifully repeated the first part, but replaced the last with 'and Jesus is his son', at which his enraged captors stole his clothes and sent him stark naked – so Wolff reports – all the way to Ghazni.

Wolff wouldn't make the same mistake twice. This time he was travelling as a 'Christian mullah'. Dressed in full canonicals: a doctor's scarlet hood, clerical gown and shovel-hat, his comedically dramatic appearance would be his unlikely protection.

It would be Wolff's second interview with the emir in 15 years, but he was no less determined to fine-tune his protocol. He genuflected and stroked his beard, and exclaimed repeatedly 'Peace to the King', until the emir, faced for a second time with this strange, prostrating clown, burst into uncontrollable laughter. Wolff's buffoonery helped him escape execution, and the emir sent him to comfortable apartments while he worked out what to do with him. 'Joseph Wolff,' said the emir, 'is neither like a Russian nor an Englishman, neither like a Jew nor a Christian, but like Joseph Wolff.' While under house arrest, Wolff searched for news of his compatriots. He found many conflicting accounts, but his memoirs present a picture – albeit heavily biased – of their fate.

As he describes it, Stoddart and Conolly were taken out of the pit up to the Registan. To the eerie sound of drums and reed pipes, they climbed the scaffold. The two men kissed each other. Conolly said, 'Tell the Ameer that I die a disbeliever in Muhammad, but a believer in Jesus – that I am a Christian, and a Christian I die.' Then he said to Stoddart, 'We shall see each other in paradise, near Jesus.' Conolly watched his companion go under the royal cleaver, before submitting his own neck.

Wolff's own description was characteristically overwritten: 'They were both of them cruelly slaughtered at Bokhara, after enduring agonies from confinement in prison of the most fearful character; masses of their flesh having been gnawn off their bones by vermin.'

With the luck that had sustained him for so long, Wolff's release arrived suddenly in the form of the Persian ambassador, who had come to bid for the missionary's freedom. Unwilling to offend the Shah of Persia, the emir decided it was time to free his European captive, arranging an extravagant 'send-off' that would exceed Wolff's wildest expectations.

The entourage that left the city's gates included a Bukharan ambassador, dispatched to explain the deaths of Stoddart and Conolly to Queen Victoria, four Persian slaves under Wolff's patronage, a thousand slaves who had just bought their freedom, an unspecified number of dervishes and fakirs, an astrologer, a portrait painter, a poet and ten sinister men attached by the emir's military advisor, Abdul Samut Khan, to murder Wolff along the way. It was well known that Abdul Samut Khan murdered everybody, and his emissaries were forever trying to detach Wolff from the main caravan.

But Wolff, who stayed close to the side of the Persian ambassador for the entire journey, had been forewarned of the precise time and place of the assassination plan, and again narrowly avoided death's clutches. With the Persian ambassador's help, the assassins were handed to the Persian governor at Mashhad for 'justice'. (As an aside, Abdul Samut Khan, who had put thousands to the sword, would eventually be cloven in twain by the khan himself for plotting against him.)

Wolff was free. He arrived with the P & O Line at Southampton in April 1845 and was reunited with his wife, Georgiana, who was now old and lonely. He wrote up his *Narrative* . . . and for a while his publishers, J. W. Parker, could hardly keep up with public demand. But Wolff's fame was shortlived. As the years passed, he disappeared from public view and died in obscurity in his Somerset vicarage on 2 May 1862, a peerless evangelist, a matchless raconteur and the luckiest missionary in history.

I walked to the synagogue that evening with Yosef beside me. I felt a kind of pride in his presence, a feeling of belonging. Nevertheless, my conscience remained irredeemably clouded, and I knew the charade couldn't last long.

Tonight was the *maariv*, the service that marks the end of the Sabbath. I reached for my yarmulke and performed the rituals more smoothly this time. One of the three scrolls was taken out and touched by all present, then the rabbi produced a sprig of basil. He pushed his beard aside and breathed it in with great concentration, eyes shut, body taut. He rubbed it over his eyebrows and let the aroma infuse his nostrils, then passed it round the small congregation.

Once again there were stifled mutters, low-voiced gossiping and the traces of an argument, but all of them – Ariel with the mop of hair, the shy rabbi, and the yellow-toothed, balding men – studiously avoided eye-contact with me. Only the bushy-browed janitor eyed me suspiciously. But never once did he inquire about my true identity.

As I walked with Yosef and Zinna to the new town, I asked them why the congregation seemed so extraordinarily shy. Was it lack of curiosity?

'No, it's not that.' Yosef dodged the question, as he often did. We walked through the *mahalla*'s streets until we reached the edge of modern Bukhara. After the warm, mudbrick atmosphere of the old town, the new centre was stark and forbidding, with its grandiose telecom towers and concrete blocks with more offices than the state could afford to light. Like so much Soviet architecture it was both extravagant and drab.

The Nilufar bar was a large concrete building shaped like a shooting star. Willowy Uzbek girls promenaded around, arm in arm. Leather-jacketed men sat in groups looking stolid and macho. A lace-clad singer strutted round the wide concrete paddock, cooing pop lyrics into her microphone like a Bosnian Eurovision diva.

We three – and a fourth called Shimon, a part-time DJ and ice-cream maker – sat down with skewers of lamb and great glass tankards of pale beer, unable to talk over the music. A small distance away I noticed an old man dancing – not exactly to the music, which was slow and sentimental – but to a jerky rhythm of his own. His chin was grizzled white, and his nose was swollen with drink. He was wearing a Soviet military jacket with service medals and was trying to serenade three young Uzbek girls, who tittered with embarrassment at his attentions. The man had to be at least 80 and his capering was unbearably – bewitchingly – undignified.

The old man came here every night, Zinna told me. He was a Russian war veteran, but had suffered brain damage when a wall collapsed on him a few years ago. Now every night he would wander among the tables, inviting young girls to dance. Undeterred by rejection, he would dance alone, and be mocked, and drink himself stupid.

Then I remembered that Yosef still hadn't answered my question.

'Tell me,' I said, 'why is it no one wants to talk to me here?'

He twirled the base of his tankard. 'You must understand,' he said, eventually, 'we are not used to outsiders, especially people asking us questions like you. In the time of Socialism, if someone asks questions it's because he wants to make trouble.'

I was silent. Yosef continued.

'Did you know that before Socialism there were 36 synagogues in Bukhara. During Soviet times there was only one, and it worked at night. So you see, even though we can worship freely now, we are still . . . suspicious of government, suspicious of outsiders.'

'But there's nothing to fear now?'

'You are right. Except . . . the synagogue has a security guard, because sometimes, you know, people come and . . .'

He flicked his neck with his middle finger – a Russian gesture that meant 'booze'.

'Daniel, *jon*,' said Zinna, grabbing my sleeve. 'Do you want to come to a funeral tomorrow?' She made it sound so appealing I didn't understand her first time. 'An old woman has just died, and we will bury her tomorrow. You will be with us. Will you come?'

'I would be honoured.'

Eighty-six-year-old Sarah had lived in Bukhara all her life. Soon after the break-up of the Soviet Union her daughters sold up and moved to Rehevoth, the district of Jerusalem settled by many of this community. This year their aged mother, bereft of her entire family, finally agreed to abandon the city of her birth and join her daughters. Her bags were packed, her documents were in order and her flight was booked. One of her daughters arrived from Israel to pick her up. But only a day later her mother had a fall on the stairs. Weakened by ill health, she died suddenly. According to Jewish law, she had to be buried within 24 hours. As she'd died on a Friday evening, at the beginning of the Sabbath, the funeral would be delayed until Sunday.

I woke on the appointed day with a hangover and a heavy conscience. Faced with the sobering reality of death, my deception had lost its savour. I dithered over whether to go or not to go. I'd been invited on the basis that I was an honorary member of the community, to offer support, to learn something of my 'roots'. I'd begun to like these people very much. I respected them.

But a Bukharan Jewish funeral? The whole community would be out in force and there were no Torahs to hide behind, no homes to slip to the moment the ceremony was over. I would be an impartial observer, invisible, and I'd come straight back to record it all in my diary. Once again, my curiosity outweighed my conscience.

The weather had turned, and the previously clear sky had broken into a restless swirl of clouds. It was colder too. I dressed warmly and slipped into the *mahalla*, making my way to the Jewish graveyard. I didn't even need to look at the old woman in the doorway. I bristled as I passed her heavy form. I sensed she was steeling herself to say something, but it was nothing more than the trembling of her elderly lips. I moved on quickly.

I joined the congregation at the start of the new town, where emirate met concrete, just as the ceremony was beginning. Ten men shuffled out of the home of the dead woman, an adobe house with a stout door. I spotted Yosef, and stood by his side just as a pair of covered feet emerged from the house, a bier, a body wrapped in a veil of patterned red cloth carried by six men.

Suddenly, the door flew open and a woman in black ran up to the bier. Her heels rang out like gunshots on the concrete. It was the old woman's daughter. She buried her face in her mother's side, causing the bearers to totter. Then she let out an unearthly shriek that rang high and sharp. It sliced through the air, then diminished to a whimper as she entwined her fingers in the seven shrouds of her dead mother. A relative from the house came forward to the bereaved woman and escorted her carefully back into the house. The stalwart bier-carriers showed no reaction. Our eyes were fixed on the mourning women. With dignity, they righted themselves, lowered their heads, and continued their march to the graveyard. The congregation broke into its customary low, almost inaudible muttering.

'She was all ready to go back,' explained Shimon, the ice-cream maker. 'It is God's will. He wanted her to be buried in Bukhara, where she belongs.'

The cemetery was one of the most melancholy places I've ever visited. The faces of the deceased were etched onto the headstones. The ancient graves, whose stones had long since flaked away, had been replaced with small concrete hemispheres. But recent burials were marked with smart stelae of polished marble: Abrahamovs, Hasidors, Moussaievs, doctors, traders, party members, mothers, twins – portraits of them in their better years scratched on the stone with short epitaphs, such as: *Your going has darkened our eyes* and *If only we had the power to bring you back.*

A plot was found. The rabbi made a signal to begin the digging. As the first shovellers began, the rest of the mourners stood on neighbouring stones. I watched quietly as Roma, a burly man I'd seen in the *mahalla*, took to the task. With his handlebar moustache he looked like a circus strongman, but his strength soon left him. He looked around to see if anyone would offer to take over, but no one did. He turned back to his digging, but when he'd reached about three feet he handed me the shovel. I looked to Yosef, who nodded, and I stepped hesitantly forward. There was a low murmur of expectation among all present.

I took doubtfully to the challenge, wedging my foot in the hole, levering the soft, sandy earth up at the feet of the congregation. There was no coffin and I could only imagine how many bodies had enriched the soft soil I was heaping at the headstone of Mrs Abramovich to my left, who had died in childbirth.

The rabbi started to gabble Hebrew prayers, faster than normal, speeding up to a climax, when all would shout in unison 'Amen'. I worked to these rhythmic responses, digging as if to a work song, anticipating the climactic coda until the prayers and my work were fused into a riff of their own. In this way I dug and dug, and sweated, and the air grew chill. I wondered what Sarah would be thinking. What would anyone think if I told them the truth?

When the grave was about five feet deep I climbed out and handed the shovel back to Roma, who patted me on the shoulder. The red covering was removed from the corpse and, wrapped in her seven white shrouds, the spindly old woman was lowered into the grave. Three concrete blocks were laid on top of her body, then covered with fine earth.

There was a strange levity among the congregation as we walked back. Yosef was up ahead with the rest, while I followed behind. I spread out my arms, feeling the wind dry my shirt, expecting any moment to be damned. Roma squeezed my shoulder.

'*Molodets*,' he said. 'Well done.'

We filed back to the house of Sarah's family, where we swelled the courtyard. A U-shaped table had been laid, crisp with white linen and loaded with a lunch of green tea and bread, boiled eggs and salt. Only four women were present, busy shelling eggs for the feast. The rabbi eluded me once more, slipping away at my every approach. But it was not a day for an interview. Anyway, a part of me couldn't face it.

He took his place at the head of the table, and began reading from the Torah and reciting the Kaddish. There were the usual vigorous amens, and then all descended into chatter.

A man next to me took my arm. I'd never seen him before. He introduced himself as Solomon from next door. He, too, was leaving Bukhara, along with everyone else.

'I went to Tashkent five times to get my papers, and I got them on the fifth time. The guy in the office was so fed up with my ugly face he told me not to worry, "You'll get your papers as long as you don't show up here again."' He chuckled, grabbing my arm roughly. 'But seriously' he lowered his voice, 'it's my son. He's young. He has his bar mitzvah next year and soon he will be married. But there's no choice here any more. They are all old, no young girls. In America he'll find a nice Jewish girl, settle down there. How long are you here for? You married? I have a daughter . . .'

I stepped for the last time into the alley to Yosef's house to say goodbye. The door was ajar and Yosef was sitting there with his legs around a kind of anvil, polishing a boot that he'd just stitched.

'Ah, friend,' he said, waving me in. '*Kak dyela*, how's it going?'

'Fine.'

'Was the funeral what you expected?' He brushed the boot with perfect, rhythmic strokes.

'More so,' I said. Yosef nodded without knowing what I meant. Perhaps I didn't either.

'Look, Yosef. I want to explain . . .'

He put down his boot and placed his polish on an elegant wooden rack.

'Thank you for everything,' I said, shying away from the admission I'd rehearsed.

He smiled widely. '*Nu*,' he said. 'Have a safe trip. Send me some photos.'

I offered my hand to shake, and he lifted his blackened palm with a grin. Perhaps it was just as well.

Away from the adobe walls of the *mahalla*, I was soon back in modern-day Uzbekistan: a dry, flat vista, dotted with white-washed farmsteads and apricot groves, telegraph wires and breeze blocks. I'd come to rely on the *mahalla*'s enveloping embrace, its shadowy, sun-absorbing mudbrick, the mystery of its alleyways and fabulously locked doors. Now I was in a taxi, following signs to high-rise Tashkent, enduring the blistering noonday sun and a molten plastic seat.

This community was not robust. The *mahalla*'s population was officially reckoned at 2,000. Even if this was an exaggeration, which it probably was, few that still lived here were of child-bearing age. I remembered Solomon's words at the funeral lunch: 'No one for my son to marry.' There was just no choice, no reason for parents to stay. What about Ari, Yosef's son? Who would he marry in fifteen or twenty years' time?

I imagined the *mahalla* would follow in the footsteps of its counterparts in Eastern Europe and the Iberian peninsula, whose historic ghettos have become living museum districts, emptied of their one-time residents, their elaborate courts enjoyed by new, rootless generations.

The day before my departure, I'd witnessed this relocation in slow motion, when I stumbled across an old Jewish merchant's house in Sarafon Street. They said it was being converted to a

UNESCO heritage site, a museum of 'former' Jewish life. Amid the overalls and banging, all the brilliant fittings of a traditional home were being refurbished, its balconies refitted, stalactite plasterwork reapplied. A frail woman stood at the doorway watching the destruction before her.

'I've lived in this house for sixty years,' she said, her eyes fixed on the builders, as if in shock. 'I was born here.'

'And now?'

'A tower block,' she said, 'in New York.' She wiped a spot of mud from the doorframe with her foot, and turned to go.

4

'The Night Air is Poison': The Germans of Kazakhstan

'Wir sind hier keine Russe und dort sind wir keine Deutsche.'
('We are neither Russians here nor Germans there.')
Russian German saying

Kazakhstan is big. It isn't just big, it is colossal. It could swallow all the other 'stans and still have room for more. Occupying an area two thirds the size of the United States, Kazakhstan's grasslands stretch from the Ural basin on Ukraine's borders all the way to China in the east, spanning almost the entire Eurasian landmass.

This vast country is many things, but its reputation in the West seems to hinge on one spoof TV journalist, the bête noire of every diplomat, PR department and self-respecting Kazakh.

Borat Sagdiyev, the cheeky invention of British comedian Sacha Baron Cohen, is the world's most infamous pseudo-Central Asian, having brought Kazakhstan unremitting humiliation with its fictional portrayal as a nation of bear-baiting, urine-swilling Gypsy-catchers. Borat is, in the words of the Kazakh Embassy in Washington, 'a one-man diplomatic wrecking ball'.

The Kazakh authorities tried to stop him, threatening legal action after watching Cohen's performance at an MTV Europe awards show. The comedian retaliated with a $250m-grossing mockumentary, *Borat: Cultural Learnings of America for Make Benefit Glorious Nation of Kazakhstan* (2006). They tried diplomacy, even inviting Borat 'home' to show him that not only could women travel on the *inside* of a bus, but could even drive. They soon realised that rational debate was futile.

Some see Borat as more of a composite 'ex-Soviet Man', created not to attack Kazakhstan specifically, but to show up Westerners' attitude to foreigners. Either way, Kazakhstan is truly on the map, and tourists (not just energy companies) really want to go there, albeit often for the wrong reasons.

For a country so large, with more than a hundred ethnic groups and climatic conditions, the nature of Kazakhstan is impossible to define precisely. To some it means interminable steppeland and tribesmen with falcons perched on their arms. To others it recalls sulphur hexafluoride gas explosions or gaudily painted wooden churches. To a great many it means terrible, wasted years in the gulag archipelago.

The Kazakhs are descendants of a predominantly Turkic people that have inhabited these expanses for hundreds of years. Yet they form only half the country's 15 million-strong population. The rest are a mixture of Russians, Poles, Ukrainians, Koreans, Finns, Chechens and Uighurs, to name a handful.

Few people have heard of the once large and prosperous German community of Kazakhstan. Even the German government was surprised to learn of its existence. They knew that their kinsmen were living somewhere in the Soviet Union, but had little grasp of the numbers, and were concerned by the 1.5 million that 'returned' to Germany after the Soviet collapse.

I say 'return' because to many of these returnees, Germany offered a quite different culture. They hadn't seen the *Mutterland* in 200 years and many Russian Germans were alienated and demoralised by what they saw. Their skills as *kolkhoz* managers or teachers were useless in a modern European country and they had to adapt radically to their new environs.

From the time of Ivan the Terrible in the sixteenth century, Germans had been in the service of the tsars as advisers, engineers and military commanders, but the first full-scale immigration campaign from Germany to Russia took place under Catherine the Great in the second half of the eighteenth century.

The *tsarina*, keen to develop her wild southern lands, invited settlers from the country of her birth. Herself a scion of Anhalt, south of Berlin, she knew Germans to be diligent, dedicated, and above all Christian, unlike the Muslim Tatars who harassed her southern marches.

The initial response to Catherine's 1763 invitation was immediate, almost frantic. Lured by the promise of a peaceful life, no taxes and permanent exemption from the draft (many were pacifist Mennonites), hundreds of thousands of Germans flocked by land and sea to Russia, armed with little more than wagons, ploughshares and wurst, all eager to escape the turmoil of the civil wars that wracked Germany's principalities at that time.

They settled mostly in Ukraine and the Volga region of south Russia, though some took to the Black Sea, the Caucasus and Crimea. There they prospered and kept to themselves in entirely German-speaking communities. They were self-sufficient and they generally worshipped in Protestant, rather than Orthodox churches.

But at the end of the nineteenth century their clannish communities were under threat. In the wake of the Russian Romantic movement, anti-German feeling became too widespread to ignore. Alexander II revoked Germans' exemption from the draft and what goodwill remained was soon diminished by the ruinous First World War.

Following the October Revolution, Germans found an unlikely supporter in Lenin, who favoured ethnic self-determination, and gave the Russian Germans their own Volga German Autonomous Republic. Whatever thaw these Russian Germans enjoyed was reversed again under Stalin, who liquidated their republic. He might even have initiated his own pogrom of Russian Germans, had the Nazis not appeared.

Stalin, who had never felt comfortable with having a German population on Soviet territory, was taken completely by surprise by Hitler's invasion of Russia on 22 June 1941. Nevertheless, Uncle Joe had taken his own precautions. In 1936, in preparation for his purges, Stalin had commissioned an inventory of every ethnic German living in his realms, almost as if a mass deportation was already being planned.

When the Red Army was finally mobilised, the Nazi forces had already overtaken 300,000 Soviet Germans between the Dniester and the Dnieper, and 'repatriated' them to Germany as newly discovered citizens of the Reich.

With breakneck speed Stalin ordered the deportation of all remaining 'free' Soviet Germans to Russia's eastern dominions, beyond the reach of Hitler or any other European power. Over a three-month period, 1.2 million Soviet Germans, predominantly in Ukraine and the Russian Volga region, were put into cattle trucks and sent to the bleak steppes of the east. It was the biggest deportation ever to have taken place on Soviet soil. More than a third would die from neglect, punishment and overwork. Amazingly, those that survived went on to underpin the Kazakhstani economy, excelling themselves as managers, farmers and professionals.

Today, a few hundred thousand Germans remain in the former Soviet Union. The overwhelming majority of them – approximately 300,000 – live in Kazakhstan, with others in Siberia, and smaller numbers in the other 'stans. Imprisoned for so long under Stalin and Krushchev, many survivors never left the environs of their former camps. As in the case of Central Asian Jews, the majority emigrated as soon as restrictions were eased in the Seventies and Eighties.

Emigration levels reached their height in the Nineties, but things have slowed down now. Few today speak German, fewer can prove their heritage to the German Embassy, and for the first time since independence, many young Kazakhstanis (as opposed to ethnic Kazakhs) see a good future in booming Kazakhstan.

Meanwhile, the elderly – the German speakers who recall the

long years of race hatred and discrimination – are on the cusp of extinction. That generation, scratching a living on meagre pensions, looks to Wiedergeburt, a German charity and cultural initiative that tries to support Russian Germans, and preserve what Germanness is left in this battered, broken community.

I arrived in Almaty, Kazakhstan's first city, with a hazy idea of where to find Russian Germans. But I had the advantage of some solid German institutions that were easy enough to locate: the Lutheran church, the Wiedergeburt offices, the German Embassy, and the use of a map of Kazakhstan that boggled my sense of scale.

Almaty is the perfect place to build a capital city. It basks in the shadow of the Alatau Mountains with its high meadows and bushy trees, and is vastly more charming than the actual capital, Astana, a characterless shamble of concrete and glass towering out of the northern Kazakh steppe.

The economic meltdown of the Nineties was over and accommodation in Almaty was no longer cheap. By dint of poverty and serendipity I found myself at the dormitory for international students at Almaty State University. I persuaded a woman who called herself the *kommandant* to take me in. She led me to a sinister-looking room called the ISOLATOR, spelt out in forbidding Cyrillic lettering. It was the sickroom. I laid out my mat and sleeping bag to avoid all contact with the bed.

For the few days I stayed I revelled in my surroundings, from the bichrome institutional paintwork to the scaldingly hot radiators. Even the seatless, urine-drenched loos grew on me, along with the perpetual gloom (the *kommandant* never seemed to turn the lights on). The one thing I never got used to was the smell of *gretchka* (buckwheat porridge) that seeped out from under her private kitchen, and even now makes me want to retch.

The poor, mostly Kashmiri, students for whom this dorm was a daily reality endured it all with inspirational good humour. I fell in with them quickly, sharing curries in their rooms and swapping stories about the evil *kommandant*. She was an exceedingly unfriendly woman, even by Soviet standards. She would stomp around in her too-loose sandals and bark when spoken to. Sometimes, out of spite, she'd lock the front door early so that students with social lives were barred from their beds for a night. She would ignore pleas to fix things such as overflowing loos and generally cast a pall over the already gloomy halls.

The one rule was that if you absolutely had to speak to her, then it must wait until the end of *Pole Chudes* ('The Field of Wonders'), the Mexican-inspired quiz show to which she and millions of Russian housewives were addicted. Interrupting this daily ritual was simply not a risk worth taking.

Before independence, Almaty was called Alma-Ata or 'city of apples'. The leaf-dappled city centre has a colonial wealth of neoclassical palazzos and pastel stucco. The most Russianised of Central Asia's cities, Almaty's churches and tram-track laid streets are decidedly Slavic. Founded in 1854 as a Cossack fort, Almaty was soon the vanguard of Russia's first Central Asian colony, from which control was steadily exerted over the indigenous Kazakh hordes.

During the tsarist period, the city was called Verney, receiving its more evocative Turkic name only after the Revolution. It was to the newly re-baptised Alma-Ata that Trotsky was first banished in 1927. His wife Natalia wrote of a city of mad dogs and leprosy, but she was charmed at least by the fruit. Famed for its wild orchards, which sprawled over the Tien Shan foothills, Alma-Ata was rumoured to be home to the world's largest species of apple.

Trees must be Almaty's most remarkable feature, not only for their fruit. It is probably the leafiest metropolis I've ever seen – choked, almost, with foliage. Heavy laden trees cluster along its boulevards, shedding their catkins and glowering over parked cars. More than once, as I strolled over the city's leaf-strewn avenues, the trees seemed to strangle out the sun.

Very little architecture has survived from before the Revolution, except for one spectacular example: Zenkov

Cathedral, a gaudy church in the middle of Panfilov Park, was apparently built entirely without nails, and it was one of the few buildings to survive the 1911 earthquake. It was to Panfilov Park that I headed that day, and in the cathedral that I would be transported to a timeless zone, as if the Soviet upheaval had never happened.

A phalanx of babushki guarded the cathedral entrance. Brushing past their outstretched hands, I encountered the smells and superstitions of a Russian country church. Here I was, only a few hundred kilometres from the Chinese border, but the building's interior was all reverence and incense, painted panel icons, and a wrought-iron chandelier suspended from an octagonal dome. Scores of aromatic candles sputtered. Scarved women genuflected at the altar, crossing and recrossing themselves while a pair of choristers sang in exquisite harmony.

I was jolted from this peace by a priest fluttering past me, his beard and cassock trailing behind him. He was followed by a tight-lipped old woman – the caretaker, as it turned out – who stopped suddenly in front of me. She turned slowly and poked an accusing finger. I strained to understand her indignation. Was it my informal clothing?

'*Nyet, nyet, nyet,*' she huffed. 'You must cup your hands like this and kiss the priest's hand when he passes. You didn't do that. Even President Nazarbayev does that – and he's a Muslim!'

She stalked off, leaving me humbled. Moments later another tourist came into the church. He wore sandals and a cap, with a large Nikon camera hung around his neck and, worst of all, his T-shirt bore the unmistakeable gold hammer and sickle on a red background – the symbol of the USSR, in whose name the clergy had been liquidated. He wore it as a statement of fashion rather than propaganda, and I was interested to see the caretaker's reaction. But the old woman passed him by without a word.

This wasn't the first time I'd found Soviet symbols accepted – even welcomed – in this part of the world. I suppose Central Asians had never been given a chance to get over the Soviet era, because it was still so present: The former party chiefs had become local strongmen, like Turkmenbashi, Karimov and Nazarbayev, and they retained powerful personality cults like their Soviet predecessors. The paternalistic slogans remained, as did the old ministries, with their thickets of bureaucracy and authoritarian agencies. Seamlessly, Central Asia had formed its own, pseudo-Soviet system, with few mechanisms to challenge it.

Yet there were sound reasons why people looked back to the 'good old days', as perhaps this caretaker did. The Soviet venture, so riddled with social and economic contradictions, gave Soviet citizens near 100 per cent literacy, free education, cheap living and an acute sense of national pride as a result of being part of a superpower.

But surely none of this could be squared with the horrors committed under the hammer and sickle symbol. In her monumental work, *Gulag: A History of the Soviet Camps* (2003), Anne Applebaum recalls a day in Prague when she was walking along the Charles Bridge, nonplussed by the popularity of Soviet memorabilia among Western tourists. She notes that, for these tourists, Nazi symbols would be completely out of the question. 'None objected, however, to the wearing of a hammer and sickle on a T-shirt or a hat . . . For here, the lesson could not have been clearer: while the symbol of one mass murder fills us with horror, the symbol of another mass murder makes us laugh . . . For some reason the crimes of Stalin do not inspire the same visceral reaction as do the crimes of Hitler.'

I took a tram down to a Soviet-themed restaurant in one of Almaty's main thoroughfares to ponder this. In the West, a Soviet-themed restaurant would be nothing extraordinary, a slice of kitsch. But as I spotted its doors on the Furmanov Köshesi, I couldn't help feeling unnerved.

The interior was a homage to Soviet imagery. Every space of wall was decked with agitprop wartime posters, airbrushed pioneers urging Soviet citizens to cleanse the motherland from the Fascist impurity, soldiers advancing 'to Berlin' or swigging vodka before the fight. It was a celebration of the Thirties and Forties, when Soviet Socialist art was at its most potent. Where they'd run out of Soviet images, the owners had thrown in a few Che Guevaras for good measure.

The benches outside were unimpeachably authentic, designed to imitate the slatted hard-class train seats and send a shiver of pain up the coccyx. The menu was laid out like a party newspaper, headed by a hammer and sickle and the Order of Lenin.

I got up to order a cup of tea, and to hunt out the manager. I wanted to know what this imagery meant to modern people and how it could be tolerated by those who had suffered from the state's brutality.

'Actually, people love it here,' she replied, surprised at my question. They come here all the time with old newspapers or record players, maybe a poster. It reminds them of a better period.'

'Better?'

'Old people who look back to times when things were reliable. Now their pensions are hardly worth anything.'

'What about the young people?' I asked. 'Do they look at the Soviet period with nostalgia?'

'Well, no,' she shrugged. 'They don't really care about history. They just come here to eat.'

It was no wonder there were such conflicting views of Stalin. Condemned and buried by Khrushchev, honoured by Brezhnev, aired by Gorbachev, forgotten by Yeltsin, Stalin's memory has lately been bleached by Putin and his protégé President Medvedev, who have no appetite for soul-searching. Textbooks now present Stalin as Russia's 'most successful leader ever', and schools are encouraged to defend the purges, the mass murder, the gulag system as 'necessary' in his drive to make his country great.

Kazakhstan, with its limitless plains and sparse population, was an ideal point of expansion for Stalin's oppression, and the gulag – *Glavnoe upravlenie lagerei* (Main Camp Administration) – was his tool. The gulag archipelago was a collection of island-like camp complexes, strewn over millions of hectares of land all over Russia and Central Asia. It provided not merely terror, but also free labour for the state. Here in Siberia and Kazakhstan, escape was almost impossible. Tens of millions arrived here at some point: thinkers, priests, kulaks, criminals, 'politicals', and dozens of ethnic groups cleansed from their homelands all over the Soviet Union, and deemed to be ideologically unsound.

Camps have been a part of life throughout Russian history. By the end of the tsarist period, some camps had become so liberal they were more like extended reading holidays, as Stalin found out several times. But the *vozhd'* or 'boss', as Stalin would be nicknamed, turned the gulags from a system of punishment to one of terror. He transferred their control from the judiciary to the secret police, and the mass arrests of the Twenties and Thirties would swell the camps to unprecedented levels. Applebaum calculates that between 1929 and 1953, eighteen million Soviet citizens passed through the gulags, not to mention another six million *spetsposelentsy* or special exiles – entire ethnic groups found guilty of treason and uprooted.

The creation of *spetsposelentsy* signalled an entirely new approach to deportation. Rather than weed out unreliable individual spies, fifth columnists and wreckers from within a population, Stalin conceived the idea of branding entire cultural and ethnic groups. His purpose was not to murder them all, as with Hitler and the Jews (and others), but to eliminate their culture. The thinking was that if a significant proportion of an ethnic group's population died – through overwork, neglect, executions – then the survivors would be cowed into assimilation, and 'forget' their ethnic origins.

Stalin would ethnically cleanse their homelands from European Russia, and use their bodies as labour-units to fuel the Soviet machine. The propaganda mill told them to talk, act and think like Russians, until they were too assimilated – or too afraid – to remember their culture. This was how an ethnic group was supposed to disappear.

Other ethnic groups deemed to be as ideologically unsound as the Germans included small Caucasian nations and other minority groups that Stalin wanted out of the way: Karachai, Balkars, Kalmyks, the Chechens, Ingush, Meskhetian Turks, Kurds and Khemshils.

The Crimean Tatars, a people of Turco-Mongol stock who had inhabited the Crimea since the days of the Golden Horde in the fifteenth century, were unlucky enough to be overrun by the 1941 Nazi invasion and forced into the Wehrmacht. Stalin took an extremely harsh view of contact with outsiders, particularly Fascists, and by the time the Nazis were pushed back, Stalin set about 'cleansing' the Crimean peninsula of this ideological threat. Within a three day period in May 1944 the entire Crimean Tatar population was packed on trains and sent east to Uzbekistan and elsewhere. Between 6,000 and 8,000 died before they arrived. The train journey was worse for the Chechens. Deprived of both food and water, 78,000 may have died before they even arrived in Central Asia.

But by far the largest deportation was that of the Germans. In September 1941 the Germans of the Volga region were condemned on a charge of 'concealing enemies'. The Supreme Soviet decreed the following: 'According to trustworthy information received by the military authorities, there are, among the German population living in the Volga area, thousands and tens of thousands of diversionists and spies who, on a signal being given from Germany, are prepared to carry out sabotage in the area inhabited by the Germans of the Volga.'

Since nobody had come forward to denounce these saboteurs, everyone was considered to be guilty of treachery: this included not only Volga Germans, but *all* Germans living in the Soviet Union. They were promised resettlement in new 'land estates'. These turned out to be camps, and would be their homes until 1956.

The deportation of 800,000 Germans was awesome in its scale, but almost no provision was made for this huge population dispersal. Fatalities caused by hunger and exposure were high. From 3 September 1941 until the end of the year, 799,459 Germans were sent to *spetsposelenia* – special colonies in the Urals, Siberia and Central Asia. More were added later from the Caucasus. With the Nazis in retreat, the number increased by another 200,000, when Soviet Germans that had been 'repatriated' by Nazis to the Reich, were now 'repatriated' by

Soviets back to the USSR. Treated as collaborators, they suffered even more brutal treatment.

Three hundred and forty-four train echelons were made ready, the bulk of them sent to Kazakhstan, but many to the Siberian cities of Altai, Omsk, Novosibirsk and Krasnoyarsk. The cattle trucks were filled to bursting point. One man recalled his experiences to the American journalist Victor Leiker in 1968:

> In Obermonjour the order came early in the morning. The people were given four hours in which to prepare for the evacuation. Anyone resisting or attempting to hide would be summarily shot, and a few were. Soldiers arrived a few hours after the order and herded the people to the banks of the river, where they boarded barges and were taken to a railhead. Each person, regardless of age, was allowed one suitcase or bundle. Some suspected that they would be sent to Siberia and took all the clothes and bedding they could carry. Others took as much food as they could assemble. In the long run those with the extra clothing and bedding had the best chance of surviving the cold in the north where little or no preparation had been made for their arrival.

With the main rail routes occupied with war-related freight, the deportation trains were often fatally slow. Deportees were given water every few days, whenever the train stopped. But the meagre supplies of salted herring only increased their thirst. In other cars, the *provodniki*, or carriage attendants, had sold the deportees' rations on the black market, leaving their human freight to starve. Crammed together 60 to a car, the bucket usually out of reach, disease was rife. When deportees died – whether of disease, starvation and exhaustion – their bodies were simply hurled from the train.

The able-bodied men were drafted into a labour army, the *trudarmia*, an alternative to active military service, where tens of thousands were sent to polar mines or forests with little protection from the elements. Meanwhile, in the *spetsposelenia*, Germans were kept under close supervision, their movements restricted to a limited zone always a few kilometres short of the nearest town. Failure to report to the *kommandant* once a month could spell a 20-year sentence in a gulag, which in many cases wasn't much worse. They were stripped of their citizenship, forbidden to speak German, go to church or even school. None had any idea when, or if, they would ever be released.

By the war's end, these peoples' previously autonomous republics were abolished and all traces of their life there were meticulously removed. Cemeteries were destroyed, towns and villages renamed, and any right of return forbidden. In 1979 not a single German was listed in the Soviet census of that year. As an ethnic group, they had been 'erased'.

I'd already spent a week in the 'isolator' and its damp charm had begun to pall. I found a half-respectable shirt crumpled at the bottom of my bag, which would have to be my Sunday best, because this morning I was going to church. It was the first step in my search for the Germans.

The question was which church. Apart from the Baptist, Presbyterian, Seventh Day Adventist and Gospel churches, there were at least three Lutheran churches. I was sure at least one of them was German.

My driver was no help at all, and the first church, the Holy Trinity Lutheran, was easily crossed off the list. It was nailed shut and the only sign of life was an old woman almost mummified by her plastic bag collection. The next one, the Missouri Synod Lutheran Church, was a possible. I thought it might be a bilateral initiative by Russian Germans who had emigrated to Missouri and were now in contact with the 'old' country (or rather the second country out of three).

The door opened to a warm community centre, fragrant with the cosmetics of the rich. Blonde, quaffed American wives sipped coffee with their husbands – the chino-clad grandees of the extractive industries. These did not look like the children of camp-sufferers. They were healthy, fresh-faced business people.

There might have been German blood there, but it was not the branch I was looking for.

I returned quickly to my waiting cab, and pinned all my hopes on the third and final one, the Almaty Evangelical Lutheran Church. I'd be lucky if the service was still going. But I might just grab the priest on his way out.

The tenements thinned, the streets sloughed off their tarmac and soon we were driving through the muddy byways of a Russian-style country village. The urban feel of Almaty had been replaced by a world of slatted dachas with painted shutters and white fences. This felt right, somehow.

The church itself was a wooden box with a corrugated iron roof. Old, harassed-looking people were just emerging. They were dressed in grey, zip-up jackets or long skirts, scuffed shoes – and they all had gold teeth. They affirmed, with lowered gazes and diffident smiles, that it was indeed a German Lutheran church, and they were all of German extraction.

The interior was very simple, German excerpts from the Bible on the walls in the ancient Gothic (or Fraktur) script, and two rows of pews that were straight and hard, brown painted, as if they'd been ripped out of an old bus. No sign of the pastor. Then, through the courtyard came a figure in a long, flowing robe.

The foot-shuffling, distracted congregation lit up at his appearance. The pastor, resplendent in his robes and white-crossed tie, had a magical effect on his flock. Tall and charismatic, with a kind, weather-beaten face, he managed to fit in a word for each person. He knew them all by name and nodded to each with a joke or a word of comfort, shaking their hands and bringing smiles to their faces. When the worshippers disappeared, he extended to me a huge, firm hand.

His ministrations over, we talked for a while, and Pastor Gennady seemed delighted at my project. He agreed to meet me when he'd finished his errands, and would show me the Deutsches Haus, an organisation based in the south of the city, which was a mine of information about the Russian Germans.

I arrived at the *rendezvous* an hour later, at a grass bank next to a thoroughly Westernised shopping centre. In the distance loomed the apartment blocks and cranes of modern Almaty, and behind, the misty heights of the Alatau Mountains. I spotted a tall figure wearing jeans and sturdy brown shoes, accompanied by an attentive Afghan hound.

'You're two minutes late,' Gennady said. 'I was here exactly on the hour.' I almost laughed out loud at the German stereotype.

'Come, let us walk up towards the Deutsches Haus,' he said, in very correct English. 'I think you'll find what you need there.'

We walked up the road towards tall coniferous trees with views of the high pastures. The air was crisp and the trees spiky and unfamiliar. Here we were in the nexus of the Tien Shan and Alatau range, and I was forcibly reminded of the island-like locale of these Germans, living a mere 200 km from China.

'My ancestors came to Kazakhstan before the deportation,' Gennady explained, straining against the pull of his dog, Julia. 'They arrived originally under Catherine, but when land became scarce they moved to Almaty in 1858. It was called Verney then, nothing more than a Cossack fortress with lots of land.'

Gennady was quick to explain that Germans who lived within the Soviet Union should be called Russian Germans *(Russlanddeutsche)*, not Volga Germans (or *Wolgadeutsche)*, as they were widely known – after their largest community in the Volga region of southern Russia. Indeed, he himself was not a Volga German, as his ancestors had mixed with Russians and Estonians at a time when many Germans lived as well-educated freemen in Russian lands before the great migration from the German states to the Volga. Thanks to his Russian blood, Gennady was raised as a 'free' Soviet citizen and spared the *spetsposelenia* that the Russian Germans endured.

Gennady had studied astrophysics at university, but after an accidental dose of radiation from an electron accelerator, he turned instead to the study of nebulae. Only in his fifties did he become volunteer pastor, when he began teaching at the seminary. Now in his sixties, he led this congregation in Almaty.

'You know,' said Gennady, 'only 20 years ago I was invited to go on radio to talk about the Lutheran church. I would have gone, but my mother protested so much. She was brought up in a different time, you see, when to be Lutheran was to be a German, and to be a German was to be a Fascist.'

Gennady explained the feeling of injustice experienced by Russian Germans. It mattered nothing to Stalin that these German peasants had no conception of Fascism. They had been divorced from European culture for some 200 years, with no experience of the Enlightenment, German unification, the Romantic movement. They were utterly unpoliticised. Despite Lenin's gift of a Volga German Autonomous Republic, most Germans never ventured outside their own villages. But in the eyes of the state, their language damned them as Nazis.

'What can I say about my congregation?' continued Gennady. 'They have learned to live in a certain way . . . to *seem* Russian.' He turned to me for a second. 'Self-preservation. So at home they may cook German dishes, speak German, but not in public. That was not the way.'

'And they managed to preserve this dual identity?'

'Too well!' said Gennady. 'A friend of mine from the GDR visited Kazakhstan once and said he could hardly understand them, as if they were straight out of an eighteenth-century storybook. He found it very funny that they used the word *brunzen*, which means to visit the lavatory. This is not a polite word.' He smiled.

'And how many remain today?'

'As you yourself saw, there are not so many now. Our congregation used to be a thousand, now it's about a hundred, though there are always a few more at Christmas. People still leave, even now. I think it would be much more sensible if they stayed here, particularly in old age.'

'But if Germany is offering them a new life, better opportunities,' I interjected, 'is it such a bad thing to be able to enjoy old age with the other returnees?'

'Not better opportunities. You will discover more about this at the Deutsches Haus.' He pointed at the buildings we were approaching. 'Russian Germans find nothing there now. Their qualifications are worth little. Do you think Germany is going to care if you arrive speaking Russian and tell them you used to be a *kolkhoz* manager?'

'And most have forgotten their German too?'

'Not completely. They speak kitchen German, what their mothers taught them. They forget.'

As we neared our destination I told him my plan to find out more, to take a train to the former camp towns and find whatever German communities were still active in the Kazakh hinterland.

'You'll be lucky to find any at all. Some villages have been completely cleared out. Here we are,' he said, pointing to an apartment block in front of us. 'I wish you good luck with all your researches,' he said. He reined in Julia, who was nibbling a thicket of weeds, and proffered his gigantic hand. 'Blessings,' he said, with his characteristic warm smile.

The Deutches Haus was a collection of offices overseeing various German welfare projects. The offices were as much as the bilateral support could muster to keep the German community alive, providing all sorts of charities for the Germans' benefit, a German-Russian newspaper and facilities to apply for German citizenship.

The centrepiece was an initiative called the Council of Germans of Kazakhstan or Wiedergeburt, a charity with offices all across the country, wherever Germans lived. It was founded to support Russian Germans, to train, educate and warm them in winter, but most of all to uphold their German identity and language.

I was very lucky that morning. Not only had I pinned down a Lutheran pastor, but I managed to find the head of Wiedergeburt, Alexander Dederer.

Dederer was the figurehead, spokesman and hope for Russian Germans. The man himself looked tired, in a creased beige suit, with mournful, deep-set eyes.

'Please, this way,' he said, eyes to the floor, guiding me to a table where we could talk quietly.

Wiedergeburt, I discovered, was a quite remarkable institution. It had managed to keep hundreds of Germans from the brink of starvation throughout the financial turmoil of the Nineties, and had successfully helped would-be returnees to apply for German citizenship. But there was a paradox. The German government, in an effort to quell the tide of applicants, believed it could reduce the number by giving Russian Germans more language tuition.

'Ah,' he said, chuckling politely, as if the issue had been knocking round the offices for ever. 'I will explain.' 'The German constitution states that anyone with German blood (*ius sanguinis*) could be repatriated in Germany. Before the fall of Communism, nobody in the West knew how many Germans were living in the former USSR. But from 1989 up to about 2000 the number was too large and they had to reduce it somehow.'

He explained that when the number of returnees (or *Aussiedler*) since 1989 had reached a million, it was clear that something had to be done. It was believed that if Russian Germans could be given a sense of community again – by teaching them the German they had largely forgotten – then their pride as ethnic Russian Germans could be restored and they'd have no need to leave Russia and Kazakhstan.

But 60 years of Soviet oppression had destroyed German solidarity. German 'pride' had been replaced with fear and the policy was worse than useless. Anyway, the skills Wiedergeburt taught only equipped Germans to fill in emigration papers.

'If they were sensible they would stay here,' said Dederer, echoing Gennady. 'Kazakhstan will soon be rich and skilled labourers are needed.'

Even in the time that has elapsed since our interview Kazakhstan's economy has continued to flourish. The few Germans with the material means to emigrate now see little point in doing so.

I wanted to ask Dederer about his own background. What had his experiences been as a German in Kazakhstan?

Dederer licked his lips and smiled. He told me that he, too, had been born in a *spetsposelenie*, and had felt the spectre of the state behind him, always checking for German speech, illicit worship, subversive gatherings. But his adolescence was spent in the post-Stalin thaw and he'd been spared the hardship of his parents' generation.

In 1956, after 15 years of indefinite incarceration, things were beginning to change. Khrushchev had succeeded Stalin in 1953 and had begun cautiously to denounce the dead tyrant's policies. Soviet Germans were declared to be innocent of collaboration with the Fascists, and they were told they were free to leave the camps. They *were* free – for what it was worth in the Soviet Union.

But, of course, it wasn't so simple. All Russian Germans were forced to sign documents promising never to revive their old communities, and life after the camps would be hard. The stigma of their ethnicity was like a brand and many labourers were denied permission to leave their *oblast'*. This was the era of the Virgin Lands project. Wheat was the new 'white gold' and German hands would be needed on the massive state farms that ploughed up the newly watered steppes.

Dederer smiled, as if recalling something forbidden. 'I remember when I saw other Germans in a group for the first time. It was the Sixties. Someone had built a German theatre. I wanted to go and my mother told me I was asking for trouble. But I went anyway and I'd never seen so many Germans in the same room – talking German together. I realised that all these people were just like me.'

Suddenly he looked at his watch.

'I have an appointment quite soon, I'm afraid,' he said, 'but first let me show you something.'

He led me towards a back room, fiddled with a key and the door opened into a tiny library. The air was musty and shot through with stripes of dusty light. Shelves buckled under the weight of leatherbound volumes, books with metal locks and thumb-wrecked binders, clinging to their pages by webs of thread.

'Please, look at any you like. People leave these for us before they emigrate,' he added. 'Call for me when you've finished.'

There were hymnals, prayer books, picture books, books for

boys on the adventures of Bismarck in the old Fraktur script. Some were beautifully illustrated. I found a book of *Morgenklänge* (matins) from 1877, whose owners had written their names in scratchy brown ink: Eduard Frick, Elise Humel and Christian Deförk. Another was gold embossed with a broken lock, thick and dusty, called *Enchiridion oder Handbüchlein von der Christlichen Lehre und Religion.* On the rough flyleaf – almost as thick as parchment – I found the year 1811 printed in uneven numerals. With the anti-religious horrors of the Twenties and Thirties, many of these books would have been transferred from shelf to hayloft. Discovery could land an entire family in a camp.

My strangest find was the *Lüneburgisches Kirchen Gesang-Buch* of 1795, a first-generation hymnal from Lüneburg. On the flyleaf was the Hanoverian Lion and Unicorn crest of George III, the British king who had ruled both these people and my own.

When I'd had my fill of burrowing I came out to find Dederer. Where were these communities of living, praying German-speaking Germans? Had they really all disappeared?

'You want German-speaking communities?'

'Is there nowhere left?'

'There is. In Karaganda, Kokshetau, Pavlodar, in the far north. Yes . . . these communities are in a bad shape.' Dederer scratched his head. 'Do you mind a long train journey?' he asked.

There was a train for Karaganda in the early evening. My interest had been whetted by Gennady and Dederer, and the German embassy had told me where I was most likely to find active German communities. From Karaganda I'd travel on to Astana and Kokshetau, not too far from the border with Siberian Russia, before looping round to Pavlodar and back to Almaty. This was the best chance I had of finding traces of German life – or Germans that had not yet thrown in their lot with the West.

I climbed into a Volga that roared off down a boulevard towards the station.

'Put your belt on,' ordered the driver. My seatbelt was just a dusty strip of plaited nylon that hung limp beside me. 'Just drape it over you.'

'What for?'

'The police.' I did as bidden.

'So why do you want to go to Karaganda then?' he asked, suspicion in his voice. 'It's all steppe, nothing to see. Just grass. Haven't you got everything you need here?'

Seconds later he slammed on the brakes. I looked up to see a woman in the middle of the road, clutching her baby to her breast. As we screeched to a halt, I braced my knees against the dashboard. There was a crunch as our rear lights were atomised by the car behind. The woman hurried off. My driver groaned. He got out, dragged his fingertips over what remained of his beloved boot, and lit a cigarette. 'What are you going to Karaganda for, anyway?' he grunted, as if I'd jinxed his taxi.

I stuffed a note in his hand and ran the rest of the way. The station was packed with travellers and drifters. Pensioners flogged sausages, boiled eggs and vegetables from their gardens, mothers clucked Kazakh to their crying babies and adolescents with gelled quiffs punched fruit machines. I fought my way through the hawkers and boarded the sturdy Soviet-era train, with just a few seconds to spare.

Pensioners were still poking their cucumbers through the windows as the train eased out of the station. The concrete high rises gave way to Almaty's gentle suburbs: kitchen gardens and overgrown cottages with shuttered windows and sunflowers. Soon we were rolling over bald land, plain and green, just as the taxi driver had described.

As evening fell I lay on my top bunk. Resting my chin on my arms, I looked out of the carriage window, enjoying the otiose speed of the train. The view was a great palette of colours, rosemary green, lavender and ochre. The sun set, leaving a thin mist over the goose grass, and the colours seemed to merge into a bluish haze.

Karaganda

Built on the plains a thousand kilometres north of Almaty, Karaganda was an industrial town of the dourest kind. The wide-set boulevards, the buildings, the statuary were functional and impressive, and what little beauty remained was half-hearted and cosmetic.

Atop one multi-storey apartment building, as brash as a motel sign, were three gigantic words, SLAVA SHAKHTERSKOMU TRUDU: 'Glory to Coal Mining'.

Beyond Gagarin Square I felt my trousers being pulled by a child beggar. I looked up and saw a group of women in patterned shawls and tresses sitting by a disused fountain. They looked like folkloric tour guides, though their faces were worn, their hems filthy. One of the old women beckoned to me. I let her take my hand, because I'd never seen a face like hers. Every inch of skin was the texture of driftwood, the crests tanned, leaving white grooves in between. Her teeth were black or gold and her grey hair had been turned into hundreds of plaits, one of which traced her hairline, like a Slavic princess.

'*Ya koldunitsa*,' she said – I am a sorceress. 'God gave me my powers, although I am an Orthodox Christian. My powers helped me escape Chechnya after my father was shot and my house washed away by a flood. Now if you give me a coin I will wish you good luck.'

I fished in my pocket for a coin, wary but intrigued.

'Now give me a note. What do you have?' She blew at my wallet and muttered some words in a different language. I gave her a small amount of tenge, half expecting to lose it. She crumpled the note tightly in her hand, blew on it, muttered something more, and when she opened her hand it was gone. She spoke commandingly.

'After two hours take a ten kopeck coin and throw it away. Then you will have good luck on your travels. Now go!' she said. Her unnaturally lined face, her elegant plaits, her odd accent, all had the desired effect. I walked away charmed by her cheap trick. But when I looked in my wallet, quite a bit more was missing.

She reminded me of the bazaars of Bukhara, where the Luli Gypsies were considered both charlatan pests and the keepers of mysterious powers. Stall-owners would drive them off with abuse, before tossing them a coin to guard against the evil eye. Hexes didn't exist, they said, but who could be sure?

It is easier to relate magic and superstition to the latecomers to the Orthodox Church, the Ossetes or Koreans or Chechens, or any number of Soviet peoples with a rich tradition of their own. But it is less easy to make this leap with the Germans.

Russian Germans have long been associated with a strong moral code, a rigid belief in their church and a simple, clannish existence. But even a century ago, magic, folklore and superstition were central to Russian German community life. When these traditions dwindled away in central Europe, many of them were transferred to the German villages on the steppes and Volga Delta. They remained preserved right up to the Soviet era by ignorant peasants who needed every protection against the threat of banditry and the winds that could ruin a crop in a single storm.

Much of today's knowledge of Russian German folklore comes from the collections of Pastor Eduard Seib, a turn-of-the-century Lutheran pastor who lived at Saratov, the capital of the German Volga region. He published his research on the spells and practices of the Germans in 1914. He would disappear in the purges in 1938.

Seib explains that the inherited knowledge, infused with augury and magic, was carried by the *Braucherin*, the woman healer, whose knowledge was passed from mother to child. Literally hundreds of practices, spells and cures were preserved by Russian German settlers in this way.

The catalogue of auguries and the folk remedies to promote well-being were compendious. The typical German house would be hung with all manner of objects, such as red beads to prevent haemorrhaging or elk hooves against epilepsy. Farmers scoured the stars and moon for signs, searching for sense in the unpredictable skies. Almost everything signalled rain, from a crow cawing or a dog chewing grass, to a cat lying on its back.

Universally feared was the *Hexe* or 'evil eye'. Any and every misfortune was put down to witches, spirits or demons, such as the *Nachgrif* (night sickness), caused by spirits wafting through a window to enter the body of a sleeping child.

Some of the folk remedies were as bizarre as they were inventive. One of the ways to test whether a baby had been hexed was to lay it onto a fire shovel and push it into the oven for a quarter of an hour. If the crying persisted the forehead of the human 'loaf' was covered three times with a cloth. If the cloth took on a salty taste from the sweat, the poor child was deemed to be hexed and herbs and prayers would be found to drive away the spirit. If the child had blood poisoning from an infection, a small live toad would be bound onto the wound and the amphibian would die, taking the infection with it. A hex could also be bought off. If cream would not beat into butter, a five kopeck coin was tossed into the batch.

I wasn't entirely convinced that the Chechen sorceress was bona fide, but like the Bukharan stallholders, who could be sure? So I threw away the ten kopeck piece as instructed.

The offices of Wiedergeburt were situated in a fine building pasted with yellow stucco, set back in its own grounds – quite unlike the Karaganda I'd seen so far. It had the faded grandeur of a chateau converted into a convalescent home. I pushed open the grand door into an empty hall. Nobody stopped or greeted me and I was free to tap through its echoing chambers. I climbed the painted stairs and crossed over the parquet floor of the ballroom.

On a door in the corridor outside was the Russian word for 'museum'. I walked into a small office, where, fixed to one wall, was a cabinet filled with artefacts and books. This was more like a little flea market than Dederer's library, full of odds and ends from inside Germans' homes. I found spinning wheels, huge conch-shaped gramophones and a hulking Mercedes typewriter that bashed out the old Fraktur script. I picked up a book called *Lichny Magnetizm (Personal magnetism)* dated 1912, a late-Imperial self-help manual designed to increase the reader's personal attraction. There were lithographs of young, noble-looking

Russians in tailcoats and waxed moustaches. They sat in a circle with their heads hanging to one side as if in a trance, while they sought to increase their *magnetizm*.

'Can I help you?' A girl appeared behind me. She had a sweet, dimpled face and spoke with perfect calm. She offered tea.

Ella Metzger worked at Wiedergeburt part-time. She, too, was German, but like most of her generation who had not emigrated, spoke little of the language. Nevertheless, she liked the idea of my project and rubbed her chin as she thought how I could best find some German-speakers.

'But surely if anyone would know, you would?' I said. 'Is there not a list of people that Wiedergeburt looks after?'

'You see, most have gone now, and the old don't come in much,' she replied, frowning. 'There used to be a part of town called Little Berlin, but . . .'

'What about this?' I'd picked up a flyer from a rack advertising an 'authentic German eating experience'. It was a German-themed restaurant called the Deutsche Küche – funded, of course, by Wiedergeburt.

'You can give it a try.' She smiled. 'But you probably won't find any Germans.'

'Why not?'

'Too expensive.'

'But worth a try?'

'Why don't you come back tomorrow and tell us what it was like?'

That evening I walked down towards the centre again, near the site of the Chechen sorceress. This time there was a crowd of Luli Gypsies, their ragged children in tow. I gave them a wide berth.

The sun was a bright orange, flickering between the identical tenements on the horizon. Locals had begun to convene for a few glasses. Young Russian men with red worn faces gathered in tent-bars, talking through gap teeth, or sitting on the street with empty stares.

I found the Deutsche Küche. A blonde waitress in a frilly Bavarian top bustled around the bar area on the street.

'Is this the German restaurant?' I asked her.

'No. This is the Deutsche Küche,' she snapped, twirling away with a tray of drinks.

I found a seat in the darkened interior and ordered a beer. This was the least German or *gemütlich* atmosphere I'd ever encountered: marble floor, chintz curtains, plastic table cloths, and not a person, let alone a German, in sight. The young Kazakh waiter brought me a plate of sauerkraut, mashed potatoes and wurst. I asked him whether Germans ever frequented the restaurant.

'Germans?' he said, alarmed.

Two men arrived while I was eating and took a table in the corner. On my way out I stopped and asked them politely if they might be German. They paused, looked at each other with a mixture of incomprehension and irritation, and showed me the door.

'What did I tell you?' laughed Ella, the next day. 'It just isn't popular. But have you thought of going to church?'

Ella wasn't religious, but she knew about a Lutheran service some way out of town. With a little persuasion, she agreed to take me. We boarded a bus bound for the outskirts of Karaganda on the Sunday morning, in good time for the service. The passengers were the usual: tight jeans, red-highlighted hair, leather jackets. But there was an exception. A strange-looking man stood at the back of the bus. In his moth-eaten frock coat, he looked as if he'd jumped from the pages of *Lichny Magnetizm*. His features were gnomish and he clutched the handrail as if it was his first time on a bus. I wondered if he might be a German, heading to the service. One by one the passengers disembarked for the huge estates on the outskirts, or for the wooden dachas further out. But he hung on.

We travelled right to the edge of the city. Karaganda here felt so ill at ease in the steppe, as if it had been parachuted onto the emptiness. On one side were the tiny wood cottages, surrounded by kitchen gardens and bluebells. On the other began the endless nothing.

I followed Ella off the bus and we joined a group of elderly passengers, babushka types in shawls and house dresses. The man in the frock coat stepped off the bus with us, walking, head bowed, along a path to the prayer house.

Like Gennady's church in Almaty, the building was as unpretentious as it could be, made from corrugated iron, its grey paint chipped by scouring steppe winds. The congregation comprised ten or so old women and three men. The older ones were haggard and lined; deportees or children of deportees.

I spoke to the man in the moth-eaten coat. His name was Zhenya Zieb and he was painfully shy, but he told me that his community had built the church in 1970. They had all pooled their resources and stood united against exorbitant taxes, and the ever-present KGB, which came round looking for evidence of religious propaganda or subversive meetings – any excuse to close the church.

Fortunately, the worship of 300-odd harrassed deportees was deemed not to be a threat to national security and the church survived. Zhenya told me there were only 50 churchgoers left. I guessed the number was much smaller.

'All the congregation are German speakers,' he said with stubborn pride. 'And God will bring more,' he added. 'Anyway, what does language matter? God speaks all languages.'

An old woman called Yekaterina beckoned me forth. She was bent and her face sprouted little copses of hair that had been allowed to grow long. 'Are you a believer?' she asked me. 'Do you go to church?'

'Not much,' I answered, truthfully.

'But you must.'

I smiled.

'You can't wait for God's love to come to you. You must suffer and strive for it.'

Yekaterina took my chin and pulled me slowly towards her.

'You must go to church once a week, and then you will go to heaven.' Her fingers tightened under my chin. 'And if you don't the opposite will happen.'

'Opposite?'

'*Hell!*'

'If you withstand religious persecution you will go to heaven,' interjected Zhenya.

'If you follow the *true* faith,' said the old woman. There was apparently a tiny Mennonite community a little way across the steppe which served as the archetype of the 'untrue' faith.

I asked about these Mennonites, wondering if I should try to talk to them.

'We don't have anything to do with them,' said Zhenya.

'They're Baptists!' shrieked another. 'They baptise you in adulthood. Barbarians!'

When the pastor arrived, everyone shuffled inside the church that was stripped to its bare essentials: a simple altar and a few rows of pews built at right angles to each other inside a painted metal frame. We sat on separate sides, the old women bundled up in their scarves and shawls, and we four men in suits and frock coats.

Zhenya and I shared the *Wolgagesangbuch*, the Volga German hymnal. But before anyone was ready, Yekaterina had taken the lead in her piercing falsetto: '*Liebster Jesu, wir sind hier, deinem Worte nachzuleben.*' Without an organ to guide us, we followed her lead like a shoal of pilot fish.

Some way into the hymn the door banged shut. A young girl with a sheaf of music hurried inside, sat at the organ and waited patiently for the next hymn. Her fingers were poised to play, when Yekaterina leapt prematurely into the first verse of the next hymn. She would not be led by the adolescent organist. She sang on, always a beat or two ahead . . . '*Daß man sie zu dir hinführe, denn das Himmelreich ist ihre . . .*' When the music ended and everyone had fallen silent, we endured four agonising seconds of a lone falsetto . . . '*iiiiiiiiiiihr*'. Ella and I did all we could to avoid each other's eye.

My visa expiry date was closer than I thought and I still had a sizeable loop to make. I boarded the sleeper train next evening to Astana, the capital, and headed on to Kokshetau, a town in the far north of the country, a mere 250 km from the border with Siberia.

I took some hot water from the *chainik* at the end of the carriage and watched the world go by from my top bunk, a prairie of wispy golden grasses. I tried to imagine the steppes beyond the horizon, this boundless, liberating, crushing space. A part of me wanted never to grasp it.

The train finally stopped at a tiny industrial town called Vyshnevka or 'place of cherries'. Rain had fallen, leaving the aromatic scent of autumn flowers and lavender. Beyond the town's factories the golden steppe still stretched into a boundless horizon.

Hours later, pylons appeared, signalling the coming of another post-industrial town, and within moments Kokshetau emerged from the steppe. It was still early August but I sensed the first breath of winter. I expected a town as colourless as Karaganda, and was not disappointed. But the city bristled with tall conifers and arctic-looking flowers. My bus bounced down the main street, passing tenements with square windows and shallow, slanting roofs, which in Uzbekistan might have been oppressive. But here they were clean and the fir trees added a brisk, tidy feel.

In amongst the grey architecture was a vision of scintillating blue – a wooden mosque from the late tsarist era. Its towers were hexagonal, built of slats, with heavy green cornices and flower carved windowsills. It seemed more like a Norwegian church or a New England lighthouse, anything but a mosque in northern Kazakhstan.

I got off the bus and walked through the evening streets, past old women wrapped tightly behind stalls of bright crab apples and purple radishes. I crossed an empty square, its concrete verges blooming with bluebells and lilacs. There was the usual slew of monuments to Soviet empire builders, and a lonely wedding photographer waiting for business with his square camera bag.

I found a clean, functional Soviet-era hotel. Ah, these Soviet hotels. How far I'd come since Nukus. Now I had grown quite fond of them. The first rule was that the name had to be extremely unimaginative: it was preferably named after the town. The one in Kokshetau was, quite correctly, called the Hotel Kokshetau. Sometimes, in a moment of rebellion, they might call it the Hotel Tourist, but it must never stray too far from the rules.

The décor of these hotels is always simple – with just a desk, a lamp and a bed. The rusting, en suite bathroom must have taps that either exhale vaporous drops or project rustwater with skin-scarring force, and the loo paper must be a hybrid of sandpaper and cardboard. There is often a *dezhurnaya*, or floor attendant, who sits stolidly on every floor, and a laundry, and the staff are either disarmingly kind or impossibly rude. And you never have to go far for a drink.

The Hotel Kokshetau had a small emporium on its ground floor, a warren of little wooden shops that tried quaintly to conceal its true purpose. There was a stationer's (which sold vodka, beer and brandy), a confectioner's (which specialised in spirits and wine) and a food-stall that provided vodka to accompany the menu. To make up for the absence of an off-licence, there was a well-stocked bar.

Svetlana, a bubbly, round woman with nicotine-stained teeth and bottle-blond hair, gave me a huge bear hug at Wiedergeburt the next morning.

'Come in, come in,' she said. I'd told her of my project the night before and now, in a small office, I found a breakfast laid for a prince. There was caviar, pickles, cold-cuts, tongue with melted cheese, tea and coffee.

'For me?' I asked, quite overcome.

She smiled with a shy tilt of her head.

Svetlana was herself a child of deportees, but she'd retained her German and had passed it to her own children. Now that anti-German feeling was finally easing, she felt it was important to cling to their roots.

'And *ius sanguinis*?' I asked her, tucking into the feast. 'Is it the right of ethnic Germans to claim their motherland?'

'What's the point?' she shrugged. 'This is their country, not Germany. They don't know or understand Germany. But,' she added, almost despite herself, 'we cannot deny our Germanness. We uphold it.'

This was of course the official line – that to instill a sense of Germanness and community among Russian Germans would help build a cohesive community here.

'Will you be here on the 28th of August?'

I told her I wouldn't.

'Shame. We have a festival commemorating the day the Kokshetau Germans arrived in the *oblast'*. We organise a party where they all get together, sing songs, play the accordian and tell of the old days.'

Wiedergeburt really did take care of their community. On top of language tuition and education opportunities, it also supplied free medical and dental work, visa help, computer training, and those with less than 10,000 tenge a month got to eat for free.

'There is one German woman in the district who is 90 years old, but she still won't accept a thing from us,' said Svetlana, shaking her head. 'She says we should give it to people that need it.'

'She lives near here?'

'Five minute's walk,' she said. 'I don't know anyone who is stronger, or who has seen as much.' She took a long drag of her cigarette, and stared past me into the street.

I'd read and talked so much about the Russian German experience, but had never met anyone who had lived through the deportation. I thought of the Soviet-themed restaurant in Almaty with its glib selection of history, and all the opinions I'd heard about the 'German situation', but this was surely the missing piece of the jigsaw.

'Can I meet her?' I said.

'We could probably arrange it,' she exhaled croakily.' Let me call her first.' Svetlana disappeared, leaving piles of food still uneaten.

Minutes later we were threading through the maze of battered housing blocks, past a concrete playground overgrown with long, damp grasses, until we arrived at one of the apartment blocks.

Irma Janssen, a thin, frail woman greeted us with a throaty yelp. We walked through into a simple but comfortable flat, with a small rug covering the floorboards, and an upright piano next to the window. Svetlana brought us tea, and when we were comfortable, the old woman made herself ready to speak.

'I've seen the whole story of the Germans if that's what you really want,' said the old woman. She took a sip of tea, the cup wobbling in her hand, and looked to the window. The soft light through the netting revealed all the wrinkles on her face. Her lips opened to speak, then she paused. 'I can't believe it,' she said. 'I'm forgetting my own language.'

Irma gathered herself and started slowly to speak in her native German. Her accent was strange, and the vowel in *Brot* (bread) was pronounced as in 'boat', like the Dutch – she told me her ancestors had arrived from the Low Countries under Catherine the Great. Then she began to find her pace, starting with the facts that popped into her head, her family, her childhood memories.

Irma was born into a close-knit family in 1914 in Ukraine, near the Dnieper river. Her father was the village teacher and doctor. He played the violin and piano, and their house – full of books and sheet music – functioned as the school. Irma showed us her medical diploma from the mid-Thirties, printed in Ukrainian, with a photo of her in her youth, hair parted in the middle: a willowy beauty.

But the rural idyll could not last long. The Thirties was the worst decade for Soviet Ukraine, where Stalin's paranoia found its full expression. The Boss wanted to break the back of the small-holders, the kulaks, and within a few years he brought the huge, near self-sufficient grain-provider to its knees. In the enforced famine of 1932–3, five to seven million people lost their lives. Ravaged by collectivisation and crop seizures, starvation haunted the land, and day after day the NKVD, Stalin's secret police, scoured the villages for new victims.

After the famine came the purges of 1936–8, where most of the remaining intellectuals, teachers and clergy were deported or shot. Then, when the ranks of the literate had been decimated, anybody at all could expect execution or deportation: farm-hands, engineers, party members, clerks, were taken away at night by the fearful *chorny voron* (black raven) prison van.

One survivor, Berta Bachmann, in the 1980s recalled the terrible aftermath of these night raids: 'When morning dawned, and the women, with swollen eyes and frightened faces ventured out onto the street in order to commiserate with their neighbours and to find out what had happened to the others during the night, they would learn that ten or twenty men had been taken away during the night.' Bachmann wrote that her own father feared to enter the street, if only to avoid the jealousy in the eyes of the other women who asked themselves why *he* had been spared.

Irma was no exception. Her father was taken one day in 1938 by the NKVD and shot, and her own husband, after only a year of marriage, was drafted into the *trudarmia* – itself a death sentence. Irma waited for him, hoping against hope. Three years later she discovered that he, too, had been shot.

Now in the summer of 1941, as a young widowed medical graduate, Irma was sent to run a child clinic in Odessa. The incessant Nazi bombing and the desperate shortage of medical staff kept her constantly on duty, rushing from wounded to wounded. But as a German, Irma would not be spared. On the first of October she and her mother, the last of her family, were deported.

'I had no time to take anything,' she said, 'the bombs would not stop. I could only put some medical supplies in a bag. And then we boarded the train . . .'

I waited for her to continue, but she only shook her head at the rush of memories that returned.

'It was terrible.' Her eyes welled. She was silent for a while, and Svetlana laid her hand on her shoulder. 'There was friendship,' Irma continued, 'We shared what we had.'

While Irma was sent to Pavlodar in north-east Kazakhstan, her mother was sent to the Altai region. Undeclared Soviet policy was to separate families to ensure that their German ethnic identity would be dispersed in exile. But now that the state had separated and killed what was closest to her, Irma would not rest until she'd found her mother, whatever the cost. With a doctor's credentials and an innate determination, she boarded a train for the Altai, shouting her mother's name over and over again: 'Amelia Janssen, Amelia Evgardova Janssen, born 1886.'

In all the chaos, Irma somehow found her mother and brought her along to Pavlodar. It was a bitterly long journey. All the main railway lines were used to supply Red Army troops at the front, and the civilian deportations would roll for months on tortuous detours.

'And we had no food at all,' said Irma. 'We could make no plans for our survival because we were totally helpless.'

They arrived in Pavlodar in early January, when the steppes were covered in deep snow. Irma's eyes lit up with faint mischief as she spoke of their arrival. 'When the train stopped I saw some Georgian Germans from another car.'

Of all the German deportees, the Caucasian Germans were probably the luckiest. Unlike the Volga or Ukrainian Germans, who had been allowed between ten minutes and a few hours to pack, the Caucasian Germans had been given generous notice. They came laden with goods from home: wine, pork, cooking oil, carpets, clothing, and experienced none of the strict rationing that the Volga Germans had. Irma begged them to take her and her mother with them.

'They asked me if I had any vodka.' Irma had nothing, no food, no water, let alone vodka. But she reached into her medical kit and took out a bottle of ethanol. It was good enough for the desperate Georgians. She was offered food and a lift to the *sovkhoz*, or state farm.

The conditions at the Kalinin *sovkhoz* were unspeakable. Irma volunteered to work at the hospital, which stank of death. Diphtheria, typhoid, scarlet fever ran rife as the sanitation was too poor and the rations too meagre to fight disease.

'The *sovkhoz* manager refused to issue rations to the hospital,' said Irma. 'Food was for the workers and fighters, not for the sick.' Irma marched to Pavlodar to beg for help from the *sovkhoz* manager.

Then a strange thing happened. A ragged group of teenagers and children from the *trudarmia* were coming down the stairs of the building where she was waiting to be seen. They had been working in the mines. Their faces were hollow and toothless, their legs covered with boils, and they, too, were starving.

'I heard one of them call my name, but I didn't recognise the voice. I turned and saw it was my brother Valentin.' Irma started to laugh and cry at the same time. She wiped away the tears with a bony hand, and stopped for a moment.

During the war, more than a quarter of all Soviet Germans toiled in forests or polar mines, including tens of thousands of children. With inadequate clothing and less than a kilo of bread per day they froze and starved. Their only hope for sustenance was the wild garlic or grasses they foraged when the guards' heads were turned. Pellagra, scurvy, malnutrition was endemic and the daily sick ration – 300g of bread – could never sustain life for long. Rations were dependent on productivity. As inmates failed to meet their targets, their bread ration decreased.

'The NKVD allowed me to care for him at the hospital,' said Irma. 'We had to walk 45 kilometres. He had no shoes and could hardly move his legs. But we got there in the end and I put him in bed and cared for him for a while. After four months, the NKVD told me he was fit enough to work.' She looked at me with tired eyes. 'I knew he wasn't fit – *I* was the doctor – and I knew what would happen to him if he went back to the *trudarmia* . . .' She took a sip of tea. 'But he did go back. And I never saw him again.'

Life after 'liberation' did improve. Irma became the head of a children's school and adopted a child. She married again in 1956 and bore four children. Like most German internees, the land of their incarceration would become their home, and Irma lived quietly in Kokshetau for the next half-century. Even now, almost a hundred years old, her memories remained terrifyingly immediate.

'*So daß ist mein Leben.* I've had a hard life and I am ill, but getting strong always.' She finished with a smile and a sniff.

In a moment of unprecedented candour the new Russian government in 1991 publicly admitted that the deportation of the Soviet Germans and other groups *did* constitute genocide. As the openness of the Yeltsin years coincided with national economic humiliation, the Putin era would erect fences around its past. There were simply too many deaths to account for, and the Kremlin saw 'coming to terms' with Russia's history as a weakening of its own authority, perhaps even dignity.

When the last survivors die – people like Irma Janssen – history will be easier to falsify, politicise and parody. Two to three hundred thousand Russian Germans are thought to have died in the 1940s. But who talks about the German genocide?

5

'Ploughshares like those of Carthage': The Yaghnobis

'Daraj-i soj-i kum, bahojash shahr-i rum'
'The valley of the river Kum, its value is the city of Rome'
Tajik proverb.

The going would get rougher now. So far I'd relied on a serviceable Russian infrastructure. There would be no more trains, with their electric kettles thoughtfully placed at the end of each carriage. From now on I was travelling by car, donkey and on foot.

In a stuffy hotel in Osh, Kyrgyzstan, I squinted to read my map. I had ended up in the messy part of Central Asia. The shapes of the middle 'stans were impossibily ill-defined. Unlike the desert borders of Saharan Africa – straight lines plotted from one co-ordinate to another – the republics of Kyrgyzstan, Uzbekistan and Tajikistan formed a devilish jigsaw puzzle. Deliberately so. They were drawn up in the early twenties by Stalin, when he was Lenin's Commissar for Nationalities.

The idea was to put all Turkmens, Kazakhs, Uzbeks, Kyrgyz and Tajiks into new republics created in their names. This was a stranger proposal than it sounds. Central Asia had never known anything like the nation state, especially one that catered to a single ethnic group.

The Ferghana Valley – Central Asia's most populous and conservative region – is a large, gently sloping basin that houses a seething eight million people. The commissar quashed its restive potential by splitting it into three republics (Uzbekistan, Kyrgyzstan and Tajikistan), welding on the lid until the inevitable explosion of inter-ethnic violence in 1990.

Staring at the map, I spotted that there were small, mysterious blobs filling the countries' shaded outlines, like cells under a microscope. These were not drops of fat from my shashlik. They were enclaves – self-contained bits of land stranded within the borders of a foreign nation.

Central Asian enclaves are not broadly uncontentious timepieces like, say, Gibraltar. They are needless little cast-offs that blight Central Asia's territorial integrity and fuel long-standing, intractable tensions. Kyrgyzstan has been lumped with three Uzbek blobs, and Uzbekistan is stuck with seven patches of Kyrgyz land. And they bicker over 40 sections of border, many of them mined.

Frustratingly, there was one good road that led from south Kyrgyzstan to northern Tajikistan. But I couldn't take it, as it seemed to skewer all the enclaves along the way, and would require visas I didn't have.

The only alternative was little better than a mule-track that took a leisurely detour around the enclaves, flinching with every arbitrary loop of the border. It was not popular with taxi drivers.

I managed to find someone willing – or desperate enough – to take me. He turned on the ignition with a sigh. By the time we'd passed every byre, barn and pig-trough in the Ferghana Valley, and felt a continuous rattle of pebbles on the undercarriage, and experienced a total loss of morale, I understood his reluctance.

I have talked a little about how Central Asia is viewed by the rest of the world. To many it is hard to disassociate the 'stans from a few brutish figureheads, some of whom we've come across. There was Turkmenbashi, who had dedicated a day of the year to the melon, and Karimov, who boiled political dissidents. Yet for everyone except hard-core Central Asian aficionados, Tajikistan remains reliably obscure.

Tajiks call themselves the oldest Persians in Asia, and their language, Tajik, is a variant of Persian. But I was also intrigued that Tajikistan seemed to be off everyone's radar. Even Iranians don't know where it is. I found educated Tehranis without the faintest idea how to locate Tajikistan on the map.

Locked between Afghanistan, Uzbekistan and Kyrgyzstan, Tajikistan has probably the least memorable shape in Central Asia. If you peer hard, it looks a bit like a molar, with two points on either side, a dip in the middle and a strange spit of land that curves diagonally across the north like a solar flare.

Ninety-three percent of the country is mountainous, of which more than half is above 3,000 metres. The Pamir Mountains in the south-east make it a dizzyingly remote place, where local Tajiks and a few long-haired, twist-horned Marco Polo sheep live a spare existence.

Owing to the efforts of their Soviet overlords, all the inhabitants of Tajikistan spoke standard Tajik. But until the twentieth century, Tajiks had lived tribally, hidden away in private valleys and mountain gorges, speaking dialects that often differed dramatically from each other. The Pamiris, for example, spoke seven languages between them, all of them incomprehensible to someone from the capital.

But there was one people that I was here to focus on: the Yaghnobis, a tiny community that lived in the blustery Fan Mountains of the west. Theirs was a spectacular heritage. They were the last surviving speakers of Soghdian, an Eastern Iranian language spoken by the undisputed masters of the Silk Road for the first seven centuries CE.

The Soghdians are the unseen heroes of Asian history. They were a people of scholar-traders who somehow managed to avoid the large-scale slaughter that future conquerors would wreak on the region. Based in Samarkand and the Zerafshan Valley, Soghdians were travellers and deal-makers, not warriors. At their peak in the seventh century CE they had established trading posts all along the Silk Road, from Constantinople to Chang'an. Like California in the MTV age, Soghdian culture was ever-present: the remotest Chinese entrepôt could be relied upon for Soghdian luxury wares: furs, silks, precious metals, horses, and piles of religious texts.

The interesting thing about Soghdian rule was its laissez-faire attitude to its subjects. Its empire was radically decentralised, and its palaces were not particularly opulent – the king was only slightly grander than his nobles. The Soghdians' passion was trade, not conquest.

They would travel any distance to exploit new markets, cross any deserts to source a good piece of silver or lapis lazuli. Rather like Latin in medieval Europe, there was rarely a town on the Silk Road where the Soghdian language was absent.

They were also remarkably tolerant in religious matters. Soghdians were not so much zealous about religions as curious about them. They were traveller scholars and evangelists, but never interested in forced conversion.

The Soghdians were successively Zoroastrian, Manichaean, Nestorian Christian and Buddhist and, once converted, they translated all of the holy texts from Prakrit, Parthian or Syriac into the local vernaculars, Turkic, Khotanese, Chinese and Uighur. Their peaceful ways were rare in those violent times, and inevitably their loose empire of walled cities could not survive for ever.

When the Arabs burst out of their desert peninsula in the seventh century, spreading Islam to their new Asian subjects, the Soghdians were given the option to convert to the new faith or flee. Many were unimpressed with Islam and found refuge in the mountains of today's western Tajikistan, a realm of impassable valleys where three ranges met: the Turkestan, Zerafshan and Hissar. While all the other mountain peoples succumbed to the influence of Persian, one Soghdian branch held fast to its ancestral language.

In 1870 a Russian orientalist called Alexander Kun – whose surname means 'arse' in modern Tajik – stumbled into the remote Yaghnob valley as part of a military expedition. He found that people there spoke an unfamiliar language, and he took copious notes.

Wild theories emerged as to the inhabitants' origins: they were Gypsies, Kashmiris, children of Alexander the Great. Kun's articles reached the attention of European scholars and, within a few years, it was discovered that these ragged people were something rare indeed. While many Tajiks can claim direct Soghdian lineage, it was only the Yaghnobis who preserved their ancient tongue. The Yaghnobis were the last link to one of Asia's greatest and most mysterious empires.

A flurry of further expeditions – Hungarian, German and French – hiked up to the site, eager to analyse the Yaghnobis' language, way of life and odd beliefs: many of which were remnants of Zoroastrianism, the dominant religion of the ancient Iranians. All noted the Yaghnobis' extreme resilience, especially their ability to grow wheat at three thousand metres.

When imperial Russia finally fell to the Bolsheviks in the early Twenties, the peoples of the new Soviet empire would experience cataclysmic changes to their lives. War, famine, collectivisation and mass deportations would inflict catastrophic suffering on the people of the Soviet Union. But the Yaghnobis somehow avoided large-scale brutality and mass arrests. They continued much as they always had done, scratching a living from the soil, herding cattle and catching wild goats in the high passes.

Until the Sixties, Yaghnobis could be said to have been the lucky ones. Their valley was too narrow for a school, their economy too humble for large-scale collectivisation, and nobody thought to teach them Russian. But they were not to be exempted from the region's upheavals, however, and in 1969, on the eve of the one hundredth anniversary of Lenin's birth, the Yaghnobis' time had come.

To commemorate this significant occasion, the Tajik Supreme Soviet wanted to impress Moscow with a bumper cotton crop. The target was 650,000 tons of cotton. More cotton meant more hands, and the Yaghnobis, who were engaged in nothing more productive than subsistence farming in a scarcely fertile valley, were prime candidates.

In a devastating manoeuvre, the entire valley was cleared of its 3,000-strong community and sent by helicopter and bus to the baking state-farms of Zafarabad and Mirzachul ('the Hungry Steppe') in the flat Tajik north. Their numbers were decimated by the shock of the deportation, the baking heat of the plains and the evil chemical run-offs in their drinking water.

The few hundred who inhabit the valley today are those who escaped Zafarabad in the Seventies and Eighties, returning in secret to the valley of their forefathers. When they came back they found their villages destroyed, the wooden rafters of their houses – so valuable in a treeless valley – burnt for fuel, and their pastures occupied by Tajik sheep herders making a profit for the state.

These returnees would endure continual crop failure and near starvation, constantly on the look-out for the authorities in their helicopters. On the eve of the break-up of the Soviet Union, any hope for their desperate situation was lost when the state collapsed into civil war. The Yaghnobis would have to manage in their time-honoured way alone in a near-empty valley.

My plan was to make my way to the capital, Dushanbe, where I could procure documents and provisions.

I clambered onto a minibus in Khojand, heading for the medieval town of Istaravshan, on the way to Dushanbe. The bus was packed with dark-browed women in curtain dresses and young men in leather jackets. But a smart-looking man caught my eye. He noticed me, too, and took his place beside me. He had very Iranian features and, like many Tajiks, a touch of the steppe in his eyes.

As we eased out of the city he began to talk to me, as I knew he would. He spoke a slow, tortured English, revealing a mouth full of small, jagged teeth like quartz.

His name was Mirzo and he was embarrassed to be caught travelling by bus. It was the poor man's vehicle, he said, cramped and undignified. Ordinarily, he would take his car, but right now his was 'being repaired,' and he trailed off as if he lacked the energy to lie.

'I used to earn $400 dollars a month,' he said, 'and I have

many diplomas: accounting, computing, management . . . and two or three others. But pay now is very poor, only $80 a month.' Every so often the whole right side of his face would quiver in a spasmodic tick. 'It is very difficult now in Tajikistan,' he said, in his slow and faltering accent. 'Pay is too low, even for people with educations.'

I was wondering if he had an agenda, but then his expression became deadly serious.

'Please listen carefully,' he said. 'I have . . . something.' He massaged the short-cropped bristles on his upper lip with his thumb and forefinger.

I sighed inwardly. I hoped he didn't want to go into business. Once in Turkmenistan an old alcoholic had badgered me to join him in gold prospecting if I provided the metal detector and all the funds.

'I have a ring,' Mirzo continued. 'It is very ancient. I found it in Penjakent. Have you heard of it?'

I looked up. 'Penjakent? One of the ancient citadels of the Soghdians? You know the Yaghnobis?'

'The ring is solid gold,' said Mirzo, ignoring the question. 'It is very precious. Very, very precious.'

'I see. Do you have it?'

He lowered his voice, then looked around for prying eyes.

'We talk in hotel,' he said, but he couldn't resist showing me a photo from his inside pocket. He unfurled the dog-eared corners of an old photograph, revealing a handsome gold signet ring, pressed with the schematic image of a stag, with stick-like horns branching from its head. It looked like a rougher version of some of the dazzling grave goods excavated from Scythian tombs in Bulgaria and Ukraine.

'Five thousand years old,' he said.

I nodded, intrigued.

'I know because my cousin is expert.'

I couldn't vouch for its authenticity, but Mirzo clung to his plan as if it were his only salvation. Perhaps it was.

'Please buy . . .' His face was pained.

I wasn't sure what to say.

'Or find a buyer in your country. No documents, no nothing. I put it on finger and walk through airport,' he clapped his hands in triumph.

We arrived at Istaravshan, an ancient city called Cyropolis by Alexander the Great. It had risen in medieval times as a powerful city state, built with winding alleys and thin-drummed Timurid mosques. The Uzbeks had called it Ura Tipah, and the Russians Ura-Tyube. But today it was filled with exhaust fumes and shashlik smoke.

'Come,' said Mirzo, manhandling me off the bus. I was making for my hotel, a dilapidated concrete building off the main road.

'I think this hotel is no good for you,' he said, trying to drag me to another. 'I think you want better, yes?'

I told him politely it was fine, and slowly twisted myself free. I asked the concierge for a room and put a note on the desk.

'No, my friend,' said the increasingly desperate Mirzo, clamping his hand on mine, 'I have money. I used to get $400 a month.'

He tapped his pockets for his wallet, checked his briefcase, and flicked through his diary. I paid the concierge and she gave me the key. But with startling alacrity, Mirzo snatched it from the counter and started striding towards my room. He opened the door to a stuffy atmosphere, thick with the smell of old socks and ashtrays. Mirzo pulled the orange cloth curtains apart to reveal a carpet, studded with cigarette burns. I couldn't deny it was grotty. But it was mine.

'Look here, you see, and here,' said Mirzo, pointing out the room's deficiencies. 'This room is no good for you. You want better room, I think.' I was silent. The man was now sitting on my bed, toying with my key, and I was officially invaded.

He wrote out the names of his four brothers, their addresses and numbers and insisted one of them would drive me to Dushanbe the next day.

'Really, Mirzo, there's no need.' He filled the paper with every possible telephone number he could think of. I walked him to the door.

He turned to me with a pained expression. 'I will come

tomorrow morning to say goodbye,' he said, and his right cheek twitched violently. But he never came.

Mirzo's ring made an impression on me. He never told me where he'd found it, exactly, but its discovery seemed to be part of a slow unearthing of Soghdian artefacts. It seems that after a lull of one and half thousand years, the Soghdian contribution to history was finally being understood.

On a Spring day in 1932 Jur Ali Makhmud Ali, a Tajik shepherd, was leading his flocks over the slopes of Mount Mugh in the west of the country when he discovered something sticking out of the ground. It was a basket, half-submerged in the earth, containing a leather document. He brushed off the dirt and found that the words were written in an unknown script. The shepherd took it to his home village of Khairabad, where it swapped hands for more than a year among the villagers, for whom its significance was lost.

By August 1933 A. A. Freiman, Head of the Academy of Sciences of the USSR, got wind of the discovery. The cache yielded 20 manuscripts on paper and parchment, and he would discover that one was in Arabic, one in an unknown language and the rest in Soghdian. Mugh means *magus*, testifying to the Mazdaic or Zoroastrian origin of these Soghdians, and the documents promised more exciting finds.

By 1933 the Soghdian language was already known from a few scraps – particularly from the so-called Ancient Letters, a cache found in a Chinese watchtower in Dunhuang by the Hungarian explorer Aurel Stein in 1907. But Mount Mugh would radically change our existing knowledge of Soghdian life and culture. Freiman went as soon as he could to the site, which was no mean undertaking. The shortest route was via the Camel's Neck Pass – which was blocked with snow – and he was forced to take the eight-day journey from Moscow by rail to Samarkand, thence by *arba* (horse-drawn sled) to Penjakent, and from there by mule track to Mount Mugh.

Months of excavations uncovered the remains of a ruined fortress and a treasure trove of documents that vindicated the old valley saying: '*daraj-i soj-i kum, bahojash shahr-i rum*' – ('The valley of the river Kum, its value is the city of Rome'). There were coins, looms, silks, bows and arrows and, best of all, 81 written documents on parchment and wood, covering a huge variety of topics. There was a lapidary or book of stones, which seems part of a shamanic rain-maker's handbook, and a reference to a 'sheep's shoulder-blade bone', apparently extracted from the Soghdian *'psßr'yc'stky*. There were also astrological texts and a short medicinal fragment with prescriptions for emetics, purgatives and aphrodisiacs.

From these artefacts scholars were able to retrace the final days of King Diwastich, the last Soghdian king of Penjakent.

Penjakent today lies in ruins at the extremity of western Tajikistan. But in the eighth century CE it was a prosperous city state, a walled entrepôt where merchants, scholars and soldiers from all nationalities jostled together. But the invading Arabs had grown tired with 40 years of resistance, and they now meant to defeat the Soghdians for good. As Arab pressure tightened, King Diwastich fled Penjakent and took refuge in his castle on Mount Mugh where he prepared to sit out the Arab siege. The new discovered documents provided a brilliant insight into life at court in those last days in 722 before the king was finally captured and put to death.

By the eighth century the Soghdians had forgotten the warlike tenacity they had shown Alexander the Great in the fourth century BCE. By now their empire was a loosely governed constellation of city states, so decentralised that when invaders came to conquer, Soghdians adapted to their new rulers without resistance. While at home they were administrators, scribes and petty aristocrats, abroad they were merchants, traders and adventurers. They discovered that those brave enough to cross the fearsome mountain ranges and deserts into China could become very prosperous indeed.

This was the age of the Bactrian camel, which would plod at two and a half miles an hour through climates not fit for humans. Their double-lidded eyes and closeable nostrils could cope with all but the worst-snow and sandstorms; they grew a special winter coat for the icy passes; and they could divine water in even the most arid conditions, pawing at the ground in places where a well could be dug.

With the camel-drivers came adventurers, with adventurers came emissaries and with emissaries came traders. In their wake followed pilgrims, mystics, missionaries and spies. The great Central Asian cities are nearly all products of the silk routes. Merv (Turkmenistan), Balkh (northern Afghanistan), Bukhara and Samarkand (both Uzbekistan), Kashgar, Turfan and Khotan (China) owe their existences to passing caravans, and every experienced trader could speak at least some Soghdian.

In their homelands in Transoxiana, Soghdians primed their children from early infancy. From the age of five boys would learn Arabic, Chinese, Turkic or Tibetan. They would grow up well-versed in the concept of supply and demand, and would buy and sell goods along their trade routes, bringing brass to China (used in the girdles of the Chinese civil service), Baltic amber and Mediterranean coral. They picked up lapis lazuli from Samarkand and on the road they could buy astrakhan, the soft fleece shorn from young karakul lambs.

Buddhism was the first religion to profit from this ancient superhighway, emerging from northern India in the middle of the first millennium BCE to find adherents across the whole of Central Asia and China. Nestorian Christianity hopped on board too, followed by Manichaeism, and finally Sufi Muslims, who found co-religionists all along the Silk Road.

From the first to the seventh centuries CE, pluralist Central Asia would become a hub for missionaries seeking to proselytise – or, more commonly, to escape religious persecution in Europe and Asia Minor. As long as the Soghdians dominated the Silk Road trade, religions of all sorts coexisted comfortably together well into the Mongol period.

We first know the Soghdians, an eastern Iranian people, as Zoroastrians. This was not the rigidly orthodox Zoroastrianism practised in Persia under the Sassanians. Rather, it was an unformed steppe religion – perhaps better called Mazdaism –

focusing on the solar deity Ahura Mazda and Savanta Armati, the goddess of earth, and other deities.

Nestorian Christianity established itself some time afterwards. Nestorianism developed as a distinct faith during the course of the fifth century, as the Roman Empire became wracked with patristic disputes about the nature of the Trinity. In 431 Nestorius, the Syrian Patriarch of Constantinople, was excommunicated by the Council of Ephesus on account of his 'diophysite stance', by which he held that Christ was not one but two persons, one divine, the other human. As Nestorius' supporters came under increasing pressure from the Roman authorities, they fled east to Persia and beyond. By the turn of the sixth century Nestorian Christianity had become the official church of Christian Asia and by 638 it had found its way to the T'ang court at Chang'an. Soghdians were key to the increasing popularity of Central Asian Christianity, translating the scriptures from the original Syriac into Khotanese, Turkish and Chinese.

Today, Nestorianism has almost disappeared, save for a tiny enclave that still survives, practising its very unusual form of Christianity near Lake Orumiyya in north-west Iran.

Nestorianism found a rival for the Soghdians' devotions in Manichaeism, a dualist religion that emerged from the Gnostic ferment of the third-century Near East.

Its founder was Mani, a canal manager from Ctesiphon, western Persia. At age 24 Mani began to preach a religion claiming to be the culmination of the partial revelations of Zoroastrian, Buddhism, Judaism and Christianity. He preached the dualism of light and dark, exemplified in the conflict between body and soul and the sins of the flesh.

His teetotal, celibate, pacifist, vegetarian priesthood was called the 'elect'. They were close to the light. Everyone else who indulged in the dark activities of procreation and meat-eating were called the 'hearers'. They were not 'enlightened'. and were enjoined to support the elect financially.

Mani died in a Sassanian prison, but his teachings spread to all the corners of the Roman empire and Central Asia. His believers even managed to convert St Augustine of Hippo, who later denounced his Manichaean years in his *Confessions* (397–400). Manichaeans, too, would flee east and took root in the Tarim Basin of central China, where they clung on until the thirteenth century.

But in 722, as King Diwastich looked over his battlements at the besieging Arab army, his pluralistic age was about to end. In a dogged seven-year battle conducted by the Arab general Qutaiba bin Muslim, the Soghdian monarchy was liquidated, and cities and villages fell into neglect.

I was relieved when Mirzo disappeared. I'd spent much of my journey alone so far. I liked it that way. I did things at my own pace and enjoyed my own company. But not for long.

The administrator clicked her fingers at me from the desk.

'An American lady has come, room number . . .' she closed her violetted eyelids in thought, 'twenty.'

I wondered what an American was doing here. I found I missed speaking English. I knocked at Room 20.

A tiny woman with wet, dark hair opened the door. She looked rather angry, as if I'd come to steal her hairdryer. I introduced myself, said I was about to have a look around town and did she want to join me? Her eyes narrowed very slightly, but hesitantly she agreed. She told me to wait while she got ready.

Anne, I discovered, was an asset manager from New York, not the Peace Corps worker or a mountaineer I'd expected. And she was not timid, as I first thought, but quite the opposite. She agreed to join me because I was the first English speaker she'd come across in days and she was bursting to recount her story of frustration and woe.

Anne and two mountaineer friends had arranged to go trekking in the remote Wakhan Corridor, a finger of land that sticks out of north-eastern Afghanistan. It's dramatic, windswept and inhabited by only the hardiest Kyrgyz and Wakhi shepherds. Her friends had cancelled at the last minute, so she was left with a ticket to Dushanbe and the desperate hope of salvaging a holiday. She was due back at work in ten days, and was determined to enjoy herself.

'This country is the pits,' she said, 'Nothing works. I tried to make an internal call yesterday and I couldn't because the post office didn't know the city code, can you believe that?'

'Yes.'

'And the guide book is completely wrong about everything. Says Istaravshan is this historic little villagey place. Look at this.' We had ended up in the bazaar where hides of mutton hung on hooks and butchers sat by a flyblown, blood-drenched tree stump. 'God, everything's so . . . *dirty*.' Yes it was dirty, but we were also standing at the meat counter of the bazaar. 'I guess that's what "adventure travelling" is all about, huh? Putting up with crap . . . Oh my god and the service. Have you ever *known* anywhere so slow?'

'You knew this was not the West,' I said. 'What did you expect?'

'Hey,' she pinned me with her outstretched finger, 'I was travelling in the Third World when you were in diapers, so don't give me that.'

We found a restaurant and I readied myself for an evening with Anne. Speaking English was not as much fun as I'd hoped. A morose waiter showed us to a table by the window, mumbling his words, and handed us menus.

'I'm sorry, but I can't eat this,' Anne said, curtly.

The waiter came back to take our order.

'Oh look, here's Mr Happy,' she said. 'Are you having a good day?' The waiter said nothing, and I didn't know where to look.

We ordered a few dishes calculated to navigate her numerous allergies, and she finally asked me a question.

'So what are you doing out here?'

I told her about my journey to find the Yaghnobis.

'What do you care about some little Tajiki tribe?'

I explained that they were the final remnants of the Soghdian Empire and one of the last peoples to be deported in the Soviet Union and . . . wondered if she was still listening.

'Yes, but what are you going to do there?' she asked.

Three Kalasha guides in Rumbur, one of the three Kalasha valleys. The author is third from the left.

Hiking up the Gambak pass between Bumboret and Rumbur, Pakistan. These hills have been badly deforested, and cedars will take hundreds of years to regrow.

Turkmen women rolling camel-hair felt in Yerbent, an oasis village in Turkmenistan. They are said to be the last descendants of the Tekke Turkmens, massacred by the invading Russians at Geok-Tepe in 1881.

Bored youths in the Kara Kum desert, Turkmenistan.

A Kalasha woman with her braids and susutr head-dress, adorned with cowrie shells.
Her community is under constant pressure to convert to Islam.

Hazara couple gathering fodder in Bamiyan. Hazaras are the only major Shiite people in Afghanistan, thought to be descendants of the Turco-Mongol army who invaded Bamiyan in 1221.

Lake Haybat in Band-i Amir, a lake complex in central Afghanistan, formed - say locals - by Imam Ali, Muhammad's son-in-law, who slew the local dragon, and dammed an overflowing river. Once a tourist destination, the surrounding roads are now heavily mined.

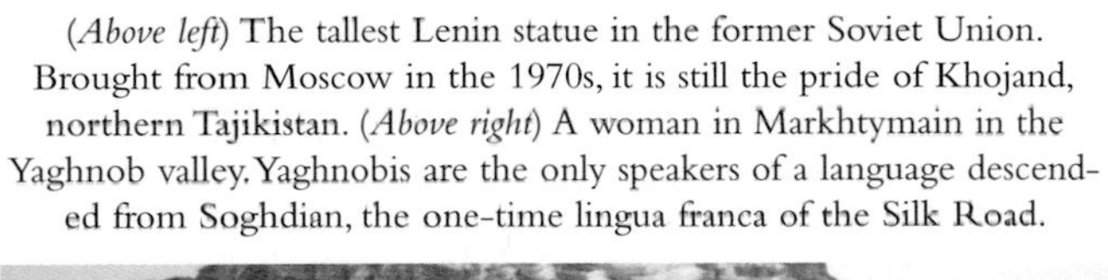

(*Above left*) The tallest Lenin statue in the former Soviet Union. Brought from Moscow in the 1970s, it is still the pride of Khojand, northern Tajikistan. (*Above right*) A woman in Markhtymain in the Yaghnob valley. Yaghnobis are the only speakers of a language descended from Soghdian, the one-time lingua franca of the Silk Road.

One of the two monumental Buddha niches, surrounded by monks' cells. Carved from the sandstone cliffs in the sixth century CE, the Buddhas were dynamited by the Taliban in 2001 as an affront to Islam.

The Shah-i Zinda ('Living King') mosque complex, Samarkand, Uzbekistan. According to legend, Qusam bin Abbas, a saintly early king and cousin of the Muhammad, is alive and well in the ground beneath the complex.

Following the track higher into the Yaghnob valley. The village of Dumzoi was never reinhabited once the valley was emptied by the Soviets in 1970-71. Many died in their new homes on the cotton fields.

Jewish graveyard in Bukhara, outside the Jewish Quarter (*Mahalla-i Yehudi*).

Mir-i Arab madrasah, built in 1537, in honour of a Naqshbandi sheikh from Yemen, is one of the few Islamic colleges in Uzbekistan continuously in use.

Constructed by the Karakhanid ruler Arslan Khan in 1127, the 47-metre Kalon Minaret was both a watchtower and an adjunct to the prison system. Captives were hurled alive from its summit.

'I don't know, exactly.'

'What do you mean you don't know?' Her attention pricked up.

'I don't have a plan.'

'You're a researcher and you don't have a plan? Do you mind telling me where they live?'

'I don't think it matters. They live somewhere near Ayni. I'll find them,' I said, without too much conviction.

'I should say it matters quite a lot.' She gazed out into the street. Then, in a small voice, she said, 'Mind if I tag along?'

Before our expedition could begin I had first to go to Dushanbe where I had an awesome amount of red tape to slash. There was my country registration (a tiresome Soviet relic that involved lodging your details with the Ministry of the Interior); my visa extension (which was apparently 'impossible' and had 'never before been issued to a tourist'); the registration for my visa extension ('absolutely necessary', despite the fact that the visa extension was 'impossible'); and the permit for the region of Gorno-Badakhshan, which by virtue of the region's 'strategic zone' status, might never arrive.

Tajikistan was still firmly in the 'Visitors Keep Out' school of tourism. Its functionaries were unpredictable, and could be corrupt, difficult, hateful and charming all in the same conversation. It was the post-Soviet experience, and hurried demands received short shrift.

But we were still in Istaravshan and it was a long and difficult journey to Dushanbe. In days past few would dare to take the road. There was a fast air to service straight to the capital. But now that market forces had shattered the Soviet-era subsidies, the Tashkent-Dushanbe highway was a terrifying reality.

Not much wider than a single carriage, the road coils round the Fan Mountains in a gravelly, ungirded corniche. Matchbox Ladas resting on their sides at the bottom of deep valleys, Moskviches that had glided over the edge now lay amid cairns of stones in the lower foothills. An aid worker once told me about Tajik villagers who roamed these mountain roads looting from crash victims. 'No point ringing an ambulance,' he told me. 'No Tajik emergency service is going to come all this way just to pick up a couple of corpses.'

Still reeling from my decision to let Anne come along, I flagged down a long-distance *marshrutka*. It seemed sturdy enough: a reliable, fuel-gorging Volga, with a claxon that moaned like an air-raid siren. Taking a bend made the usual precautionary honking a doom-laden whine.

We seemed to circle forever into the Turkestan range, taking long detours that zigzagged many times up the mountain. As we climbed higher we approached the flossy underlay of the clouds, increasing our general feeling of unease.

The road was serviceable while the traffic remained light. But I had a feeling that if any vehicle larger than ours were to come along, there would be trouble. And there was trouble. A fruit truck appeared in the distance, chuggling along with a huge load of watermelons. I reached for my seatbelt, but found only a fluffy, broken-off stump.

'I think we have a problem,' was Anne's assessment. Abdullo, our driver, reached for his claxon again.

'Oh Christ!' she said. 'Will you stop that? I *think* the guy can see you!' But Abdullo wasn't listening. He was leaning out of the front window shouting obscenities at the other driver. The truck driver revved his engine in response, and we faced each other in a game of chicken.

Being the smaller of the two vehicles, the pleasure of passing on the cliff-edge side would be ours. Abdullo muttered inaudibly. I looked out of the window. The drop was not sheer, but steep enough to keep the car tumbling for a fatally long time.

Abdullo pulled in his left wing mirror so it lay flat, then squeezed past in tiny bursts between the truck and the abyss. At last we were clear and Abdullo slammed his foot on the accelerator, jerking the wheel hard back into the safety of the road. He was too proud to show his fear. But I noticed he gave his brow a quick mop with his handkerchief.

*

Dushanbe

Seven hours later, we were speeding through Dushanbe's main axial road, Rudaki. This was the prettiest Central Asian capital I'd seen. Originally a small market town at the confluence of trade routes to the Pamirs, Afghanistan and Transoxiana, Dushanbe was developed by the Soviets in 1921 to be the capital of the then Autonomous Soviet Socialist Republic of Tajikistan.

Far from the drear conurbation I expected to find, Dushanbe sparkled. It had charm. There were neoclassical buildings in pink, violet and yellow stucco and rows of flowerbeds and plane trees.

Local clothing was a parade of conflicting cultures: Muslim Central Asia versus atheist Soviet modernism. Women wore floral curtain dresses and Bactrian-style beaten gold earrings, or strutted about on clicking heels displaying exaggerated cleavages. Young men smoked on street corners with gelled hair and high-belted waistlines, while their grandfathers sat dozing on park benches in body-length *khalats*, black boots and emirate-era cummerbunds. There seemed to be a peaceful parochialism about this tiny, spotless capital.

Of all the 'stans, possibly Tajikistan has suffered the most. For years it was merely an adjunct to its powerful western neighbour, Uzbekistan. It was just short of the million people required to qualify for full republic status. When it was made a republic in 1929 (having lost its twin cultural heart – Samarkand and Bukhara – to Uzbekistan) Tajikistan was never considered an economic success. Its mountain peasantry were often resettled to state farms on the lowlands, and the country staggered along on Soviet subsidies.

By 1990 all of the 'stans looked to Moscow for direction and support, so that independence from the Soviet Union was at best unexpected and at worst unwanted. But when the Soviet republics were finally cast adrift in December 1991, most paid lip service to a transition to democracy.

In Tajikistan, however, democracy was neither offered nor promised. The Tajik Communist Party refused to relinquish its power and ignored the people's pleas for reform. The Seventies and Eighties, decades of pent-up calm, culminated in full-scale civil war. A motley coalition of Democrats, Nationalists and Islamists formed the United Tajik Opposition – united in their desire for change, but little else. They stormed the Presidential Palace in August 1992, installing their own president, a Pamiri called Akbarsho Iskandarov.

But the Tajik Communist Party would not be outdone, and fought tooth and nail to wrest back its old power. Russia and Uzbekistan, fearing an opposition they perceived to be Islamist in character (though Islamism was only one strand of the opposition), were soon backing their old allies in government with offers of arms, troops and finance.

The Tajik Civil War has been cast as Communist versus reformist and secular versus Islamist. But in reality it was a war of regionalism. Dushanbe and the rich north had always held the keys to the country's wealth, and the relatively poor southerners had suffered the continual agony of Soviet relocation policies, forced to accommodate streams of mountain peoples arriving in their southern cotton fields. Here was where the worst fighting took place, under the banner of the Government's strongman, Sanjak Safarov, a convicted murderer, hardened by 23 years in jail.

By 1994 the Government and its allies had beaten their way back into the Presidential Palace with unprecedented ruthlessness. The opposition was flushed out of Dushanbe and retaliation parties rampaged through the south, razing villages and butchering families. It was the worst violence seen in Central Asia in recent times. The war dead numbered 60,000 and refugees close to a million.

When government forces had the upper hand, a near-unknown appeared from within their ranks, Emomali Rahmonov, a former chicken farmer. He was sworn in after staged 'democratic' elections (from which the opposition had been banned), and a precarious power-sharing agreement was brokered. The peace survived until 1997 when the war was officially declared over, and Rahmonov – who changed his surname in 2007 to Rahmon to sound more Tajik – ruled on, skilfully avoiding the bind of democracy.

The Tajikistan of today is not an obvious holiday destination. It is desperately poor, suffers from endemic corruption and is one of the main conduits for Afghan opium smuggling. Nevertheless, the atmosphere in Dushanbe was peaceful and courteous, and as I looked over the genteel aspect of Rudaki with its painted facades and neat flowerbeds, the place felt further from trouble than I could imagine.

But this is not to say that Dushanbe was problem free. Its attractions were often only cosmetic, as I discovered on the way to the visa office (OVIR) when a gleaming green trolleybus stopped beside me with a sharp bang. The overhead cable snapped and a single live wire slapped the roof of the trolleybus before hitting the curb. The passengers, inured to decades of collapsing infrastructure, simply got out of the inert vehicle and waited quietly for the engineer to arrive.

That day and the next (and possibly the day after that) would be devoted to document fixing. My registration, Anne's registration, my visa extension, registration for my visa extension, a GBAO permit and an Afghan visa were clearly not going to arrive in decent time. Certainly not before Anne boiled over, and I'd already witnessed something of her hot temper.

The air outside the OVIR was heavy with despondency. People waited for their papers with quiet reserve, often for days, only to be told *nyet* or to be faced with a higher bribe than they could afford. A guard emerged from the office and pointed a baton at me. It was my turn.

'*Davai, davai!*' Yekaterina Danilova was a woman with a bowl haircut and a row of brown ceramic teeth. She grabbed my passport from underneath the grille.

'Where is your invitation?' she barked.

'I have none. I was told it was not necessary.'

She loosed a stream of Russian, which amounted to the fact that I was in deep trouble and that Tajik bureaucracy was not at fault for forgetting to give me one. I was batted to another OVIR office.

This 'other' OVIR was even more oppressive. All supplicants focused on the 'hatch' which opened with maddening irregularity. When it did, everyone would surge forward to try and attract the attention of the man in the darkened room behind it.

Having finally elbowed my way to the front, I was sent to yet another, more obscure outlet of Tajikistan's bureaucratic apparatus to fill in more forms; then to tourist offices to process my invitation; to banks to process my payment; and to photographic shops to procure the exact dimensions of the portrait.

After three days I found myself back in front of Yekaterina Danilova's perspex screen. She flicked through my documents, making tutting noises. Then, unexpectedly, she picked up her giant stamp, bashed the papers with its rubber butt, ripped sections off with a ruler, and slapped the forms in front of me.

'Is that it?' I asked, aghast that the woman was satisfied.

'*Nu* . . .'

'Thank you so much, I . . .'

'You're blocking the others,' she snapped.

Next day the jeep arrived to take us part of the way to Yaghnob. It was the first part of our excursion, and we'd packed our rucksacks with as much food and water as we could carry.

As we drove north, Anne told me, matter-of-factly, that I hadn't been pulling my weight.

'Are you joking?' I said.

'What *exactly* did you *do*?' she asked, with a piercing look.

'You want to know what I did?' My voice was controlled, but I was close to anger. 'I found you a place to stay in Dushanbe, got your registration because you were too ill, negotiated for you, translated for you, and let you come with me to Yaghnob.'

She slumped in the back seat, staring at the horizon, and after a few moments, she said with sulky insouciance, 'OK, all right.' And I turned my attention to our driver, Kabud.

Kabud was a Pamiri, and he told me of his years as a driver in Badakhshan. He would get us safely to Ayni, he said, but he had no illusions about the state of the road.

'It's all right until the turn-off to the President's dacha,' he said. 'After that it's shit.'

But it didn't matter. Our hired car was like a tank and pebbles pinged off the tyres like deflected bullets.

The lush fruit trees and grasses of the lowlands began to disappear as we rose into the Zerafshan range. The grasses became shorter and tougher until they covered the slopes like bright green fur. The flinty rock of the lower landscape now lay in ruddy chunks down below, and the rocks above were pitted with rivulets of last winter's dull-coloured snow. In the rarified, blustery air, boulders everywhere suddenly grew skins of lichen, flaky turquoise or volcano red, and mosses like short-cropped velcro. People lived and flourished in this environment, they said, but I wondered how.

This whole region of western Tajikistan was once known simply as Kohistan: 'place of mountains'. It was an area of high ridges and petty princedoms, where Iranian clans had lived in near isolation for millennia. Lowland Tajiks had a special name for these highlanders. They called them *Galtchas*, after the crow that descends to the plains when hungry and retires again to the mountains.

The sheer remoteness of these regions was enough to persuade nineteenth-century anthropologists that *Galtchas* were the 'original' Iranians, or 'Aryans', as they called them – the progenitors of the great European civilisations. One surprised traveller, Bento de Goés, a sixteenth-century Portuguese Jesuit, described these Mountain Tajiks as having 'blond hair and beards like Belgians' – an observation that would provide grist for the Aryan theorists centuries later.

Though the term 'Aryan' was later hijacked by the Nazis for their own racist ideology, there is little doubt that these Mountain Tajiks had had a greatly reduced contact with the stream of Turkic, Hunnish and Mongol outsiders that had entered the bloodline of many of the lowland Tajiks.

One scholar, convinced of the Mountain Tajiks' Aryan ancestry, was Karl Eugen Újfalvy von Mezokovesd, a Hungarian orientalist of minor nobility who was captivated by the blue- and green-eyed peoples he'd heard of, travelling to Turkestan to settle the question of their origins.

With measuring tape in hand – and his wife Marie not far behind – his plan was to determine the cephalic (cranial) index of 58 Mountain Tajiks of varying tribes: Maghians, Falgars, Fans, Matchas and Yaghnobis. After a difficult and dangerous tour, Újfalvy found that despite being somewhat distinct from one another, Mountain Tajiks were mostly all *dolichocephalic* (having long skulls) and this – according to him – was proof enough of their Aryan ancestry.

When not measuring crania, Újfalvy noted a curious aspect of these highlanders: a strong reverence for fire. 'A Galtcha never blows a candle out,' he observed, 'for his breath is impure.' This bore a striking resemblance to Mazdaism – the pre-Zoroastrian religion of the steppe-dwelling Iranians – according to which fire was the essence of purity and any contact with the human breath was strictly forbidden.

Újfalvy also found that Mountain Tajiks treated fire as a kind of panacea, as vodka is treated in present-day Central Asia. A sick person, he wrote, was enjoined to walk round a burning log three times, and then to jump over the fire three times. If the patient was too ill, he would stare fixedly at the fire while being beaten on his back.

Many other scholars were aware of the layers of pre-Islamic belief that existed among these peoples. By Újfalvy's day, Tajiks would unanimously identify themselves as Muslims, but up here in the Fan Mountains orthodoxy frequently wavered.

The early Soviet anthropologist M. S. Andreev bore testimony to these local strains of Islam. In his fieldwork he discovered a panoply of demons that dwelt alongside Yaghnobis. He wrote of the *ajina* or elves that appeared in the form of small five-year-old girls, and were said to gather at night and dance to the sound of tambourines; as well as the terrifying figure of Ol or Olbasti, a tall woman with long hair and blue eyes, a ripped pelt dress and 40 breasts, who came to harm women in childbirth or suckle small children to death.

Andreev's research trips to Tajikistan were often fraught with trouble. The handover to the Bolsheviks had been a painful period in Central Asia, and the Basmachi Rebellion – a grassroots resistance movement that staged attacks on the Bolsheviks throughout the Twenties – had proved difficult to quash. One day in 1925 Andreev was tipped off that Basmachis had occupied the Anzob Pass in wait for him and his party, and he narrowly escaped with his life.

But banditry was not the only danger. The banks of the Yaghnob river were so steep that cows, sheep and even people could easily tumble into the abyss. Once, crossing a disintegrating section of mule track, Andreev's Yaghnobi guide lost his footing and he, a horse, and his baggage asses tumbled into the ravine. All of Andreev's Yaghnobi research – his notes on the Yaghnobi language, his observations, transcriptions of local stories, his herbarium of local botany, and his camera – were lost to the broad-gushing river.

Nevertheless, in the notes that did arrive home intact, all travellers testified to the extreme simplicity of the Yaghnobis' lives. Yaghnobis had no blacksmiths, shops, schools or roads. They had no design or ornamentation of any kind and no medical help save semi-literate mullahs who wrote out spells to ward off disease.

All the scholarship, knowledge and sophisticated artwork for which the Soghdians were renowned, had disappeared. Andreev found among Yaghnobis a litany of bizarre folk remedies. Syphilis, he discovered, was treated with child's urine, drunk three times a day, while smallpox was relieved with a mixture of milk and water – only considered effective if the remedy was served very slowly, and the spoon lifted high in the air.

The Yaghnobis' poverty was well known among the few scholars to visit the region. Újfalvy had found living conditions of almost Neolithic simplicity, noting their 'ploughshares like those of Carthage'.

Sent in 1896 by the Imperial Geographical Society to study the glacial phenomena of the Bukharan Emirate, the geographer V. I. Lipsky was equally horrified at the Yaghnobis' grim living conditions, their basic clothing, lacerated *khalats* and bare legs. 'Such dirt, such poverty, such ragged inhabitants I'd never seen before,' he wrote. Lipsky was also unimpressed with Yaghnobi bread: 'A black stoney mass,' he called it, 'only suitable as a collector's item, as there is really no place for it in the stomach.'

Nevertheless, Yaghnobis would enjoy, at the very least, a kind of autonomy, a de facto independence from Moscow. While the Tajiks of Khojand and Dushanbe felt the first assault of Soviet state policy – the five-year plans, the population movements – Yaghnobis continued much as they always did, their valley neither profitable, strategic nor close to any major centre of Soviet power.

As Tajikistan was slowly dragged into the twentieth century, hydroelectric plants were built, dams constructed, roads laid, and the curse of the cotton crop hit the country's lowlands. As the crop grew, hands were needed. Massive state farms absorbed large labour brigades, forced from their homes in the mountains. But everyone forgot about the Yaghnobis.

One by one the mountain Tajiks felt the pressure to join the *sovkhozes*. The first to be resettled were the people from the Gharm and Qarategin valleys in the late Twenties. By the Fifties, Soviet methods of enticement were more coercive, and an entire Mountain Tajik tribe called the Matcha (or *Mastchoh*) was settled in three large settlements near Proletarsk, after which their villages were levelled by tanks.

Then, in 1958, when it was decided to water Mirzachul, the much larger, drier region known as the 'Hungry Steppe' – a flat piece of land shared by Kazakhstan, Uzbekistan and Tajikistan – more hands were needed for the cotton-picking. For the time being, the Yaghnobis were safe.

By the Sixties, the Tajik Council of Ministers was scouring the highlands for more labour. The entire republic had been given the Order of Lenin, the highest honour of the USSR, for its valiant contribution to the white gold reserve. But local labour could never meet production targets. The finger of GosKomTrud – the State Committee for Labour and Social

Problems (whose first function generally caused the second) – finally pointed to the Yaghnobis.

It was late afternoon when we reached the Anzob Pass. The scene was wild and beautiful, as I'd imagined from the pages of Újfalvy and Andreev. The Yaghnob river was swollen with snowmelt and the wheels of the car danced over a potted mud road. The outline of a village finally appeared, its wooden columns and turf-piled roofs rising above a distant ridge.

'Is this the Yakoby Valley?' said Anne, deliberately getting the name wrong.

It wasn't. It was Margheeb, the last Tajik village before the trek up to Yaghnob.

As we pulled in, the entire village streamed out of their huts, women in velveteen dresses who stared while rocking their babies, old men in *dopilar* caps and children capering around on the earth slope.

We paid the driver and we found ourselves alone in the village surrounded by unfamiliar faces.

'OK. What do we do? They're staring at us,' said Anne.

A man materialised in front of the crowd, beckoning to us come with him. He turned out to be the *rais-i mahalla*, the head of the village, and he led us to one of the larger mudbrick houses, where we sat on his veranda and were served bread and tea and dried apricots. Children gawped at us from behind the poplars.

The *rais* spoke fairly incomprehensible Tajik and his Russian was poor, but I managed to communicate our plan to go to Yaghnob. He responded as if foreigners turned up every day looking for Yaghnobis. For my own sake I hoped they didn't. But I'd encountered this non-reaction more than once in Central Asia.

I told the *rais* we were looking for a guide, and asked if he knew anyone to take us.

He twiddled his moustache thoughtfully, then turned towards the house.

'Sadriddin,' he called. There was no answer.

'Sadridddiiiiin!' he shouted again, the veins swelling on his tanned-leather neck.

Seconds later a young man sloped onto the veranda. He was a raffish version of the *rais*, with a small, oiled moustache and boots made of strips of leather swaddling.

'Sadriddin will take you,' said the *rais*, his posture as straight as a ruler.

'Tell him I don't trust him. We want someone else,' Anne said.

'I can't do that,' I replied, but for once I agreed with her.

'What about you *āghā*?' I suggested deferentially to the *rais*.

'Sadriddin will take you.'

'Anne, I don't think we have a choice.'

A jeep was made ready, we piled in our rucksacks and provisions. Sadriddin had brought nothing.

'He realises we've hired him for a week, doesn't he?' asked Anne.

'I hope so,' I said.

We rumbled slowly over a schisty track cut out of the cliff-face. It ran along the steep banks of the Yaghnob river, bringing us ever further from Tajikistan's famously ambivalent emergency services.

As we climbed, the trees were replaced by fleeces of tough, heather-green ferns. Mountain tops towered and rock faces appeared, denuded to an iron peach and grey. The air was thinner.

'*Zdes' sobaki zliye,*' said Sadriddin at last. 'Here the dogs are nasty.' I wondered what he meant, when suddenly, as if out of the rock itself, a pair of ferocious hounds leapt at the jeep, snapping and snarling at the wheels, leaping up to the window with froth-flecked jaws. 'Only guard dogs,' said Sadriddin, smiling.

It was pitch black when the jeep stopped. We opened the doors to a blast of chilly air, light rain falling in gusts. Above us a fern-covered hill rose up in a steep gradient, at the top of which we could make out the faint twinkle of a lantern.

'The village of Markhtymain,' said Sadriddin, grabbing our bags and charging up the bushy hill.

We followed, straining to keep up with him. The fuzzy outline of a homestead appeared amid a tiny grove of trees. They were the last trees we'd see for a week.

'Village?' I said, out of breath when we got to the top. 'But it's only one house.'

Sadriddin pointed to the opposite bank, where a single cottage seemed to cling to the rock face.

'And that is the village of Bedev,' he said.

Sadriddin rapped on the window with a stick. A stocky, ruddy man called Niyoz appeared, and we were shown into a tiny room lit by a single bulb. Three old men sat trussed up in their dark green *khalats* and blue turbans, their faces shrivelled and wrinkled like nectarine stones. Anne was led, somewhat unwillingly, into the women's quarters.

These Yaghnobis were fairer than Lowland Tajiks, and their eyes were uncommonly green and blue. I was struck by the woman who brought in a tray of *shorbo* (greasy meat soup). Her face was so pale, her nose so straight and her hair parted so neatly in the middle that I could only think of a Greek vase painting.

All my reading had prepared me for the near monastic simplicity of the Yaghnobis. Nevertheless, I couldn't help thinking of the frescoes of the ancient Soghdians and their palaces at Samarkand and Varakhsha. Their palace walls were decorated with colourful and dramatic scenes of Iranian, Greek and Indian myth: the hero Rustam fighting supernatural devas, battles of Amazons, Hindu Brahmans playing dice. Soghdians produced some of the most vivid wall paintings of the era. I was naïve even to seek traces of them here.

A little boy had spotted the instrument that I kept hooked onto the top of my backpack. He was Niyoz's son. I noticed he had red bites all around his legs and ankles. 'What is it?' asked Niyoz.

I tried to explain: 'It's a uk—'

'It's a guitar,' said Anne, rolling her eyes. 'He's not going to understand ukulele.'

I ignored her and described the instrument to Niyoz with slow defiance. But the boy was too eager for a performance.

'*Musighi*,' the boy cried, at which all the other children – about ten more had joined us – all shouted '*Musighi! Musighi!*' in unison. I made my way with Anne to the adjoining room, which was full of young women and their children, grandmothers, sisters, crouching on the voluminous folds of their home-sewn dresses. '*Musighi!*' the children squealed, their mothers smiling with anticipation.

I played a Johnny Cash number, 'Ring of Fire.' It didn't go down well. When I finished I looked to find a crowd that was still smiling, but . . . not quite so much. One of the women pointed to Anne.

'I think she wants us both to sing together,' said Anne.

This was a terrible idea. The idea of singing 'New York, New York' (Anne's suggestion) to our Yaghnobi hosts made me shudder.

'C'mon, it's Sinatra, they'll love it.'

We performed a woeful rendition of the old favourite, without the right lyrics, rhythm or harmony. Our audience looked at us in bemusement. The smiles had vanished. It had become – possibly prematurely – time for bed.

We were all put together in the room where I and the old men had sat – Anne, Sadriddin and some family members – and were given thick quilts. The wind rattled the single pane of glass.

I lay in thought. It struck me that no one but Yaghnobis had wanted to live here. The Tajiks of Ayni who had enserfed the Yaghnobis over the last few centuries were content to rule from afar, where fruit trees and crops grew without back-breaking toil. Up here, where heavy snows blocked the passes for more than six months a year, their Yaghnobi language was left to crystallise. The wind suddenly abated. The pane stopped rattling and a silence descended like a cloak. I could almost hear the valley breathe a sigh of relief.

We rose at dawn the next morning, woken by a tray of home-baked bread and green tea, and a bowl of freshly churned cream. It was the same vase-painting woman of the night before. She smiled shyly and retired to the other room. The bread was soft and milky.

When we were ready, Sadriddin wound the leather straps of his boot round his ankles. We managed to hire Niyoz's donkey for the trip and tacked it up for the road ahead. The plan was to go as far as we could and come back for the *sunnat* a few days later. This was the circumcision ceremony that would be performed on Niyoz's son, the seven-year-old boy with the ankle bites. It would be quite an event, said Sadriddin, and the whole valley would be invited.

It was late August and the sun shone brightly behind fast-moving clouds. The air thinned again and the land unfurled into a glorious vision, cradled on all sides by the Zerafshan and Hissar ranges, dancing with the shadows of the clouds that passed overhead. The whole of the left bank was lit up, revealing its rocky clefts in sharp relief. The right bank that we followed was an unpredictable series of smooth curves and dead drops into the river. Every patch of flat earth was harnessed for peas and wheat, catching the valuable rays of summer sun. One false turn I avoided led straight down a beetling rock-face into the blue-green river below. I thought of Andreev's Yaghnobi guide and the danger of growing too comfortable on the track.

Sadriddin was an enigma. Our initial impression of him, Anne and I both agreed, was wrong. He was not the sneering youth we'd taken him for, but a genuinely reliable and likable man. When we asked him for advice on our travel plans he would smile sweetly, and say, with a slightly bowed head, 'Whatever pleases you.' When we wanted specific information, such as distances, or facts about the weather, his answers would be vague and contradictory. Most often he would smile serenely, point to the sky and say, '*Khodo khohad havo khub shavad*': 'God willing the weather will be fine.'

Sadriddin was unconcerned with details. He planned nothing and abhorred predictions. He accepted whatever happened, even if he'd caused it to happen, and preferred to sit on the back of the donkey singing Tajik folk songs in his high, clear voice. He was religious in the Tajik way. Occasionally, he would stop at the bend of the track or at a particularly strange-shaped rock or bush, mutter a prayer and pass his hands across his face. He explained that a *hojja* was buried there, a holy man. When we asked about the identity of the *hojja* he would invariably reply, 'A very great man,' or 'That's just what we do.'

One time Sadriddin dismounted by a heap of rubble by the side of the road. He knelt down and muttered a prayer.

'Is it the shrine of a *hojja*?' I asked.

'No,' he said, 'This is the village of Dumzoi.'

I looked to see where Dumzoi was on the map that Sadriddin had drawn.

He'd carefully indicated all the village names in biro, but I noticed for the first time how some of them had been struck through. It dawned on me that these were the villages abandoned in the deportation of 1970 and never re-inhabited. Their ancient walls were left to crumble, their mosques overgrown.

'They never came back,' said Sadriddin.

We wandered through the remains of Dumzoi's thick-walled homes of slate and stone, windows deep set against the winter cold, and ceilings impossibly low. Wild berries and rhubarb grew in rooms where people had once slept and prayed, the wooden rafters having long since disappeared.

In 1969 geologists arrived in Yaghnob with hi-tech equipment. Following some preliminary measurements, they announced that it was a 'geo-dynamic' zone, in imminent danger of an earthquake. But Qarategin and the Pamirs were in far greater danger of avalanches and earthquakes. Yaghnobis were unconvinced.

Determined to harness Yaghnobi manpower, the Tajik Supreme Soviet passed a resolution that all 3,020 registered Yaghnobis from 22 villages that should be resettled 'voluntarily' on the lowlands.

The first helicopters descended in early March 1970, when the snows were thick and there was nowhere to run. Pskon was the first village to be evacuated, followed by Kashe and Dumzoi.

Instructed to bring pelts and clothes – nothing bigger than a suitcase – Yaghnobis were herded into the helicopters. Those who resisted were beaten. Their flocks were requisitioned, their hard-won grain left to rot, and their prized wooden rafters – so precious in a treeless valley – would be burnt for firewood by Tajik shepherds soon after the Yaghnobis had left.

In a bizarre twist, the notes of the late M. S. Andreev were published in the same year, causing a stir in academic circles. Muhammad Asimov, President of the Academy of Sciences of Tajikistan, was impressed by Andreev's research and petitioned GosKomTrud to make a documentary film to record the last days of Yaghnobi life, now only weeks from annihilation.

A plan was hurriedly approved to document the life and customs of the 'Tajik-Soghdians' in order to demonstrate the Communist Party's efforts to improve the cultural and living standards of the country. Billed as an educational film, it was supposed to document for posterity the very anthropological phenomenon that the authorities were trying to destroy.

Life in Zafarabad was, predictably, not the labourer's utopia the Yaghnobis' were promised. They were relocated to a vast, flat, dusty plain, where chemicals forced cotton out of thousands of hectares of land. Many of the drab, identical houses had been built without doors or windows, and families were crowded together in tiny rooms.

The Yagnobis' green world had become grey and the cool wind of the mountain tops was exchanged for the stifling air of the lowlands. Yaghnobis reported hearing the clicking of heels on concrete for the first time. Powerful, deadly fertilisers washed into drinking water and were sprayed on to workers from planes, killing scores of people.

The first Yaghnobis to escape their Zafarabad prison in the early Seventies and begin life again in Yaghnob were condemned to an existence of almost Stone Age simplicity. Survival was a daily challenge. Many of the cows they'd brought from the lowlands were unaccustomed to Yaghnob's steep banks and perished in the ravines. Wolves, too, were a constant threat and preyed constantly on the frightened guard dogs.

The authorities would hunt the escaped Yaghnobis in the valleys, launching search parties on foot and by air, flying back to the old Yaghnobi villages to scoop up whomever had returned. Yaghnobis would break out again, and again the helicopters would hunt them down. Eventually the authorities turned a blind eye to the returnees, but damned them to excommunication from the Soviet Union. This meant that they were denied access to foodstores or healthcare and were no longer issued birth certificates. They were stateless in their own land. But by 1973 few Yaghnobis cared about their civic rights. By then half their number was already dead.

The scenery seemed to shift constantly once we'd left Dumzoi. We began to dive down a scree of gunmetal schist. Swollen with meltwater, the Yaghnob river washed a clean path through the slate, snaking from the mountain tops in a bewitching cerulean green.

Soon the grassy hills fell away and we were left in a stark canyon, surrounded on all sides by nude stone cliffs. We hopped across the low slatey river, through a pass that shut out the sunlight, following the sure footing of our donkey.

Over the hours we spent walking, I came to see a more gutsy side to Anne. She told me she'd spent her twenties doing risky NGO work in the West Bank and China, and recalled a day trip she'd made to Iraq in 1990, ten days before the allied bombing.

'I just hopped over the border into Iraq for tea,' she said. 'Everyone knew America was coming, but they treated me with such respect. The guy at the border put a stamp on a separate piece of paper, because he knew it would be trouble and just said "a souvenir from my country" – a country we were about to bomb the shit out of. Can you imagine us doing that to an Iraqi?'

'Didn't you worry you might get arrested?'

'Hell, I'd just come from China. Remember Tiananmen Square? I was still organising pro-democracy demonstrations when the tanks were rolling in.'

'You were doing *what*?' I realised I had completely misjudged her. 'So what happened? Why didn't you carry on working abroad?'

'As I got older, time got scarce and the Third World just got up my nose. I don't like delay and I don't like incompetence, as you've probably noticed.' We chuckled. 'Though I can't say things are necessarily better in the West. We can be completely useless. I used to work as a consultant for McKinsey on a lot of start-ups and I was once called in to give a presentation in D.C. on employment in global non-profit organisations. You know all these guys had lived in the system for years, all had trust funds, hadn't got a clue about the realities of job creation. So I come in, talk for an hour, and what have they understood? Not a goddamn thing. That's America's biggest problem – insularity.'

By late afternoon the sky was swirling into wispy darkness. The haphazardly winding mule-track followed the shallow-sloping right bank, furred with tawny-green heather. The left bank was a barren, chalky slope that sustained little life. We suddenly caught sight of a village.

Pskon was a jumble of box-like one-roomed huts, surrounded by patches of farmed land, short wheat stalks of waxy yellow and pale-green beans. Half the village seemed to perch on a precipice. A woman sat with her child on the edge of a sheer rock face, dangling her legs while she shelled her pea pods.

'Ho!' shouted Sadriddin, announcing our approach.

A tall man dismounted from a grey horse and strode over to meet us. His name was Rakhmatkhan, a hulking figure with dimpled cheeks and a handlebar moustache. He said little, and appraised us as if we were horses at the *mal bazaar*.

Rakhmatkhan asked us nothing, neither our names nor intentions, but beckoned us to his house. Like Niyoz, he seemed to display a total acceptance of whatever came his way. His hut was made of stone and mudbrick, with some folded quilts and one or two shelves on the wall. It was completely without ornament – with one exception: a flat woodcarving, inscribed in Tajik: '*Khona fonus ast, mihmon sham' ast, man parvon-am*': – 'The house is a lampshade, the guest is a candle, I am the moth.'

Within minutes, a haggard old woman arrived with a tray of bread, cream and green tea for the unexpected guests. Rakhmatkhan signalled for us to eat, while he chewed his barley stalk.

It was quiet outside, except for the faint gushing of the river below, and the sound of panting. An ancient figure appeared, as bent as a figure of eight, with a high stack of brushwood strapped to his back. He released a buckle and let it fall in a heap with a whimper. I stared at my unearned cream-dipped bread.

Rakhmatkhan read my thoughts. 'Winter is long here,' he said. 'We must prepare.' In Yaghnob it was still summer.

In the early evening the sky burst as it had threatened and the slopes were bathed again in showery night. The single window pane rattled in its sill. A lantern was lit and some neighbours arrived. The door was battened and we crouched around the floor with more bowls of *shorbo* and tea.

Rakhmatkhan asked me suddenly: 'Do you have cotton in your country?'

I told him we didn't, as our weather wasn't right for it. He nodded and turned away. Then, without prompting, he spoke about Zafarabad and the fertiliser planes that flew low over the fields. He made swooping gestures to illustrate and fluttered his fingers up and down his arm to indicate the chemical irritants, defoliants and pesticides.

'It fell on our heads, arms, legs. The water was no good. Up here the water comes from the glacier. Down there the water killed us.'

I asked him what happened to the Yaghnobi community on the lowland.

'We built a cemetery, and within five years it was full.'

At night everyone disappeared, including Rakhmatkhan, leaving the three of us to bury ourselves in quilts. But in the morning, after scratching all night, I realised I had company.

I'd picked up bedbugs in Markhtymain and they were multiplying in my sleeping bag. I showed the bites to Sadriddin, a man who'd walked and slept in the same clothes for days. He examined my bitten arms.

'*Kayk*, we call them,' he said, smiling. 'They're harmless.'

Typically, Anne was utterly indifferent to my *kayk* problem and told me to stop being such a child. I had been prepared for this response, but I noticed something new: Anne hadn't complained about the discomfort or the weather since we reached the Yaghnob Valley, even though this was the hardest part. I learned that it really was inconvenience she objected to: the non-fulfilment of plans, the impossibility of long-distance calls, the slowness of public transport. When it came to the physical realities of cross-country travel on foot, she was remarkably tough.

Our plan that day was to visit the village of Gharmen. Even smaller than Pskon, it was on a bit of a branchline, sitting on the banks of a tributary river a couple of hours' walk away. Andreev had written that according to Yaghnobi tradition, the people of Gharmen had 'eyes like sheep', and it was the last village we would see if we were to get back to Markhtymain for the *sunnat*, the great circumcision ceremony.

We set out under a bluff, marble sky, backtracking until we reached the veiny tributary of the Yaghnob river. These were not the sheer cliffs of the main river valley. The land seemed to roll in manageable folds and it was a lot greener here.

In the distance we could see a promontory and the tops of terraced homesteads on a slope, patched with mint-green farmed land. Some children were running barefoot over the terraces. A guard dog soaked up the season's dying sun. It had a white coat, a long snout and tufty cheeks, and was probably three generations from a wolf.

A little way up the slope was a *mihmonkhona*, the Tajik mosque-cum-meeting-house. It was constructed in the old Bukhara style, a single column of wood supporting a roof of crushed ballast, shot through with girders. But the roof was heaped with the white-bleached skulls of deer, their rough, pitted antlers still attached to their smooth skulls. I thought of Mirzo and the ancient ring I'd been shown on the bus from Istaravshan.

I knew that this had been an ancient Central Asian practice, to place ram or gazelle horns by mosques and holy sites. The origin of this was disputed. Could these antlers be the last vestiges of Soghdian tradition, which outlasted the Arab invasion, centuries of seclusion and a devastating deportation?

A bear of a man strode up from the lower fields. He wore a leather jerkin, had a bristling beard and large, calloused hands. But he didn't have 'eyes like sheep'. His name was Sangin Murod and he gave Sadriddin a powerful hug. We were ushered with Yaghnobi etiquette into his house with gruff, silent generosity, and brought bowls of *shorbo* and bread, followed by thick slices of liver. Anne heaped them onto my bowl, and reached for her rice cakes.

I shot her a pleading look.

'What? What is it?' Anne bristled.

Sangin Murod looked at Anne's bowl. 'Why will she not eat her meat?' he asked.

'She cannot eat meat,' I replied.

He was appalled. 'But she must. I eat a kilo a day, and if there is enough I will eat five kilos. Tell her if she doesn't eat meat she will not bear children.' Judging by the number of small children running around the hut, there seemed to be no shortage of meat in Gharmen.

Sangin Murod told me he was two years old at the time of the great deportation. He studied in Dushanbe, learning (on top of Tajik and Yaghnobi) Uzbek, Russian and German. I asked him about the antlers on top of the mosque.

'I don't know. I am a Communist.'

But I persisted. Did he know anything at all about the significance of the antlers? Was it an old Soghdian tradition?

'Deer is a clean animal,' he said. 'Antlers are the sign of a mosque.'

Sangin Murod didn't really know, but I thought of Újfalvy, who noted that a 'Galtcha never blows a candle out for his breath is impure.' All over Central Asia and Iran the new year festival of Nouruz (or here Navrus) is a continuation of the ancient Zoroastrian festival. Here in Central Asia, the periphery of the Muslim domain, it was yet another substratum that poked through the patina of Islam.

'But I tell you this,' said Sangin Murod, with incontestable conviction, 'there were once magicians in this valley that turned people into cats. With Allah as my witness it happened.'

We spent a second night in Pskon. Inside our hut, the eiderdowns were warm against the bracing air, but my *kayks* were tormenting me. I fidgeted all night like a cat in a bag, inviting scorn from Anne and warm smiles from Sadriddin.

But the walk back to Markhtymain was epic. The sky was inscrutable as ever, a great capricious vault that constantly changed its mind. Infused with ink, clouds swirled around the mountain tops with restive indecision, threatening to disgorge themselves. Then without warning, the sky commanded that today there would be no rain, and the clouds would skulk away to brood until the next opportunity.

Sadriddin walked in front and Anne strayed far behind. Again, she was quite uncommunicative, but she no longer sulked. Anne spent long hours on her own, and every so often I saw her smile.

Rakhmatkhan trotted ahead to Gharmen to pick up Sangin Murod, while Sadriddin pressed on. He sat with a contented look, rocking back and forth on the donkey. He took my ukulele, fiddled with the pegs and struck up an old Tajik song. In the clear valley air, he sang as sweetly and contentedly as a character from pastoral verse.

Yo mavlon, dilum tang omadast
Shishe-i dilum zir-i sang omadast
Bulbul ba sar-i chashma chi kor omadei,
*Yo tishna shudi, yo ba shikor omadei . . .**

*'Oh holy one, my heart is heavy, the glass of my heart has come under a stone. Nightingale, why have you come to the spring? Are you thirsty, or are you hunting?'

We passed more ruined villages like Dumzoi, but I no longer tried to investigate. The path now took a steep tumble down to the river. The donkey, fully loaded with kit and Sadriddin, negotiated the descent with great care, placing its hooves in wide, safe steps. As we reached the ford we bumped into an old man in a dusty *khalat*. He'd come all the way from Kirionte, a Tajik village several hours' walk at the far end of the valley. He was tiny and bent, and took slow, purposeful steps. Just one tooth remained attached to his gums, and it gave a whistling, indistinct quality to his impenetrable, high-pitched Tajik. He was 72 years old and was making a journey that would tax a far younger man.

When we reached Markhtymain around dusk, the *sunnat* was underway. The child himself was nowhere to be seen and the mullah had been delayed by a day. Two dozen Yaghnobis stood round a bonfire, while loud Iranian pop music blared out from a sound system rigged up to a generator. They were rough, country types: threadbare woollen jumpers and scant teeth. Rakhmatkhan sat alone, chewing a stick. Sangin Murod stood apart, staring moodily into the valley, in a Seventies cream corduroy jacket with elbow patches. Perhaps the *sunnat* was not cause for merrymaking.

Inside the men's quarters, steel platters were carried back and forth, piled high with rice and meat from a freshly slaughtered cow. The 72-year-old we'd met sat crosslegged, dwarfed by his *khalat*. To this day I have no idea how he'd managed to arrive before us.

A Yaghnobi from Dushanbe was holding court. He was a smart city type in a suit. He'd brought his own tea bag and its string hung ostentatiously over his cup. He was educated and spoke like an orator.

'Which is better,' he asked the crowd, 'knowledge or money?'

'Knowledge,' they all mumbled.

'Knowledge, I tell you, is the wine from the cup of life.'

'*Durust ast. Durust ast,*' they said, automatically. 'That's right, that's right.'

The women's quarters were, by contrast, a riot of joking and laughter. Twenty women were crammed together, clad in garishly floral dresses with puffed-up shoulders. Children were passed around to be fed, clothed and coddled.

Then, a woman called Said Mo, a strikingly beautiful mother with fine skin, changed her daughter's dress to reveal red *kayk* bites all over the toddler's legs and stomach. The little girl had cried herself sick.

'What is there to do?' asked Said Mo, resigned. 'She won't sleep. Only cries.'

Another woman with a gaunt, withered face was cradling her child's head. His eyebrow was grossly swollen and shining red, as if he'd been bitten by hornet. She offered him to me to cure, like a beggar seeking the King's Evil.

'Please,' she said, pitifully.

'I'm sorry,' I said. 'I'm not a doctor.'

'From the Government, then?'

'No,' searching hard for what I could offer.

'I'm ill, he's ill, we're all ill.' She nodded her head round the room of apparently healthy women. 'We have no doctors.'

That night Anne and I were put in a hut a little way down the hill. It was a freezing night and the plastic covered only part of the window. A youth was lying in a dirty bed in the corner, scratching. The blankets reeked of urine. It felt like a makeshift hospital for the war wounded.

All I wanted to do was climb into my sleeping bag, pile it high with the smelly blankets, and drift away. But Anne was keen to eke out the last hours of the *sunnat*, though she spoke not a word of the local language. She darted off up the hill, while I fell into a shivering sleep.

Hours later, Anne shook me awake. I blearily came to.

She was alive with excitement.

'That room we were in, with the women. It was amazing,' she said, agitated. 'One of the women dressed up as a man. She danced round like it was the most normal thing in the world. She had on this red and gold mask, banging a platter like a drum. Then all the other women got up and danced and tried to sing songs together. None of them could think of the right words and so they couldn't finish them. And then you know what they did? They started crying. They all sat around and they were crying like it was a funeral or something. Seriously, it was intense. I wanted to cry myself, but I didn't know what I'd be crying about. Man, I wish I spoke Yakoby!'

The remains of the bonfire glowed in its white ashes as we got up for breakfast. Guests sat with cold *shorbo*, talking in the same deadpan manner, and the women returned to their day to day tasks, as mothers, cooks and laundry women.

The donkey was returned to its owners, and we packed our things up very high on our shoulders. It was to be a 25 km walk back to Margheeb.

When I thanked Niyoz for all his hospitality, his eyes expressed little, as if thanks were an irrelevance. I consulted Sadriddin afterwards.

'Was it very inconvenient for them?' I asked.

'You could have stayed forever if you'd wanted,' he said, without irony.

With every step to Margheeb, the air became thicker and denser. The trees returned slowly and soon we were walking through habitable landscape. Three times we crossed streams that had burst their banks and gushed over the road.

Arriving in Dushanbe the next day, tender in the calves, we felt quite tired and were keen to eat anything but *shorbo*. As I scrubbed the layers of sweat from my body I could examine for the first time the bites on my skin. These 'harmless' *kayks* had bitten me 170 times. I washed my clothes and cleaned all of my kit.

Anne prepared to leave for New York.

'Thanks, I had a blast,' she said in her inimitable way. We hugged. Uncomfortable with the sudden intimacy she wagged a figure at me: 'And don't go to Afghanistan!'

I spent the next few days convalescing in sunny, civilised Dushanbe, slowly getting used to a world without Anne. I did little. I walked along Rudaki, bought some Georgian wine and read novels in the comfort of our old Sixties flat. It was like being in suburbia again. I was alone at last, a state I'd longed for day and night. I had no one to shout at now or translate for; no more errands to run or tempers to soothe. I no longer had to check my words before the withering look on her face told me I was a complete idiot. I was free. And more than a bit concerned about the next step.

6

'Slaying the dragon': The Hazaras

'Sag-e Aughu kas dāra, ādam-e Azrah nah'
'Even a Pashtun dog has a protector, but not a Hazara.'
Hazara proverb

Recalling my first few steps in Afghanistan, my strongest memory is a surge of new senses and smells. They were the most evocative of any country I've visited, and different from the rest of Central Asia. I will never forget the aroma of steaming *qabuli pilau*, green tea with cardamom, rain-pattered wool, and the stinking dust of Kabul's streets.

I'd carefully planned my entry point. I didn't want to take the direct route across to Shir Khan Bandar, via southern Tajikistan. Instead I flew to the town of Khorog, in the Autonomous Region of Gorno-Badakhshan, the impoverished and remote part of Tajikistan's extreme south-east, from where I would cross to one of Afghanistan's safest provinces – Badakhshan, a quiet, rural country where shepherds spoke Persian and there were no Taliban. This last detail was important.

From Faizabad, the regional capital, I'd head to Qunduz, and thence to Kabul: a tortuous route, perhaps, but I felt that if I made it safely to the capital, I'd be well prepared to strike out into the interior to visit my next people, the Hazaras, Shiites of

Mongol descent who lived in the parched central hinterland known as the Hazarajat.

Relying on my straggly two-month beard, and my shalwar kameez, retrieved crisp and starched from its packet, I was as ready as I'd ever be. I walked to the end of Khorog's main road, girding myself for trouble, bribery, interrogations. But the border post was like a country tollbooth. Teenagers in fatigues took pains to scratch 'torist' onto my visa and ushered me through with enthusiastic smiles.

Entering Afghanistan was like being plunged into the thirteenth century. The tarmac disappeared into earth tracks, the concrete houses made way for mudbrick huts, and the only transport seemed to be carts and crudely tethered asses. Western clothing was discarded for exotic-looking wool *patous*, waistcoats, shalwars, and beret-like *pakul* hats. Unlike the mostly clean-shaven Khorogis, here men sported magnificent black beards as soft as lambs' wool. And the women, unlike Khorog, were nowhere to be seen.

The nearest village to the border was Shugnan, a jumble of huts and rutted roads, where men lounged on tea-beds, sucking their teeth and eating *qabuli pilau* – the standard fare of rice with meat and raisins. I took a Toyota minibus to Faizabad, an eight-hour journey, driven by Aman, a dour, jowly taxi driver. He said little and rarely smiled. He also had a filthy temper, and if I didn't understand whatever he was saying he would shake his head and sigh heavily. But he seemed to want to teach me about his country, and would give me practical advice about how to act and speak, and how to avoid unwanted attention. I felt protected by him.

The road was terrible. We bounced and swayed over giant potholes and boulders. But this time I didn't mind. I slid open the window and felt the cool Badakhshani air on my face, breathing in the green of the high meadows, the hardy mountain flowers, the lichen-bitten boulders and grey slate.

A light drizzle began to fall and some way along a mountain corniche, flanked by a shingly stream, a young shepherd appeared by the road. He flagged down our vehicle with his crook. The boy opened the sliding doors and I was immediately aware of the odour of rain on wool from his chocolate *patou*, still greasy with lanolin. He sat down and shivered. His eyes, I noticed, were a brilliant green, and his skin was already showing signs of roughness. He couldn't have been more than 15. I asked him his age, and he stared at me as if no one had ever asked him anything so irrelevant.

'*Namedānam*,' he said. 'I don't know.'

When the rain stopped he tapped Aman's shoulder, slid open the doors, and strode off along the meadow towards the snow-dusted hills beyond, to a byre out of view and off the map.

The matt white sky had darkened, leaving us a single headlight to navigate the road. Around a sudden bend came the faint glow of naked bulbs. A large tent had been erected, chugging with the sound of generators. It was a makeshift restaurant, where drivers, shepherds, dealers and traders sat on the ground next to plastic tablecloths, bunched up in dirty shalwars and cloaks, shovelling handfuls of pilau into their mouths. We found a place among them.

A small boy came over with stainless steel platters of rice with lamb, and side dishes of cold okra. Every time I tried to scoop up the rice, the grains fell apart and spilled all over my front.

Aman's eyes flickered away in embarrassment.

'Look,' he said, holding up a pinch of rice. 'You do it like this.'

The trick, it seemed, was to compress the rice between the three fingers, pushing the meat and rice together until compact.

'Now,' he said, leaning in, 'there is another thing.'

'What?'

'You told me in Shugnan you were English. From now on you are Iranian, OK?'

I'd considered the identity change myself, but wasn't sure if I'd pull it off.

'They will believe you,' he said. It was taking me some time to get used to Dari, Afghanistan's Persian dialect, and I was still speaking the language with a heavy Iranian accent. 'The important thing,' he said, 'is that you are not English, understand?'

'Why shouldn't I say I'm English?' I asked.

'Because you English don't like Muslims.'

'That's not true.'

He did not like to be contradicted.

'Then why are you fighting us on our land?'

'The British are fighting the Taliban, not Muslims.'

He shook his head as if I'd completely missed the point, but I didn't contradict him again. He told me that during the anti-Soviet jihad he'd launched a number of raiding parties against Soviet supply lines, and had 'killed many men.'

I couldn't help asking how many.

'I don't know,' he said gruffly. 'You ever fought in a war? Ten, twenty, fifty.'

He went quiet, swirling his fingers and thumb round the plate for the last of the rice.

'The Russians hated Muslims too,' he added.

We arrived at Faizabad as the muezzins were calling their dawn *fajr* prayers. Cartwheels churned the morning mud and shopkeepers set up stalls on the messy, unpaved streets. Aman led me to his house, an upper storey wooden apartment with a row of wood-latticed windows that looked over the town. He showed me a soft sheepskin and left me to sleep. He closed the door softly and I lay on my back, wide awake, my nostrils heavy with pinewood and lanolin, my senses still taut, my eyes still wide.

When I awoke a couple of hours later, I opened the latticed window and watched the town outside. The rains had formed small pools of brown water. I listened to the squelch of flip-flops and goat hoofs. The air was infused with the smell of baking bread and animal ordure.

Instead of rows of wood or brick, van-sized metal containers had been dragged on to the main street, their roofs heaped with earth, and the interiors filled with produce: spices and roots, headless carcasses, woollen *patous*. The stock was often oddly specific: one shop sold only fly-swats, another sold only partridges in wicker cages. One other had a comprehensive range of firearms and stereo systems.

The public lavatory, it seemed, was a rubbish tip at the foot of a steep hill not far from Aman's house, where both men and women were taking their morning shit. The men were screened by the flaps of their shalwars, and the women modestly cocooned in their burkas, although they squatted only feet from each other.

I bought a cream *pakul* hat – one of the woollen caps with a rolled rim, popular among Tajiks – and found a taxi to Qunduz. I walked up the slippery main street. An old man with a long grey goatee pointed his stick at me.

'*Az kojā hasted?*' he asked. 'Where are you from?'

'*Irān,*' I replied.

'No you're not.'

'*Cherā,*' I said. 'Yes I am.'

'You're lying. I can tell a Turk, an Uzbek, a Pashtun. I know an Iranian when I see one, and I say you are American.'

A small crowd began to form. One smirked.

'*Az kojāst?*' asked one, pointing at me, 'Where's he from?'

'*Āmrikā, Ingilis, Farānseh?*'

'*Khāreji-a, farqi namekona,*' said another. 'He's foreign, what's the difference?'

Quickly, a crowd of young men formed a circle around me. This was exactly the kind of situation I wanted to avoid. I backed away, relieved to find a long-distance taxi rank, where I met my next protector: Rasul.

Rasul had the dry, worn face of a long-distance driver, though he was only in his mid-twenties, like me. His vehicle was a battered Toyota corolla, a yellow hatchback with a crushed left headlight and hairline cracks in its windscreen. For six years Rasul had negotiated these difficult roads, but he'd managed to retain a certain youthful enthusiasm. He had a thick, country accent and I strained hard to understand what he was saying.

Faizabad was linked to nowhere. The few, terrible roads were the key to the region's inviolability. Badakhshan was one of the few provinces in which the Taliban never gained a foothold.

Crawling up a stony mountain road, we hit a problem. A truck had broken down, blocking all the Faizabad-Qunduz traffic.

The only alternative was a winding track that led up the mountain slope, a path rumoured to lead eventually, days hence, to Qunduz. We reached the turn-off, a thin, steep track with a metre-deep hollow in the middle of the road. I asked in disbelief: 'This goes to Qunduz?'

'*Ensha'allah*,' Rasul grinned. 'God willing.'

Like a seasoned boxer who refused to fall, the Toyota, like its driver, took pleasure in every challenge, leaping over moon craters, scrambling up dust-screes, and when its tyres lost their purchase and its chassis thudded heavily on rock, it soldiered on. Rasul leapt out every half an hour with spanner in hand, tightening the bolts and tapping the engine until it was ready again.

Meanwhile, there wasn't a squeak out of my travelling companions, a middle-aged Afghan-Tajik couple and their teenage daughter, who sat together in the back. I turned round to commiserate over the journey, but my attempts at small talk were met curtly. 'I can't keep putting on my *rusari* all the time,' bridled the old woman, for whom hours in the back meant valuable time away from prying eyes. Chastened, I focused on the road ahead for the remainder of the journey.

In the late afternoon, as the poor car sputtered its way over the dry, ragged rocks of this unforgiving country, the engine was beginning to wheeze. Its next challenge, a steep dust slope, proved too much for the tired Toyota. Rasul did what he could, rattling levers, pushing pedals, but with an exhalation of fatigue, the car sank slowly and dispiritedly back to the bottom of the hill. Within minutes, the entire male population of the village had emerged from their huts, slightly misshapen men, some with harelips and hunchbacks, all gathering to push the car as it spewed sand from its tyres. The engine squealed, the tyres spun, and Rasul murmured incantations until the old Toyota reached the top. The mother and daughter, who had hidden modestly in the shade, appeared as if from nowhere, climbed in and the car burst into life again.

Later still, the mountain trail gave way to better tracks, but they could hardly be called roads. We passed countless mudbrick villages, where time seemed to stand still. In the village of Argo, every rooftop seemed to be piled with dark-red poppies, their stalks like the shafts of cannon brushes. It had been another bumper harvest.

'I used to live in Argo,' said Rasul, 'but I fled when the Taliban came to Qunduz. The Taliban never made it to this village, but it is very traditional here. They don't listen to music. They say it is a sin.'

We arrived at night in Qunduz, a small city in the Uzbek north. I salvaged my kit from the oil-filled boot of Rasul's Toyota, blackened and covered with a fine dust. I found a filthy, overpriced room, inflated my camp bed, got into my sheet sleeping bag, and fell into a long, bone-buzzing sleep.

When I awoke it was midday. Emerging into the street, I had my first taste of urban Afghanistan. The air was filled with the smell of woodsmoke and dung, and the sound of jingling bells. Horse-drawn gigs charged through the streets at a furious pace. Small Kataghani horses were draped with bells and pompoms like Christmas sleighs. Peddlars vyed politely for room: a grocer squatted by sacks of cardamom and an old devotee was encamped in the middle pavement on his *kilim*, offering his *zohr* prayers. Women in sky-blue tents sat in threes on the backs of horse-drawn gigs, or walked with husbands in the street, their eyes obscured by a tiny gauze.

The final stretch to Kabul was less daunting than I had expected. The road was metalled and it was a question now of waiting and sitting, and there was no need to worry about what to do in case of a breakdown. My taxi was yet another Toyota Corolla, and when it was full, we set off on the four-hour journey to Kabul.

As we snaked through the Hindu Kush, via the Salang Pass and Baghlan, there were the constant reminders of the jihad, the ten-year struggle against the Soviet Union, between 1979 and 1989. With superior manpower and all the latest technology, the Soviets had been routed by an alliance of militiamen known as the mujaheddin, which has now come to mean 'holy warriors'. Round every bend in the road and scattered across the slopes were small Soviet tanks, strewn like discarded toys. There were personnel carriers and armoured snow-ploughs, their tracks torn off and turrets half-attached. Every few miles rocks were painted with crude red crosses that winked in the headlights, like cats' eyes, a warning of live mines. There were still tens of thousands of unexploded mines around the country, which in the last two decades have killed and injured 70,000 Afghans, as well as sheep and cattle.

You could see Kabul from miles off. Smog lay over the city like an oppressive mantle. Soon we were immersed in a sea of yellow cars, drifters, hawkers, amputees, and street children selling bottles of ditch-water through car windows.

Kabul is a plunging, foetid pit. Faecal matter was dumped on street corners all over the city like an evil *potpourri*. The exhaust from a million cars cut visibility to a few metres, turning the sunset an apocalyptic orange. Within days my nostrils would be furred with a dry black gunk. Wearing contact lenses was particularly unpleasant.

There was a time, presumably before the combustion engine, when Kabul was quite lovely. Babur, the Timurid prince ousted from Samarkand by the Shaybanids, made Kabul the capital of his new Mughal capital in the early sixteenth-century. He writes nostalgically of gardens and palaces, an excellent climate, succulent fruit and streams of caravans bringing luxury goods. One Indian poet, Haidar, was equally effusive: 'Dine and drink in Kabul,' he wrote. 'It is mountain, desert, city, river and all else.'

A string of modernising kings brought universities, an educated elite, and a middle class that shopped. Marks & Spencer opened its first Central Asian outlet here in the Sixties. In the decades of peace under Zahir Shah (who assumed the throne in 1933 and died aged 92 in 2007), the Government demolished much of the old city. In the name of progress, Soviet planners were invited to remodel it with prefab apartment blocks and concrete pavements.

Nothing, however, could compare to the destruction caused in the Nineties, when warring factions of the mujaheddin competed for control of the city. Whole areas were flattened.

The western district of Demazang got the worst drubbing, fired on by two opposing sides, and largely reduced to rubble. Kabulis, who found themselves surrounded with building materials, but few buildings, turned to recycling. Steel was picked out of heaps and sold; mud was scraped from rubble and fashioned into new houses, and the starving, pummelled populace kept some areas inches from obliteration.

In the years following the fall of the Taliban in 2001, Kabul has seen an unprecedented building boom. Property prices have rocketed and today cheap sleeps were strangely hard to come by, particularly for foreigners. It was a question of security. Hotels without the means to protect their guests would often rather refuse them than attract dangerous attention.

The hotels that did accept foreigners usually had electric generators, hot water, food, and knew that their patrons could pay. I found myself in a place that had no security, no food, only a few hours of electricity and charged foreigners whatever they thought they could get.

It called itself The Plaza. It was in the poor end of town, in the hurly-burly of the Salang Wat, one of the city's main arteries, choked with traffic and pedestrians. The railing that bounded the pavement had buckled under the weight of peddlars, blind men, amputees, beggars, watchmakers, phone-card sellers and petty entrepreneurs. I became fixated with the ice-cream sellers who rolled great cubes of ice along the dungy pavement, hacked them into shards, and massaged them by hand into a delicious-looking paste. The results sat curled in elegant glass bowls, belying the botulism they inevitably concealed.

The range of headdresses on the Salang Wat was as fascinating as it was theatrical: black-turbaned sayyeds, white Pashtun turbans in artful heaps and vertical flourishes, there were *pakul* caps in cream and brown wool, white skullcaps and black karakul hats of curling lambs' wool. Each headdress was a statement of identity or tribal affiliation.

The management of the Plaza were impossible to haggle with. I gave up quickly. They showed me a spare and very expensive room: wooden floorboards, a plank on stilts with a thin mattress and a bedside table, bearing an unexpectedly random aluminium spittoon. The bare walls were run with cracks from the bombing, and the upper half of one of the walls had been converted into a row of windows, rendering the room totally open to view. There was no water or electricity either.

But I hadn't come for the five-star treatment, I had my inflatable bed, bottles of mineral water for my showers. I was determined to enjoy my stay at the Plaza.

If you ever walk around the streets of north Tehran, one thing you cannot miss is the building site, the omnipresent drilling and banging, creating marble and concrete mini-palaces for the Iranian elite. Amid the dust is the familiar sight of the young Afghan boy in his soiled overalls and baggy shalwar. These tend not to be just any Afghans, but Hazaras: Shiite Afghans of Mongol origin who fled to Iran in their tens of thousands during the turbulent Nineties, seeking refuge and employment among their co-religionists.

Shiites differ from Sunnis chiefly in that they reject the first three Caliphs after the Prophet, and consider Ali (the Prophet's cousin and son-in-law) and his successors to be the only rightful heirs of the Prophet. But sharing a common branch of Islam would not shield the Hazaras from repeated discrimination from other Shiites.

I remember once asking directions from a young Hazara labourer in Tehran. I showed him the address on a piece of paper and he waved his hands at me, signalling that he couldn't read. Then he furtively backed away, as if expecting to be hit. Many Hazaras were mistreated by their Iranian employers, who exploited them for cheap labour and taunted them for their illiteracy, Mongol features and thick accents. '*Afghānī*' is one of the commonest insults in Iran, and effectively it means 'Hazara.'

But if Hazaras were strangers in Iran, they could be equally uneasy at home in their native Afghanistan. Numbering about a million (300,000 in Bamiyan province and 700,000 in neighbouring provinces – not to mention the hundreds of thousands in exile), Hazaras have long played the role of 'untouchables'.

Informally called the Hazarajat, the Hazara homeland is a rugged stretch of high plateaux and dry valleys, running alongside the western spine of the Hindu Kush mountains. Once covering a much larger area, the Hazarajat of today covers the Middle provinces of Afghanistan: Bamiyan, Orozgan and Ghur, where the roads are completely unserviceable and the entire region is cut off for six months a year by snow. The tenth-century Persian poet Ferdowsi called this wild region *barbaristān* – place of barbarians. So remote was the Hazarajat that Afghan central rule consistently failed to assert itself there and the region was governed by its own rigid feudal system.

Its villages were constantly harassed by Uzbek merchants from Qunduz' slave market, demanding tribute in the form of money or humans. Ensconced in their central haven, Hazaras were little understood beyond units of labour, and their status as Shiites only legitimised their enslavement to Sunnis.

Hazaras are thought to be descended from the Turco-Mongol armies that swept across Asia in the thirteen century – their name meaning 'thousand' in Persian, a Mongol military division. Arriving in 1221, the Mongol conquerors wiped out the local Iranian population, supplanted the locals' forts and garrisons and, curiously, decided to stay.

The Mongols learned much from their Iranian neighbours, not only in the adoption of Persian, but also the old Zoroastrian reverence for fire. One traveller in the Fifties recalls observing the practice of Eid-i Mordo, 'festival of souls', when lamps were lit and dedicated to the souls of the dead, to help the departed to the next world.

The Hazara language is a difficult Persian dialect, a heavily accented Dari called Hazaragi, 10 per cent of which is derived directly from Mongol. Elsewhere in Asia the memory of the Mongol horde recalls savagery and destruction, but the Mongol image in the Hazarajat recalls nobility and strength of character. Today, a Hazara mother will tell her slouching son '*Moghūl beneshin*' – 'Sit like a Mongol.'

But it would be wrong to award the Hazaras exclusive rights over the Mongol heritage. Uzbeks, Kyrgyz and Turkmens all have varying degrees of Turkic and Mongol blood. Hazaras are, however, the only ethnic group in Afghanistan that adopted Shia Islam en masse, following the dominance of the Shiite empire of the Persian Safavids that ruled this part of Afghanistan from the sixteenth to the eighteenth centuries.

To protect themselves from hostile Sunnis, Hazaras would practise *taqiyyah*, or 'dissimulation'. This uniquely Shiite practice enabled the devotee to protect himself within a Sunni society, leaving him free to accomplish Sunni acts while remaining true to his faith. But even *taqiyyah* couldn't immunise the Hazaras from trouble.

After 600 years of near total self-reliance, Hazaras would, towards the end of the nineteenth century, endure the bitter rule of Abdur Rahman Khan, a British-backed potentate known as the 'Iron Emir', who came to the Afghan throne in 1880.

The arrival of the Iron Emir signalled the end of the Hazaras' isolation. A Pashtun himself, his cruelty was indiscriminate. None of his subjects was exempt, regardless of their ethnic background. Kafir, Uzbek, Tajik, Pashtun: all quivered at the emir's wrath. He once boasted to an Englishman in Kabul that he had executed 120,000 of his own people.

The emir particularly hated Hazaras. He was suspicious of their autonomy, covetous of the mineral wealth beneath their land and, as a devout Sunni, he loathed Shiites. He hated their resistance to his centralising rule, and his offensive would be the most violent and sustained against any of Afghanistan's peoples.

Hazara grumbles and basic opposition to Abdur Rahman's regime eventually grew into a full-scale revolt in 1892. This gave the emir the *casus belli* that he had dreamed of. Appealing to a fanatically Sunni *'ulema* (or clerical elite), the emir declared an all-out jihad against these Shiite infidels, promising his levies a place in heaven, booty, women, and Hazara slaves for all.

The emir assembled an enormous army: 30,000 foot soldiers 10,000 cavalry and 100,000 levies. Hazara bravery was no match for the emir's numbers and modern British weaponry. Their defeat was near total. Decapitated rebel heads formed towers by roadsides and thousands of men, women and children were forced into slavery. The Hazarajat, already subject to the depredations of slave traders, became one of Asia's greatest sources of human labour. Broken and impovished, some Hazaras saw slavery as the only alternative to death by starvation. In the 1890s an average 7,000 Hazaras were sold annually, some for as little as 70 kg of barley, and the Hazara population was reduced by more than half.

The tax burden on the remaining Hazaras was increased, and many of their lands were requisitioned for Kuchis, Pashtun nomads loyal to the emir. In an effort to extirpate all vestiges of Hazara autonomy, Abdur Rahman summoned every local leader, both spiritual and feudal, to Kabul. All sayyeds, sheikhs, mirs, maliks and khans – dignitaries in the complex Hazara hierarchy – were ordered to leave their lands and move into the watchful orbit of the emir.

Exhausted but not defeated, in early 1893 the Hazaras would stage another rebellion, ejecting government functionaries from their posts in the Hazarajat. It was an act of suicide, given what they knew about their ruler.

There was no immediate response. But the emir's counter-attack, when it came, would be deadly. Abdur Rahman sent his men again to rampage through the central lands, enslaving and executing Hazaras wherever they were found, and driving another 15,000 into exile. All grazing lands were given to Kuchi nomads, leaving Hazaras with virtually no source of livelihood. The subjugation of the Hazaras was complete. It would be another 100 years before they dared to assert themselves on the national stage again.

The abolition of slavery in 1919 made little difference to the Hazaras. Those who had avoided enslavement found work as labourers and seasonal workers, forming a new national underclass, reviled as 'mouse eaters' and 'load-carrying donkeys'. Right up to the 1970s Sunni Pashtun clerics declared that the killing of a Hazara was an accepted way of securing God's favour. '*Sag-e Aughu kas dāra, ādam-e Azrah nah*,' went the Hazara proverb: 'Even a Pashtun dog has a protector, but not a Hazara.'

By the 1980s, as the mujaheddin prepared to face down the USSR, the Hazara fighters remained excluded from the resistance. It was with great effort, and not a little savagery on their own part, that they forced their way into Kabul warlordism under the *Hezb-i Wahdat*, one of the post-jihad, civil war factions in the early Nineties, all of whom were swept away by the Taliban in 1994.

If the Hazara region is known for anything in the West, it may be due to Bamiyan, the Hazarajat's unofficial capital, where on 1 March 2001 the Taliban – a matter of months before they themselves were toppled by the American-led coalition – dynamited some of the greatest examples of Buddhist art: the 1,500-year-old colossal statues of the Buddha. The international community erupted at this act of philistinism. Others were disgusted that it took an atrocity of archeology, not of humanity, to open ordinary people's eyes to the Taliban's inhuman regime.

My plan was to travel to Bamiyan, the very heart of the Hazarajat, the site of the great niches that once held the giant Buddhas, to visit this famously tough and remote people. If I was able, I wanted to see the countryside around the fabled Band-i Amir lakes, believed by Hazaras to have been miraculously created by Imam Ali himself, and try to understand what life was like for a people who had known for so long only the very bottom rung of society.

Before setting off into the hinterland I had an old school friend to look up. He was a journalist called Jack, an English freelancer who'd come to Kabul for fame and adventure. I hadn't heard much from him in recent months and I wondered what had happened to him.

The last I'd heard, Jack was making a decent living in Pakistan, hopping from one journalists' party to another, filing stories on the Tribal Areas and the North West Frontier Province. But eventually, bored with the stale atmosphere of the journo circuit, he decided to get a taste of some real action and head for Kabul. Unlike other ex-pats, he'd eschewed the cosy community of Shahr-i Naw – a safe-ish district of the city where expats lived in armed compounds – and opted instead for the Zarnegar, a pit of a hotel only two doors down from my own.

Wading through clouds of kebab smoke, I made my way up to the second floor of this uniquely horrible hotel. A forlorn-looking houseboy called Mohammad, whose lodging was a dusty sofa on the first floor landing, took me up to a garret room.

'Mr Jack!' he shouted, pounding the door a dozen times until his lungs were spent. He took another deep breath. 'Mr Jack!' More bashing.

'Maybe he's not in?' I suggested.

Mohammad looked at me with dead eyes and some hostility. '*Hast*,' he said. 'He's there.'

He continued the banging until we heard a scuffle, a sniff, and a muffled shout. 'All right all right!' It was an undeniably Jack-like voice.

Mohammad turned without a sound and retired to his bed on the first-floor landing.

The door opened a fraction, releasing a wave of fetid air. A cadaverous figure appeared, with puffy-eyes and yellow teeth.

'Just give me a second,' he groaned.

I sat on the landing for a good five minutes. How had Jack let himself get into such a state? Finally he emerged looking brighter-eyed, his shalwar kameez rolled up to the elbows, and lit cigarette in hand.

'Hey, how are things?' he said brightly, shielding his face from the light of the window.

'Fine. What's up with Mohammad?' I said.

'My rent's late again, that's all. Let's get something to eat.'

We crossed the road to Jack's daily haunt: the restaurant at the top of the Spinzar, a warhorse of the hotel circuit, as blithe to the disasters of the last quarter century as its unshockable top-floor waiter, Hassan, who'd worked there since the Sixties. Hassan guided us to the table with one word: '*Arshak*?'

Aršhak – leek dumplings with yoghurt – was all Jack had been eating for the last three months.

We sat by a window looking over the Salang Wat as the daily fog rose. The waiter brought the food on stainless-steel platters, and a pot of green tea with cardamom. Jack picked up his fork in a half-hearted attempt to summon an appetite, but reached for a Marlboro instead.

'This place isn't healthy.' His face was all gloom, his eyes sunken.

'Jack, are you all right?'

'Me? Oh, fine.' He watched his food listlessly. 'Just hate Kabul that's all.'

'Why?'

He took a deep drag on his cigarette, exhaled and said nothing. I wondered if he'd heard me.

'I'll tell you,' he said, eventually. 'Life as a freelancer isn't easy. It's not like Islamabad. There you have a ready-made circuit, you've got an English press, you've got people who respect you because you're educated. They're snobs, which is infuriating, but at least they're professional. Here no-one reads, so, you've got to sell abroad. That involves getting yourself in gear, hiring a photographer, getting an interpreter, and once you've done the story someone else has done it first. So, that leaves you to salvage what you can from what's already published, until you end up a vulture like everyone else, churning out stuff you'll probably can't even sell for a fee that you'll never get. It's very, very tiring.'

'What about the other journalists? Have you made any friends?'

'I used to . . . Well, it doesn't matter,' he said. 'Anyway, I'm sick of it.'

He confessed he hadn't been getting the pitch right lately.

'Lately?'

'For the last three months.' He smiled guiltily.

'But what have you been doing with yourself all this time?'

'Hanging round here. And the Zarnegar.'

'What for?'

'I've rediscovered sleep.' He gave a throaty chuckle that developed with a coughing fit. 'It's quite underrated.'

'Go home, Jack.'

'Hmm, you're probably right,' he said, but I wondered whether he could summon the energy.

'Listen, Jack, I'm going to the Hazarajat in a couple of days.' I told him of my plan to explore the region. 'What do you know about the Hazara population?' I asked.

'Hazaras?' he asked aloud, tea-cup suspended. 'Buddhas, blown up by Taliban. Descendants of Mongols. They're Shiite – which is always a problem. Who's their leader now? Mohaqiq. Hasn't got a chance. Only Hazaras will vote for him. I don't know that much about them, actually.'

'You seem to know quite a lot,' I said. This was the frustrating thing. Jack had a brain like a compendium and I'd never known him to be short of an answer. When he felt like it he could be devastatingly persuasive. With three dreadful A levels he'd still managed to talk his way into Oxford, a decision his tutors would bitterly regret. When in nihilistic mode nothing could put that mind of his to creative or protifable use. I asked him if a trip to the Hazarajat might get him out of his rut.

'What, and leave Hassan?' he said in mock outrage, while Hassan sat contentedly in front of the TV, picking his teeth.

'Come off it.'

Jack stared out of the window, slowly chewing the last of the *arshak*.

'Do you know, they've stopped selling peanut butter in Shahr-i Naw.'

'Jack, are you coming or not?'

'Yes, I'll come. Maybe I could interview some child soldiers or something.'

'If you want you could come with me to the lakes.'

He frowned, swallowed his last forkful and said: 'How we going to get there?'

'Not sure,' I replied, with a mouthful of flatbread.

*

Jack really didn't need too much persuading. It was a way out of his cesspit at the Zarnegar, now knee-deep in clothes and ashtrays. His sheets were, as he put it, 'brittle with the fruits of my frustration'. We planned to leave as soon as I got my visa extension.

That afternoon I hailed a yellow taxi to take me to the requisite ministry. The driver wore the white cap of a pious Muslim, starkly offset by his black beard and dark robes. He negotiated the traffic with the stern concentration of a cleric with a second job. I wasn't sure if he'd appreciate talking to a foreigner like me, so I refrained from conversation.

The elections were only a few weeks away now and at every turn we were bombarded with the posters and billboards of the presidential hopefuls. Only the big men made it on to Kabul's posters: goat-faced Hamid Karzai, the current incumbent, in his karakul hat; Yunus Qanuni, the Panjshiri warrior turned suave politico, with brushed hair and glasses; Abdul Rashid Dostum, the pudgy, bristly commander of the Uzbek north, who ran one of the most efficient smuggling circuits in the country. Dostum had reduced his beard to a weasly moustache, changed his flak jacket for a suit, and told journalists he was uncomfortable with the term 'warlord'. But his boozer's face, glistening pink, made him distinctly unappealing.

'It's all politics,' muttered my driver. 'All these idiotic politicians. Nothing ever changes.'

'What?' I responded, pleased and surprised that he was talking.

'Beards, *burkas*. No one can be what they want to be. You ever seen a woman walking with her hair out?' He looked straight at me. 'Where are you from?' he asked.

I told him I was half-Iranian.

'Iran,' he sniffed. 'Bad government. They force you to be a Muslim even if you don't believe.'

This was not what I expected.

'I suppose I can tell you because you're a foreigner,' he went on. 'I am a Marxist.'

'A Marxist?' I was extremely surprised to hear anyone admit that they were, or ever had been, a Marxist.

'I fought for the PDPA.* What can I say? I believed in progress.' He threw up his hands momentarily. 'Problem is, so does everyone else.'

'So why are you dressed as a believer?' I asked.

'When the Taliban came there was trouble. I had to be "devout", praying, saying the right things. I had to do everything I could to show that I was one of them, or else . . .' He made a slash across his neck with a forefinger. 'Now I'm in the army, and I've got the same problem. They've all got beards, they all pray. I don't believe in Islam in my heart. I don't even believe in God, but if I told them that, they'd probably kill me.'

He told me of the anxiety he felt when the Taliban came. Somehow, in the chaos of the civil war after 1992, he'd managed to avoid recognition as a former Marxist fighter. But when the Taliban took Kabul he lived in terror of denunciation. Secession from Islam, which is outlawed in the Koran, was now punishable by death. He grew his beard long, wore the right clothing and learned all his prayers by heart. He called himself hajji, one who has performed the pilgrimage to Mecca, and cleared his house of anything incriminating: old Marxist tracts, his PDPA documentation, ID cards. At prayer times he would devoutly stop his car, as was the law, and perform all the rituals.

'But it was all a performance,' he said. 'That's how you survive in Kabul. You have to seem to be something. The only rule is . . .' and he gave me something approaching a wink, 'don't get found out.' He turned his head to the road and we both smiled.

The Taliban have become so intimately associated with Afghanistan it is hard to imagine a time when they were never a presence. But despite their ultra-traditionalist values they are a tragically modern invention.

Nobody predicted the Taliban's emergence. They appeared as if from nowhere – a tight, disciplined, military force that seemed unstoppable. Who were these ill-educated flotsam, these

*People's Democratic Party of Afghanistan, the Soviet-backed puppet government in Kabul.

returning refugees who swept everything aside in the mid-Nineties? It was not the Taliban, after all, but the seasoned mujaheddin who had managed to fight off a ten-year assault by the USSR, then a world superpower. But a mere three years after their first appearance in 1994, the mujaheddin were being routed by a group of illiterate, inexperienced adolescents, some of whom had never fired a gun.

In the Eighties, Afghanistan had galvanised a motley but effective fighting force from many different tribal backgrounds. The task had not been to make a government, but to get the Soviets out. They not only succeeded, but precipitated the downfall of Communism – something the United States had failed to achieve for decades.

But in the years following the Soviet exit, agreement between the different factions proved impossible. Western funding dried up. All were heavily armed and none would cede their hard-won fiefdoms to Burhanuddin Rabbani's government in Kabul. Ismail Khan held the western province of Herat; Abdul Rashid Dostum the Uzbek north; Abdul Ali Mazari the Hezarajat; Gulbuddin Hekmetyar held some outlying provinces of Kabul, and various Pashtun warlords occupied much of the south and east. All vied for power in a bewildering sequence of shifting alliances and betrayals, bombing Kabul from all sides.

In the terrible years between 1992 and 1994, the country sank deeper into chaos. The mujaheddin, who fell to looting from the country they'd so bravely defended – hijacking food convoys, swiping telephone wires – rapidly lost the people's support.

It was then that a soft-spoken minor cleric called Mullah Muhammad Omar began to gain attention. From his madrasah in his home town near Kandahar, he railed against the chaos and corruption that was ruining post-jihad Afghanistan. Messianically, he preached the necessity of the perfect Islamic society, one that he promised to bring to the country. His plan was simple: to unite Afghanistan, bring stability and impose Sharia law – which, as interpreted by Omar, would be the strictest ever known in a Muslim society.

The ranks of his students swelled and they were soon

militarised into a committed fighting force of 12,000. With Pakistani backing Omar drafted new cadres in great numbers from madrasahs and refugee camps on Pakistani soil. These were the children of the jihad, orphans and refugees who had grown up in strange, all-male environments, where they were fed nothing but extremism, told to be martyrs, to fight to the death for a perfect society. By winter 1994 Mullah Omar had occupied Kandahar.

While the Taliban was preparing for total war, Rabbani's government was an embattled shell. Kabul was under constant attack, bombed from the east by Hekmetyar, from the south and west by Mazari's Hazara troops, and by Dostum from the north. As Rabbani watched the Taliban's sweeping victories with horror he forged a ragbag coalition of warlords. By now it was too late. One by one the provinces fell, and the warlords who'd proved themselves so valiant in the jihad, fled. In September 1996 the Taliban poured into Kabul. Rabbani and his defence minister, Ahmad Shah Massoud, moved the Government and its arsenal to the rugged Panjshir Valley in the north-east, where they remained barricaded and helpless. By the time of the allied invasion in late 2001, the Taliban occupied 90 per cent of the country.

By now Afghanistan was shattered. The nation had been stripped of its fabric, its old loyalties and tribal leadership. Much of the *'ulema* was discredited and scattered. People were displaced and brutalised. Cities were wrecked and much farm and grazing land mine-ridden: the perfect conditions for the Taliban to build their new society.

Their original aims – to unite the country and wipe out corruption – were noble ambitions, but their creed, a Deobandi-Wahhabi hybrid, was a brand of Islam that had no precedent in the region and was the most severe ever to be enshrined in law. With Pakistan's blessing, the Taliban concept of unity was virulently pro-Sunni and pro-Pashtun. It was not a good start for a multi-ethnic and multi-sectarian society.

In September 1996 Dr Muhammad Najibullah, the former Marxist puppet president, who had been taking refuge in the

UN compound since his downfall in 1989, was beaten senseless and dragged from the back of a jeep near to the presidential building, where he was castrated and hanged.

A new Taliban ministry for the Promotion of Virtue and Prevention of Vice criminalised a long list of pastimes, such as television, videos, kite-flying, and all sports and games. 'Religious police' ranged the cities with cables and whips, flogging people for the smallest transgressions. Girls' schools were shut and women banned from leaving their houses without a male relative. Houses were forced to blacken their windows so that women remained unseen. Every man was obliged to wear a beard, or else face imprisonment. Sentences were issued with summary abandon, and many of the new prisoners had no idea when or if they'd be released. Money changers in the bazaar were ordered to cease charging interest or be imprisoned for – according to Taliban law – 'a long time'.

As the Taliban advanced through the country, they became increasingly aggressive. Their revenge attack on Mazar-i Sharif, an attempt to flush the Hazaras out of the north, was one of the worst massacres in recent times. Aid agencies were expelled and ordinary Afghans increasingly alienated. When Saudi Arabia finally withdrew its support, embarrassed by the Taliban's cruel and erratic behaviour, only Pakistan – which has a large Pashtun population of its own – remained as its chief backer and financier.

On 7 September 2001, just weeks before the allied invasion, the Taliban Minister of Justice enjoined Afghans not to associate with foreigners on the grounds that 'Islam prohibits friendship with infidels.'

Once again, the Taliban showed an utter disregard for – and ignorance of – their own history. Afghanistan has been the home of many great internationalist empires – Greeks (Alexander's descendants) ruling from Bactria, the Kushans from Kapissa, the Ghaznavids from Ghazni, the Mughals from Kabul. The Gandharan school of art at the turn of the first century was the unique fusion of Greek, Iranian and Indian styles to celebrate the Buddhist form. The Taliban movement had plunged the country into a dark age the like of which it had never known before.

The sad postscript to all of this is that the Taliban are back. The US-led coalition to topple their regime in 2001 brought initial success, but the last few years have seen a gradual resurgence of this Islamist force. From 2006, when NATO re-established itself in the south, where central authority is weak, the Taliban has been a perpetual thorn in the side of the international community.

But as the years roll on, NATO seems no closer to expelling the Taliban and winning the confidence of ordinary Afghans. Jaded by unending instability, they are confused that the West consistently fails to win. The problem now is time. It is becoming increasingly difficult to keep Afghans onside, while persuading Western governments to surrender their own citizens for a seemingly unwinnable conflict. Eventually the international presence must depart, leaving Afghans the necessary but unenviable task of filling the vacuum.

The streets were empty when I returned to my hotel. Jack and I had been up drinking whisky at a Chinese restaurant, which he confided also doubled as a brothel. By ten o'clock the streets were empty, and a few dim headlights lit up the clouds of dust like swarms of midges. Stray dogs were the only visible life, picking at rubbish, some limping around on three legs. The Plaza was locked with a security mesh, which I rattled until I roused one of the staff. Out of the darkness came the weak blue flame of a paraffin lamp, followed by the hand, then the face of a bleary-eyed man with a bunch of keys, who tutted at me for coming back late.

In the flickering light the Plaza exuded a very different feeling. Its vast maroon-painted lobby resembled an Edwardian music hall broken open after a century of neglect. The porter led me up a mirror-covered staircase across a creaking passageway, handed me a lit candle and pointed to my room at the end of the dark hall, where I walked precariously.

I found my mattress, doused the flame and settled down to

the tremulous chorus of mosquitoes that began to close in.

I woke at 3 a.m., startled by the short scream of a firework, which landed with a thud. My heart pounded. Fireworks don't land, I thought to myself. I fumbled for matches and lit the candle. I wandered down the hall of mirrors to the maroon foyer, where I expected to hear another missile, but I didn't. It was just a one-off. Returning to my room, I realised my T-shirt was bathed in a cold sweat. It was painful to walk. I stopped on the stairwell, surrounded by six mirrors. The flickering light from my candle revealed a ballooned throat, a pair of hooded eyes and a haggard face. I was ill again.

As the morning sun heated my room I felt like death, but Jack never came. I lay on my bed in a kind of delirium. All the parts of my throat seemed to have fused overnight into the shape and consistency of a golf ball. As a hot morning turned into a baking day, I felt like a prisoner in that airless room, while passers-by shamelessly peered through the windows.

I was running a temperature and my mind was swimming. I attempted to read an Iranian novel I'd picked up in the bazaar about a young Iranian who went to Nazi Germany to become a spy, but seemed to spend all of his time going to burlesque shows. It was pretty dreadful, and I drifted in and out of consciousness, still aware of the dull rumble of Kabul's traffic, and the stifling smog that penetrated the Plaza's porous walls.

By late afternoon my breathing was laboured and I was beginning to worry. I needed a doctor. It took me ages to dress, but I dragged myself, wheezing, to the Zarnegar, just two doors down. It was as if I were in a dream world, where none of the voices on the street were connected to any bodies, they were just packages of noise without a source, hovering and floating in the heavy, hot air. I made extremely slow progress to Jack's garret room and beat my hand on the door.

He woke at last from his 16-hour sleep.

'I need a doctor,' I said. He rubbed his eyes, blinked with surprise at my state, and immediately grabbed his kit. We made enquiries in the street and a boy of about twelve guided us through some backstreets, past bazaars I'd never seen before, and endless buildings of concrete and dirty glass, wagons of upended produce, until we came to some steep stairs. I forced my way up to a tiny practice in a slant-ceilinged attic room.

Doctor Azimi was a small, ferrety man in late middle-age who'd studied in London in the Sixties. He had a quiet but busy manner and looked as though he was able to work anywhere, under any conditions. His office was small and triangular with barely enough room for his patient to lie down. Every inch of floorboard was taken up with periodicals, files and table legs. The walls were pasted with flimsily framed certificates and newspaper clippings. An articulated skeleton swung from the ceiling like a hanged man. I lay down on Dr Azimi's examining board and he poked at my throat with an aluminium tool like the claw of a praying mantis.

He furrowed his brow and clicked his tongue.

'My friend . . .'

'What is it?' I mumbled, the claw still in my mouth.

'You have serious problem. Hmm. It seems you have throat infection. It's bad, and it's spreading to lungs. I write prescription.'

'But why? What is it?'

'Kabul air. Not uncommon.' He frowned, covering a piece of paper with illegible Dari scribbles. I asked him to translate his prescription.

'Nine pills a day?' I exclaimed.

'You wanna get back alive or what?' he asked.

It took a few days for my cartload of pills to take effect. In the meantime, I lay and slept and read. Sometimes Jack came round to play chess and bring water, but mostly I slept. It was a lonely business, getting better, and it gave me a lot of time to think. I wondered if either of us was in any fit state for the journey.

Initially, I doubted the provenance of these pills, but, post-2001 Afghan pharmacies were well-stocked and supplied their customers well, providing you could pay. The golf ball in my throat softened and soon I could swallow again. By this time I was heartily sick of the Plaza. I desperately I wanted to see the countryside.

But just as I was packing my things to check out, the Plaza

management started hammering on my window. They'd already doubled the price of the room, mid-stay, and were unmoved by my condition. Now they gave me half an hour to leave on the grounds that a government delegation had booked out the entire hotel. I wasn't sure I believed them, until I suddenly noticed a train of flowing cotton billowing up the stairs: Pashtun grandees with turbans as high as laundry heaps, *patous* slung over their shoulders, kohl-rimmed eyes and hennaed beards. They filled the hotel with soft Pashto chatter, adjusting their headgear and sipping from cans of Zam Zam Cola.

Jack, too, had outstayed his welcome at the Zarnegar. He'd defaulted on his rent for the last time and was finally ejected. We met, homeless, in the Salang Wat.

We managed to find a night's refuge with a dodgy friend of Jack's, a Chicken Street carpet trader who'd done particularly well out of the recent economic boom. Behind his modest shopfront was a den of vice: a plasma TV with satellite, flowing whisky, and the air thick with the barbecuey smell of opium.

Before the call for morning prayers, the next day we tiptoed around the empty bottles and ashtrays, found the pre-dawn minibus to Bamiyan and zipped out of Kabul into the clean air of the countryside.

I was pleased at last to be heading towards the home of the Hazaras, because as yet I'd met very few. I'd seen them in Kabul, performing the lowly jobs they were renowned for, as hotel-sweepers, cooks, labourers and assistants. So far, I'd only snatched a few brief conversations with taxi drivers and carrot-juice makers, but I found their manner different from Tajiks and Pashtuns, who were confident and frank, open-armed or proudly dismissive. Among Hazaras I sensed the same kind of timidity I'd encountered in Iran. They spoke softly in their difficult dialect, performing their tasks with an ingrained diffidence.

The road to Bamiyan took seven hours to negotiate, though it was only 250 km from Kabul.

Moving slowly on potholed earth roads, we nevertheless had

a magnificent view from the window. Entering the Koh-i Baba, a range which runs east-west for about 80 miles (130km) at the western end of the central Hindu Kush, we passed orchards of lime and plum trees, and lemony wheat fields, their dwarfish stalks shivering in the wind. There were walled villages of rusty brown, set a little distance from the road, where villagers gathered vetch and hogweed from their fields and piled them on flat roofs for the fodder to dry.

As we shuddered through the high-walled roads, the minibus halted to make way for a flock of goats scrambling along the earthy road. A young Kuchi girl followed behind them, whacking the strays with her leather crop. I'd never seen such girls in Afghanistan, walking bare-faced in patterned green shawls and vermillion robes, draped with jewellery in star and lozenge patterns.

Hours later, the narrow road widened and the serried walls of the farmsteads disappeared. The land became dry and tawny, the mountains languished in a heather-haze backdrop, with the high Koh-i Baba rising high behind in an almost fairy-tale dusty white. Every river valley seemed to possess its own lonely fort, an old mudbrick structure with watch towers that the Hazara barons or *mirs* once inhabited, keeping an eye out for Kuchis or government troops.

The Kuchis that the Iron Emir settled here would be a source of continual tension, as the adventurer and travel writer Wilfred Thesiger once witnessed. He describes seeing a Kuchi straying on to a Hazara field, and the Hazara farmer giving him a good thrashing.

Thesiger was disenchanted with the Hazaras. Having just spent six months in a boat with the Marsh Arabs he needed the summer of 1954 to 'stretch his legs' on the Koh-i Baba, but 'was left with the impression of a tough people, hardy, industrious and honest, but close-fisted, inhospitable and rather dreary.' He wrote that whenever he needed shelter they always pointed to the next village, which he found 'disappointing'. Given their years under the Iron Emir it was a well-earned suspicion of strangers.

As the minibus progressed through the land, the earth became drier and redder, the villages squarer, more carefully fortified. The mountains had lost their dry, tawny hue and were now magenta-red. Strange growths were visible in fingers of rock-like termite hills. More forts, also made of the same rock, perched over fearsome vantage points, camouflaged from a first viewing. The tallest and best was the Shahr-i Zohak or the Red City, a garrison that stands over the convergence of the rivers Bamiyan and Kalu, the ancient sentinel of Bamiyan.

Bamiyan new town was nothing more than an earthen thoroughfare lined with one- or two-storey shops. It had a Wild West feel, with a brisk movement of donkey-carts and bicycles. Weary shopkeepers threw pails of water on the road in a vain effort to control the dust. It was early October now. Though the sky was a deep blue and the afternoon sun was high, there was a definite chill in the air.

I saw them immediately, the icons of the Hazarajat: the great Buddha niches cut into the rock face, this giant megalithic centrepiece of the Bamiyan Valley. Behind them were the wrinkled folds of the high Koh-i Baba mountains, hazy purple in the far distance. As soon as we'd checked into our hotel, I knew I'd have to hike up to the cliff faces while the sun was still high.

The Hotel Zohak was a simple place with springy beds and cold running water, run by a friendly Hazara teenager who kept no notes about what you'd ordered and would write out seemingly random invoices. I packed a small bag and got ready to explore the Buddha niches. Jack was already sprawled on his bed, asleep and unmovable.

I set out towards the niches, crossing the line of shops, and followed well-trodden paths through a patchwork of mud houses and clover. Willows and poplars grew by small pools of water. The rock face simply rose out of the ground. It was a strange and arresting shape: horizontally striated, rising at the top into little towers like the roots of a giant celeriac.

Meanwhile, the base of the cliff face was pocked with hundreds of grottoes and niches. These were the caves where

Buddhists once worshipped, surrounded by their long-disappeared devotional frescoes. And there in front of me were these two enormous niches, where the monumental Buddha statues once stood: 55 metres for the big one, and 38 for the 'little' one. They were now starkly empty – bottle-shaped holes like toy sentries that had left their boxes. When they dynamited the Buddhas, the Taliban had ripped the heart out of the city.

I opened my copy of *The Valley of Bamiyan* (1967), the classic Sixties guidebook by Nancy Hatch Dupree, the doyenne of the Afghan travel guide, and examined some of the old photos of the Buddhas. In my mind I tried to place them in ancient Bamiyan, when the city was the ceremonial, commercial and spiritual centre of Buddhist Central Asia. In 400 CE a thousand monks were said to inhabit the rocks in silent meditation.

In spite of the bicycle bells and barrow-wheels of the far-off street, I could visualize a place of infinite peace. The bizarre rock formations, the lush valley and cool air made the spot ideal for religious contemplation.

The statues were the largest – and perhaps best – examples of Gandharan art, a fusion of the Indian, Iranian and Romano-Greek artistic traditions that coalesced in Central Asia in the first few centuries CE. They were a classic product of the Silk Road, the place where four worlds met, where each great civilisation contributed something of its own artistic heritage. The Greeks gave the Buddhas their human form, the Indians their rigid frontal position, and the Romans their drapery. The paintings that originally lined the grottos bore depictions of the Cyclops of Greek myth putting on a local workman's cap, and the Iranian god Mithra, wearing Phrygian headgear, in communion with the Buddha.

Despite their commitment to a simple life, monks soon grew rich on passing trade. Bamiyan was a natural caravanserai, where travellers would find physical and spiritual refreshment. They would pray and buy and sell goods from the China-Byzantium route. Entering Afghanistan at Balkh, these men would travel south to Bamiyan and then to Kapissa and India through

Peshawar. Rome would provide gold and silver plates, glass vessels, coral and linen, and Silk Road traffic would send a continuous stream of merchants, philosophers, scientists and missionaries to Bamiyan's bazaars. Meanwhile, Buddhist pilgrims could always rely on Bamiyan for indulgences in a bid to escape samsara – the endless cycle of death and rebirth – by buying merit from bodhisattvas, who through their saintliness had much to spare.

King Kanishka of the Kushans was one of the greatest champions of this era of cross-cultural enterprise. Ruling from Kapissa in eastern Afghanistan in the second century CE, Kanishka was open-minded about faith. He flirted with most of the religions on his doorstep, beginning with the Greek gods of his predecessors, the Graeco-Bactrians, who had ruled this region until the first century CE, and from whom he appropriated the Greek alphabet for his coins. Other Kushan coins reveal an interest in the Iranian god Ardoxsho, and the Indic god, Shiva.

Eventually, Kanishka would become one of Buddhism's most lavish patrons. He set up *viharas* (monasteries) and stupas (shrines) all over his empire, stretching from the Aral Sea to Tibet, and called for a grand conference in Kashmir, where it was decided to translate all the vernacular Buddhist texts from the Prakrit into the high Sanskrit language. This was one of the great turning points in the Buddhist literary canon.

The encroachment of Islam was especially slow in this remote part of Asia. The Arabs first pushed into Kandahar in south-east Afghanistan at the turn of the eighth century, but it would be another 300 years before Islam fully took hold in the Bamiyan Valley, creeping in finally under the Ghaznavids of the eleventh century.

The arrival of Islam spelt financial disaster for Bamiyan. Once the Arabs had secured victory over the ruling Western Turks, long-distance trade came to a halt, and Bamiyan, whose lifeblood was trade, became a backwater. As trade dwindled, devotees stayed away. Without the means to restore their monuments, Buddhism fell into terminal decline and the monks protected their wall-paintings with layers of mud. Over the centuries, iconoclasts would deface the paintings, and nature would do the rest.

At the end of the twentieth century, by which time the Buddhas had resisted 1,500 winters, the Taliban arrived. They declared that since the Buddhas were idols, and idols were proscribed under Islamic law, the Buddhas must be destroyed. Their first volley bore the unmistakable signature of the Taliban: they dynamited the head of the small Buddha and machine-gunned its groin. Three years later – after the leadership had announced that not a single statue in Afghanistan would be spared – they were back. Demolition experts were consulted, Chechen sappers were hired and Hazara forced labourers spent three days digging a trough to make space for the explosives. On 1 March 2001, front-row seats were booked for the supreme smashing of idols. The Taliban regime, which branded all video as an abomination, recorded the demolition on film and had them printed on memorial calendars to be sold in the bazaars of Kabul and Peshawar.

As I scrambled around the foot of the cliff I heard a murmur of voices from one of the monks' cells above me. A Hazara soldier peered out of the cave and waved me in. I climbed the precarious path and he hoisted me up. It was an old monk's cell hacked deep into the rock, with smooth, dark walls, its frescoes long faded, and rugs on the stone floor. A crowd of Hazara levies with wispy beards and leather jerkins beckoned me into their niche.

'*Be waqt āmadi*,' said one. 'You've come on time.' One had heated up a dark broth for lunch. They set me down in the corner, where they plied me cheerily with questions.

Apparently, they were former fighters of the Hezb-i Wahdat, the main Hazara faction that had made its name in the civil war.

Ali Heidar seemed to be the leader. The rest listened respectfully when he spoke, and it was he who put a bowl before me. He picked apart a sheaf of bread, throwing pieces into the gravy to form a sticky goo, something I'd seen a Yemeni student do at the Tehran dormitory.

'You are a good man, I think,' said Ali Heidar. 'In New Zealand there are many good men.'

In 2004 the Kiwis formed the bulk of the main NATO reconstruction team in Bamiyan. With the toppling of the Taliban in 2001, NATO became a well-respected guarantor of Hazara autonomy.

I decided to tell him I was from England.

'*Inglisi*,' he said, rubbing his chin thoughtfully. 'You are the good guys,' he said, 'Not like those damn Iranians, who abandoned us.' I'd judged wisely. 'But don't forget,' he continued, 'NATO will need us one day.'

'One day?'

'When the Taliban come back.'

There was a general feeling that the Taliban were never far away. It had only been three years since they'd reclaimed their town and Hazaras had long memories. Twice the Taliban had taken Bamiyan, and twice they were driven back.

The Taliban had tried to conquer the Hazarajat in 1997, starving them out by blocking all the roads. The inevitable offensive came in September 1998, at which the Wahdat leaders, weakened by infighting, were routed to the Koh-i Baba, where they plotted their comeback. Months later, in spring 1999, the Wahdat drove the Taliban out of Bamiyan in a dramatic reversal. But the victory was temporary, and before long the Taliban were to return and rule the Hazarajat with brutal oppression until the US-led invasion.

I asked Ali Heidar about the Taliban invasions and he perked up instantly. He described the foreboding every Hazara felt when the Taliban swept in at the end of summer 1998. Most of the population fled as they came, burning and destroying everything before them. In one village 50 old men were killed in cold blood.

'When they came they destroyed all the houses, killed anyone in sight. We flew to the hills, to the loneliest part of the Koh-i Baba. We took whatever we could stuff in our pockets – beans and dry bread – killing al-Qaeda behind us as we ran. We went to the mountains and the villagers gave us food, whatever they had.'

A small man on the far side of the cave provided a running commentary in comic mime: two shaking fists, one in front of the other; a sub-machine gun; a finger across the throat; his tongue hanging out of his mouth and eyes bulging. He was like a court jester, relieving the intensity of these morbid recollections. Ali Heidar quelled the mirth, raising his hand:

'We have to stick together, because no one thinks about the Hazaras. We have been betrayed by everyone – Iran, Massoud, America. We are on our own. We have to be strong.'

There were earnest mumblings of agreement.

'How old are you?' asked Ali Heidar, making his next point. I told him I was 25. 'In the last quarter-century your country has been learning many things: technology, science, house-building. All the while we, my friend, have learned to be *ādamkoshān*: killers of men.' The cave fell silent as we all ruminated on this.

On my way back to the hotel I was struck by how proud these Hazaras had been, how humorous and talkative. They were a far cry from their cousins in Kabul and Tehran, and I was convinced it was because they were on their home territory, for which so much blood had been shed. There was no one here to exlude Hazaras, to insult them as infidels and beasts of burden. Here in the Hazarajat, their historical problem – from the feudalism of past centuries to the civil war of the Seventies and Eighties – was their treatment of each other.

The next day, as I lay on my well-sprung bed, I took out *The Valley of Bamiyan* by Dupree. Jack was still snoring on the other side of the room. He had an extraordinary capacity for sleep.

I started reading about the Bamiyan Valley. This whole region was full of myths that related to the miracles of Imam Ali: his damming of the flooding river (that became the Band-i Amir lakes), his slaying of the dragon (that now became a strange-looking rock formation that supposedly resembled the vertebrae of a dragon).

I got ready to make the short walk up the main road, where a mound appeared, a stark reminder of Bamiyan's misty past. The citadel – which had nothing to do with Ali – had never been reoccupied since its total annihilation by the Mongols in a revenge attack by Genghis Khan after the murder of his favourite grandson, Mutugen. Every man, woman, child and animal was said to have perished in the slaughter. One Arab historian, visiting a century later, found the city still uninhabited.

The citadel today is called Shahr-i Gholghola or the City of Screams. From afar it looked like an enormous termite hill, but on closer inspection there were many reminders of a brilliant past: a recognisable squinch or niche, or some latticed brickwork, but most of the decoration had been whittled down by violence, wind and sand, and rounded and shrunken like a melted snow sculpture.

In another era, hundreds of people would have inhabited the citadel: soldiers and civilians, mullahs, court poets and chamberlains. Situated on a natural outcrop, its position was vital in times of war: the nooks were filled with shell-cases and magazines now, and doorways had been turned into gun batteries. The path was daubed on all sides with crude red crosses, signalling the presence of uncleared mines, and on the summit was a lonely military post, where two soldiers smoked and drank tea. What were they doing up there? I wondered. Keeping watch for the returning Taliban?

According to myth, the entire calamity was blamed on the actions of a single woman: the king's daughter, Lala Khatun, Bamiyan's Helen of Troy.

As described by Dupree, the story went like this: King Jalaluddin Manguberti of the Khorezmshah Dynasty had several daughters, but none could compare to Lala Khatun. A dazzling beauty, she was cruel and jealous of her father's attention. When the widowed king made plans to remarry, Lala Khatun withdrew in a rage to plot against her future stepmother. She pleaded with her father to build her a palace all for herself 'far from the intrigues of the court, which may impair my delicate health.' He consented, hoping to end their estrangement, and in an enchanting garden a palace was built with four corner towers and dizzying ramparts, which was called Kalah-i Dokhtar, the Castle of the Maiden. Lala Khatun filled it with beautiful furniture, luxurious carpets, precious stones and chests bursting with silks.

But while her father's wedding preparations continued, the princess grew more and more unhappy with the situation. She shut herself inside her castle and refused all visitors.

Meanwhile, the army of Genghis Khan was approaching, encamped in the nearby Kakrak Valley and preparing to besiege the citadel the following day.

Lala Khatun sent a treacherous message to Genghis Khan. There was an underground canal that supplied the city with water. He should throw chopped straw into the river and follow it downstream until it started to eddy. This was where the underground canal began. Once the opening was blocked with felt matting, the town, deprived of water, would soon surrender. The plan worked perfectly. The Mongols surged in, butchering everything in sight, and were soon beating the gates of the citadel. Lala Khatun, who had fallen in love with the Mongol invader from afar, assumed she would be his bride, and ordered her old nurse to dress her for the wedding day. She was massaged, anointed with perfumes, oiled and bejewelled, her fingers hennaed and a veil of flower-decked gold was draped about her head.

When at last the Mongols arrived, the princess was neither offered marriage nor thanked. She was dragged ignominiously into captivity. 'What have I done?' she cried. Genghis Khan answered: 'That girl deserves no mercy. She must be punished for having betrayed a father who was too good to her.' Lala Khatun and her aged nurse were sentenced to death by stoning.

Meanwhile, the king had been in the midst of his wedding festivities in Ghazni. On being informed of Genghis Khan's attack he rushed back to Bamiyan to gather an army. But it was too late. The news of his city's destruction and the death of his daughter killed him as if by a bolt of lightning. From that day forth the Shahr-i Bamiyan took the name Shahr-i Gholghola, City of Screams. The Mongols had their own name for it: Mao Balegh – the uninhabitable city.

I wanted to find the remains of Lala Khatun's castle, which, according to Dupree's 1967 guide, you could still visit. This

Kalah-i Dokhtar or Stronghold of the Maiden, was in the village of Saidabad, a small distance outside the town.

I asked a small boy on a donkey for directions. He led me over parched fields where old women, bent double, were collecting winter fodder. He pointed me towards an alleyway, before veering off into a dry field. I followed the path and ended up in a sort of maze amid the ramparts of a fort. Dupree refers to a 'very large building with four corner towers and ramparts of such giddy heights as to excite the wonder of wayfarers'. Something wonderful had clearly existed here a long time ago, but the village had obscured it like ivy on a drystone wall.

Convinced this must be the palace, I continued through the *iwans* and courtyards, dead-ends and passageways and ended up, lost, in a sequestered farmyard. A donkey stood braying and a lone karakul sheep waddled up to me, swaying its hefty bottom and nuzzling my hand in search of food.

Next to cube houses of mudbrick, built up against the wall was an unmistakebly Medieval rampart. There were bricked-up portals, arched windows and the stones, though weatherbeaten, were fine and even. Further up was a good latticed window with arrow-head recesses. The tops of the battlements were high, but rough and sawn off like broken toast.

Two horribly bent villagers stood on their huts, chopping dry grass with a sickle.

'Do you live here?' I asked.

'I wouldn't call it a life,' said one, grimly. His voice was rough and two teeth poked out of his lower gums. I asked if he'd ever heard of Lala Khatun, who once owned the castle.

'We don't know,' he said. 'We have no education. But I've heard it was a palace once.' He stood up straight and I heard his spine click into place. He pointed to the streets beyond the courtyard and said, without any emotion: 'The Taliban set it on fire.'

The last and most inaccessible spot I hoped to visit was Band-i Amir, the site of five lakes sacred to Shiites, located hours further into the country's interior. According to tradition, after a devastating flood Ali created the lakes by building a great dam.

Each of the five lakes was named after different chapters of his heroic exploits.

Once popular with tourists and bathers, the lakes sat in sheer bowls of rock 3,000 metres above sea level, their sapphire-blue waters replete with health-giving properties. Band-i Amir was still an important pilgrimage site, though, and I wondered what state the lakes were in after the wars.

The question was how to get there. The only way was by jeep (which Jack and I didn't have) and there were certainly no buses. But if I could have picked a travelling companion more reckless than myself, it was Jack, so against all the advice we were given, we decided to hitchhike.

We found two thick duvets from a clothes-dealer who appeared to be selling foreign donations, two Chinese-made haversacks, which fell apart within 24 hours, five carrots and two bars of chocolate.

With the sun still high in the sky we made the first leg of the journey by bus. Villages clustered on defensive hilltops, then disappeared. Trees vanished, too, after a while, and the further we moved away from human habitation the dry grass thinned to nothing, revealing little but black earth, cooled by a fine, streaking dust. This was not a place to be stranded in.

The bus took a left turn and Jack and I got off at a crossroads. Hours passed, the light faded and a knot formed in my stomach. Our morale plummeted. We ate all of our chocolate, and railed at our naivety.

Suddenly, Jack jumped to his feet. I looked up, shielding my eyes from the whirling dust.

'I see something!' he said. A fuzzy speck appeared in the distance, more like a swarm of gnats than a vehicle. But it was a truck, certainly, and we shrieked with joy.

'I'll jump up and down waving my scarf and you throw yourself in front of the wheels,' Jack said. But there was no need. The truck shuddered slowly up, stopping with a hiss of hydraulics. The drivers, two wizened Hazaras, offered us pride of place with them in the cabin. They were going to Yakawlang.

But we decided to climb on top. Our morale soared. It had

been a good idea to hitch after all, we agreed, and not so rash to have eaten all of our chocolate and half of our carrots. We settled down on hundreds of packed bottles of cooking oil, each one bearing a label that read: *A Gift from the People of Luxembourg.* We thanked the people of Luxemburg, laid out our duvets and felt uncommonly alive.

The land around us was either black or steel brown. It was bleak, dry and life-sucking. I recalled an article I'd read about a famine in the Seventies when supplies were blocked and hundreds were left to starve. Even in times of peace supplies to this remote area could fail. And it was getting more remote.

The earth became ever finer now, forming shelves of sand on the dune banks, whisked by the tyres into our eyes and mouths. The sun hid behind clouds and a wind came up, drowning out our voices. The skies opened and a heavy rain fell, turning our dust-caked clothes to mud. A fast, modern jeep zig zagged up the road behind us, then zoomed past. 'Don't think it,' said Jack.

Drenched, cold and blackened, we came to a halt. It was dark. There was no moon. The wind had stopped, so we could hear our teeth chattering. We prised open our eyes, glued shut by the dust and the rain. A few feet away a hurricane lamp hung from the roof of a small mudbrick building. It was a pitstop, a barely electrified caravanserai of old. To one side lay a derelict Russian tank. We swung down stiffly from the top.

The drivers looked up at us with injured pride. 'We offered you a place in the cabin and you sit up there,' one said. We followed them into the caravanserai, as primitive and bare as a medieval inn. A small boy busied himself in front of a great stone hearth, shovelling dung on to the furnace and ferrying trays of *shorbo* to guests.

Jack and I found a corner by another fire and let the heat do its work on our sodden clothes. The boy handed us bowls of soup and green tea, which we poured down our throats as he heaped the fire with bracken.

As our limbs slowly warmed, we began to feel human again, contented and quiet. Every so often the wooden door flew open and bedraggled Hazara truckers or shepherds, cold and dripping, joined us in a circle by the fire.

One young Hazara took his place next to me. He hung his *patou* under the smoky eaves to dry.

'Salaam,' he said to us, giving his name as Hamid Reidi, a young shopkeeper from Yakawlang. He had deeply pitted skin, a sparse beard and his black eyes danced with the fire's reflection.

Jack did not stay awake for long, but Hamid Reidi and I talked late into the night. He told me he'd been on his way to pick up produce in Bamiyan when he ran out of fuel.

'Who are you? A soldier?' he asked.

'No, I'm a traveller.' He seemed satisfied.

Inevitably, the subject veered to the struggle with the Taliban, the most desperate conflict in recent Hazara memory. But the story of his capture and escape from the Taliban's clutches was told with a strange innocence, as if he was recalling days of scrapping in the playground.

He explained how he'd been living in Yakawlang when, one quiet September day in 1998, he saw the Taliban coming: a sea of Toyota pickups crammed with armed teenagers. The townspeople panicked, grabbing whatever they could, before they fled. The attack had been long expected, but Wahdat forces were no match for the Taliban troops this time.

The Taliban's orders were not simply to conquer. Hazaras were *monafeqeen* (hypocrites) said Mullah Omar, and deserved to die as heretics. Hamid and his family escaped to the Koh-i Baba, the exposed mountain range, where Hazaras waited out their exile. Once his family were safe he returned to join the defence. By this time, Wahdat forces were scattered and only the most defiant continued to make guerrilla attacks on Taliban encampments.

'The Taliban caught me and put me in jail. They beat me every day with sticks. I still don't know why they didn't kill me. One night I and some of the other inmates waited for the guard to fall asleep. Then we broke a window and escaped. Two days later they caught me again, and I thought I would definitely be killed this time. But I survived, thanks to Hazrat-i Ali. But they hurt me – look.' He showed me his hairless chest, which still bore long streaks of lurid scar tissue.

Hamid Reidi escaped once more and found a car to the Iranian border. This time it was the Iranian police that arrested him, not the Taliban. He was beaten again and locked in a metal container for two days without light, food or water.

'I thought Iranians were our Shiite brothers,' he said, 'but they were no better than the Taliban.'

'I don't understand,' I interjected. 'Why did the Iranian police treat you like that?'

'They hate Hazaras.' He pointed to his Mongol nose.

'They put me in prison for a month and then one day they let me out, told me to go back to Afghanistan. I went back, but I knew I couldn't stay. This time I was more careful. I lay near the border and when the time was right I went back into Iran. I joined some other Hazaras there and worked on a construction site in Qazvin. I stayed for three years, always wondering what had happened to my family. When I finally returned to Afghanistan so much had changed, but my family was alive, thanks be to Allah. They had fled to Mazar and they had just come back to Yakawlang. Yes, these were difficult times.' He grinned again, but his smile was not so wide this time.

That night Jack and I ended up in a tiny mudbrick room with a rattling wooden door. We hardly slept, because of the roar of the trucks leaving at different times. I'd told the staff to wake me when one left in the direction of the lakes. Hourly came a shake of the door, the shout of '*Āghā!*' and I would stumble into the car park to find the truck had gone, or was going back to Bamiyan. By dawn, all of the drivers had departed. Only we English travellers remained, like party guests who have outstayed their welcome.

There had to be some way to get to the lakes. We asked if we could hire the management's donkey. The owner, a suspicious man who avoided all eye contact, seemed half open to the idea, but, after an hour of bargaining, he revealed that he didn't actually own a donkey, so we trudged, exasperated, back to the road, where I was put on look-out duty.

It was an exact repeat of the day before. A morale-sapping wait. Nothing moved. The horizon extended to the hazy peaks of the Koh-i Baba. The sun rose slowly in the sky.

After two hours I noticed a blurry image in the distance. Soon the speck turned into a minibus, which drew to a halt to allow its passengers to get off for tea. I took the driver aside. He told me he was heading for Yakawlang. For a small fee, we persuaded him to make a detour, which would add an extra hour or two to the route. I felt bad for the passengers, but nobody seemed to complain.

Shortly after we'd taken the turn-off for the lakes, I noticed the appearance of red crosses by the road. Our route led right through a minefield. The driver kept to the middle, not veering to left or right. We passed another minibus on its side, a blackened shell. The passengers craned their necks to get a peek, sighing and tutting.

'If we hit one,' said Jack, solemnly, 'we've got a lot to answer for.'

Gradually, the crosses began to disappear and our bus descended into a large hollow surrounded on all sides by sheer cliffs. We seemed to have entered a white moonscape and, turning a sharp corner, a mirage of sparkling blue suddenly appeared. It was Lake Haybat, sitting on a raised terrace about 20 metres high, filled with the bluest and clearest water I'd ever seen. Islamic architects had striven for centuries to capture the effect of blue sky against buff stone, but their attempts paled next to this, nature's original.

At the water's edge, by a modest shrine to Imam Ali, three chadored women sat beseeching the holy one for his beneficence. Next to the shrine was a small, decrepit restaurant with plastic furniture and umbrellas. A sad fleet of swan-necked pedalos bobbed by the jetty, but there wasn't a boater in sight.

We watched the bus depart and tiptoed over thin runnels of water on the white earth towards the café tables.

The stillness and the beauty of the place banished all of our anxieties. Even Jack looked happy as he gazed at the distant cliffs over the surface of the lake. We got some tea and sat down.

A young Hazara in foreign clothing was the only other person at the restaurant. He eschewed Afghan dress for square-toed loafers, tight black jeans and an open-necked shirt. He looked very out of place, and very bored.

It turned out he'd left the lakes as a teenager and had been studying engineering at Tehran University for the last nine years. Now, against his will, he was back with his family. His accent was pure Tehrani. I noticed his necklace. It was a silver *farāvar* talisman, the Zoroastrian symbol often worn as a quiet protest against the Islamic republic.

I asked him why he was so hostile to Hazara culture.

'Because they are such backward people. I suppose you can't blame them – the war halted progress. But they are so superstitious. Look at the shrine up there, see how it needs repair.' I looked up and it certainly appeared in need of a patch-up. 'Iran offered the money and expertise, but Hazaras rejected the money. Said that if Iran helped, they'd lose control of it. They don't want to be educated.'

His name was Ehsan and he was one of millions of émigré Afghans who left for Iran at the start of the war, got diplomas, started businesses, embraced modern life, only to be evicted a quarter-century later, forced to return to near-medieval villages.

As evening fell, we and the restaurant staff went off in search of firewood. We piled into a speedboat – myself, Jack, Ehsan, Azim and Hossein, the cook and the boat's owner – and shot over the marbled surface to the other side of the lake.

Having moored at a place where wild mint and bullrushes grew, we meandered along the white-earth beds between natural terraces of varying height, spilling water in beguiling streams. One terrace was two metres high and its water as clear as glass, nurturing saplings of buckthorn and willow. We filled the boat with roots and bark, enough to build a fire for the evening. Hossein, the owner of the boat, lay down in a depression by a rock and retrieved a small, compacted dark red rock and a hollow biro from his waistcoat pocket. He heated a filament under his lighter and pressed it on to the block until a fast-curling smoke appeared, which he sucked through the biro. He and Azim sat in an opium-induced torpor as the day waned. We remained there, quietly, listening to the susurrations of the streams and enjoying the dying sun on our skin, until at last Hossein took us back to fry the carp that he'd caught earlier.

That evening Ehsan invited Jack and me to dine at his family home. He led us to a small wooden cottage a little way along from the restaurant. His father Ismail turned out to be a mullah and a sayyed – a descendant of the Prophet. In his black turban and green *khalat* girded at the waist, he was a complete contrast to his modern, wayward son.

The sayyeds were once a formidable force in Hazara society. A rigidly endogamous caste, they were long considered to be ethnically distinct; not of Mongol descent, but Arab. Ismail's features were notably non-Hazara, with rounded eyes, a straight nose and a thick bloom of white stubble.

Over a plate of battered, salted carp, I asked Ismail about the lake and the power Ali was rumoured to exert over the Bamiyan Valley.

'Rumoured?' said Ismail, 'there is no rumour about it. Three times in my own lifetime Hazrat-i Ali has saved our valley from destruction.'

I saw the faintest look of fatigue in his son's eyes.

'Once,' continued the sayyed, 'Lake Haybat was rising and rising. Every day the water got closer to bursting its banks. We all went to the shrine and read about the martyrdom of Hazrat-i Ali and his sons Hussein and Hassan, we sacrificed cows and sheep, and by morning the water had receded.'

He looked at me, then at Ehsan, to see if we needed further convincing.

'This is the work of Imam Ali. The sick and helpless come to his shrine and they walk away cured. If your faith is strong enough you can rely on Imam Ali.'

'Even in wartime?'

'Especially in wartime,' he said. 'Once, many years ago, at the beginning of the jihad, some Russian planes came over. We went to seek help at the shrine. We fasted and prayed. Bombs fell, hundreds of them, but Imam Ali came and made sure none of them exploded.'

Ehsan sat to one side, shelling sunflower seeds.

'And did Ali help the valley when the Taliban came?'

Ismail was more muted about this. It was fresher history and more painful to recall. But later, over tea he spoke about it.

'The Taliban did terrible things here. When they came to Yakawlang in winter, they set up a base not far away. They butchered 300 people. They made it an offence to bury them, and the bodies were left to rot for ten days. Hazrat-i Ali never helped the Taliban.'

During the political upheavals of the Eighties, the sayyeds experienced a dramatic loss of authority. Until the end of the last century, they had wielded great power and influence. Along with other feudal grandees, the *mirs* and khans, they were landowners, slave-owners and occasionally despots. But the convulsions following the Soviet invasion saw a sea change in Hazara society. While the rest of Afghanistan was fighting off the Russians, the Hazaras were busy fighting each other. In a vicious struggle, the sayyed leadership was broken from within and a modern political party emerged, the Hezb-i Wahdat, which for the first time provided fighters from all strata of society and struggled for a stake in national power.

The appearance of a unified Hazara fighting force was unprecedented. To most Afghans, the Hazara were usually no more than road sweepers or houseboys, not fighters. But when Wahdat forces appeared in Kabul after the Communist collapse, occupying an entire quarter of the city and coming head to head with the other warlords, the Hazaras were finally taken seriously.

The power of the sayyeds today is spiritual rather than material. A passer-by will kiss the hands of a sayyed as a guardian of the Prophet's blood, but sayyed kinship is no longer a passport to political office. I detected a note of regret in Ismail's voice.

'Everyone ganged up on us,' he said. 'All the Hazara factions:

the Sepah, the Niru, the Harakat. Black turbans make us easy to spot.' He tapped his chest. 'My family has ruled in the Hazarajat for seven centuries. I can prove it.' He pulled out a huge tome from a shelf, a compendium of the world's sayyeds, to prove his ancestry. I noticed that Ehsan was sitting with his legs to his chest, his head buried. Ismail's world was as foreign to his son as it was to me and I wondered how long Ehsan would stand being home.

In the morning, having spent the night on the restaurant floor – its air, its rugs and furniture pungent with opium smoke – we gathered our few belongings and cadged a lift in a jeep that was heading to Bamiyan to pick up a UN official.

I was quietly amazed to have got to Band-i Amir. Jack and I had weathered hours of uncertainty, dust storms, torrential rain, a mini minefield and had got back to Bamiyan in one piece. But the final test was still to come. After our last night in the Zohak we planned to catch the 6 a.m. minibus to Kabul. But by morning Jack wouldn't move. His belongings were strewn round the room and next to his bed were the results of a toffee binge the night before. He'd spent the night chomping through a bumper-sized packet. I counted 64 wrappers. I tried to wake him, but all I got was: 'Give me ten minutes.'

Four more hours passed. I told him I was leaving – with or without him. Still trussed up in his duvet, savouring every last drop of sleep on his sprung bed, he said, in a small, raspy voice, 'OK, see you in Kabul.'

I walked off on my own.

The minibuses had all gone. There was only one thing for it: hitchhike alone. I walked to the edge of the town, found the turn-off, and waited. When a potato truck appeared after an hour in a haze of dust, I noticed a small figure in a backpack running towards me. The truck stopped and Jack jumped up beside me with a smug smile.

'Git,' I said.

I tried to stay in a bad mood with him, but couldn't. There is nothing so uplifting as open-air hitching, with its breathtaking views and the illusion of complete freedom. We were now in a land of steep gorges, termite-hill rock formations, tinkling rivers and mudbrick castles.

We laid our duvets over the potatoes and watched Shahr-i Zohak glide by, chameleon-like, on its magenta plinth. We found a couple of black and white checked keffiyehs, which we draped around our heads to keep off the dust. As night fell, the moon rose over the Hindu Kush and we could hear the faint echo of exploding missiles.

It was the right time to leave Afghanistan now. I wanted to be clean again, to breathe some fresh air, to drop my guard. I found I could hardly stand the stifling heat of Kabul after a week on the cold central plateau.

I hated the grime, the corruption, the feeling that every act was a chore, the vagueness and obfuscation that greeted every request for information. Yet there was something I loved about Afghanistan. There was the *ta'ārof,* of course, but the acts of kindness that a conversation could inspire, wherever you were, in a ministry or a taxi or a shop, would always bring the country close again. Security guards, clerks or shopkeepers would become your unexpected friends, your unbidden protectors for as long as you needed them. It was a part of the country that was impossible not to love.

I'd saved a brand new shalwar kameez for the last leg of my journey, and bought some second-hand novels. Jack and I parted at the Salang Wat, getting into different taxis. He was soon hitchhiking west across Asia to Europe. I was heading east into the thick of Taliban country.

7

'The Lost Tribes, or something like it': The Kalashas

> *'Look at their eyes – look at their mouths. Look at the way they stand up. They sit on chairs in their own houses. They're the Lost Tribes, or something like it, and they've grown to be English.'*
>
> Daniel Dravot in Rudyard Kipling's 'The Man Who Would be King' (1888)

The taxi rank was obscured by a cloud of dust, though the barefoot children still spotted me. I found a car and shut the door. They tapped on the window with loose-topped bottles of mineral water and phone cards, and pathetic outstretched hands. The driver shooed them away as if they were stray dogs, and we were soon speeding out of Kabul, heading for the Khyber Pass to Pakistan.

It was a long way to the high passes of northern Pakistan, home of the sixth and final peoples I'd been looking for, the Kalashas. In the interim, I would cross a wild band of territory in eastern Afghanistan, straight across the Tribal Areas on the Pakistani side, a land of fiercely independent Pashtuns (or in Pakistan, Pathans), and into Peshawar, capital of the North West Frontier Province (NWFP), an area considered high-risk by the UK's Foreign & Commonwealth Office.

This border territory was the breeding ground for the Taliban and their extremist allies. I can't say I was thrilled about travelling through this part of the country, nor was I particularly happy with my travelling companions, who made their sympathies known.

'Who do you want to win in the elections?' I asked the rotund Pathan next to me in a mixture of sign language and Dari.

'Taliban,' he said, with a thumbs-up and a grin.

To boot, my travelling companions spoke no Persian, only Pashto, with its distinctive, palatal retroflexive common to the Indian subcontinent. It was the starkest reminder that I was leaving the Persian-speaking sphere for good.

A world away from Badakhshan's mountain air, fine white dust clothed everything: roadside shrubs, spiky trees, and families of bedraggled road-repairers, breaking rocks for a few worthless afghanis.

But the fleets of Pakistani buses, lit up with their extravagant decorations, were strange and wonderful things. Every inch of their metal bodies was covered with swirls, patterns, fish-eyes and paisley, their chassis hung with a thousand chains like a Turkmen bride, and they always bore amusing messages, cloying and romantic, like WE'RE ONE and FEEL THE LOVE, or brilliantly offbeat, such as one I noticed that said simply: DISAPPOINTMENT.

Darius the Great of Persia had marched his army this way to reach his far-eastern satrapies half a millennium before Christ. In Silk Road days, the caravan route led from Balkh in northern Afghanistan down into India to plunder its fabled riches.

During the Raj, the British put the Khyber Pass under stringent watch, intent on keeping the Russians as far away from India as possible. It was the Great Game era, when the British exerted increasing pressure on Afghanistan's leadership, sponsoring its Pashtun kings in an effort to keep Russia at bay.

But Afghan resentment, which had been rising steadily under British domination, led to a massive uprising in 1842. Weakened by a total failure of the colonial power's diplomatic and military nous, the entire British occupation was forced into headlong flight, powerless against Afghan cunning, unfamiliar terrain and mountain snipers. In the retreat, 16,000 soldiers, sepoys, camp followers and army wives perished, picked off one by one from the clifftops and ambushed in the snow.

Only one Briton, army surgeon Charles Brydon, managed to survive, riding hard to the British garrison at Jalalabad, where his horse expired on arrival. Thereafter, the Khyber Pass became a nightmare in popular memory, entering cockney rhyming slang for 'arse'.

A mass of people and vehicles appeared ahead, which usually indicates a border. Rows of buses slowed and parked in an orgy of colour. Families streamed out with sacks, baskets, Thermoses, women trailing burka hems in the dust. Suitcases were lashed to trolleys, and crowds of Pathans crossed through the oil-slicked dust towards Pakistan.

The border was a straight marker, like a finishing line in a race, flanked by unfriendly guards with berets and rifles. Passports didn't seem to be an issue. Travellers either crossed unmolested or inexplicably were dragged to one side and beaten with sticks. I walked beside my two hefty Pathans for protection. One of them handed a guard a discreet wad of cash, and we were through.

Secure in the next taxi relay, we sped towards Peshawar without looking back once. My Pathan neighbour fingered my passport with curiosity.

'But, you Muslim?' he asked, with worried eyes.

'No,' I said, too tired to lie. He never spoke to me after that.

Peshawar was a paradise after the sun-baked plains. The air was balmy and vastly preferable to the stink of Kabul. I received an overpowering, welcome blend of spices, drains, exhaust, fritters and hashish. This was no longer Central Asia or part of the Persian-speaking world. I was now in the Indian subcontinent, a land of obsessive ornamental detail. Every space was painted, inscribed, chased or adorned with lurid posters, Koranic surahs, advertisements for toothpaste, caramel or Capstan cigarettes, a British wartime favourite. Shalwar kameezes billowed in every direction. Pathans, Sindhis, Baluchis, Punjabis, Chitralis,

Uzbeks, Tajiks and Hazaras strolled hand in hand
about on motorbikes or sold reams of soft fine w
evening bustle.

Peshawar also sounded very different from Kabul. Wh
Afghan capital growled with car and bus engines, Pesh
beeped. Three-wheeler rickshaws zipped around on engines fit for lawnmowers. Tonga carts lashed together from wooden beams clattered along the streets, drawn by lean, flea-bitten horses. Animals abounded, not only stray dogs that lived on crap heaps as in Kabul. Here goats and sheep reclined on street corners like territorial shop owners, and shiny water buffaloes forded streams with giant, unhurried steps.

One of the nicest things about Pakistan was its professional hospitality. The ex-Soviet 'stans had an ambivalent attitude to the paying guest. Afghanistan was still too wrecked to cope, but in Pakistan I found a very modest room at the Spogmay Hotel, where a friendly Punjabi chowkidar led me to a room with a shower, hot water and crisp, clean sheets. I shuttered the humid air out of my room, turned on the air conditioning and fell back on my bed, where I napped, as if in heaven, to the whirring of the fan above me.

When I awoke an hour later I was ready to sort out the next and last stage of the journey. I ordered and devoured a good lamb curry and two cups of milky tea from the hotel restaurant. Then I went back to my room to rummage around for my papers on the Kalashas.

It was probably Rudyard Kipling who brought the Kalasha people (whom the Chitralis traditionally called the Kalash) to a world audience. His short story 'The Man Who Would be King', (1888), is the engaging tale of two adventurers who travel to a remote corner of the Hindu Kush. Stumbling into a distant valley, they discover the lost descendants of Alexander the Great's army. In a moment of hubris, one of the two (Sean Connery in John Huston's 1975 film) allows himself to be worshipped as their anointed king – the son of Alexander – with predictably dire consequences.

The tendency of travel writers to link the Kalasha people with the lost descendants of the ancient Greek army is as fanciful as the claim that they are one of the Lost Tribes of Israel, as some Bukharan Jews used to believe. Since their ethnic origins are unknown, and their culture is so unique, the Kalashas are anything you want them to be.

What is remarkable is that the Kalashas are the only non-Muslims in a fervently Islamic region. More than that, their culture is unlike their neighbours'. Their striking garb, carved wooden effigies and home-made mulberry wine are a tour operator's dream.

The Kalasha people – a community of just 3,000 souls – are in actual fact the last survivors from a region known until the end of the nineteenth century as Kafiristan or Place of Infidels, a loose confederacy of villages in hundreds of small valleys on the Afghanistan–Pakistan border. In the west, the savage raiders of the Waigal and Bashgal Valley were called the Red Kafirs, while the Kalashas (the quieter and less warlike eastern branch in today's Pakistan) were called the Black Kafirs, due to their black clothing.

That the Kalashas preserved anything of their ancient culture is owed in part to the British. In 1888 Sir George Scott Robertson, a surgeon turned political agent, was sent to the wild Bashgal Valley in Kamdesh to see how the north-west frontier could be defended in the event of a Russian invasion. Fascinated by the people he met, he returned to live with the Kafirs for a year (1890–1), and wrote a vivid account of his stay among this pagan, warlike people. In *The Kafirs of the Hindu-Kush* (1896), he noted a pantheon of gods and fairies, strange, totem-like wood carvings and lavish 'feasts of merit' in which entire herds of goats were slaughtered to secure a higher place in the social hierarchy.

These Red Kafirs had been a scourge on their Afghan neighbours for centuries, launching devastating raids into the Panjshir and Kunar valleys, looting passing convoys and returning with the ears of the slain.

Kafirs were so fearsome that Tamerlane – the most savage

Asian conqueror after Genghis Khan, whose empire stretched from eastern Turkey to the borders of India – failed to subordinate them, even though they were on his doorstep. Crossing the Panjshir Valley in 1398 his detachments were ambushed and slaughtered and, within three weeks, he was forced to order 'victorious retreat'. But the Kafirs would meet their match with the Iron Emir, the scourge of the Hazaras: Abdur Rahman Khan.

Soon after Robertson's reconnaissance mission, tensions between Russia and Britain were relieved by the Durand Boundary Agreement of 1893, under which the borders of Afghanistan were formally demarcated from the Russian and British empires. Afghanistan was to be a buffer state within the British sphere of interest, and any invasion by the Russians would be considered an attack on Britain.

The Durand Line would be a consistent source of tension for Pathans, as it effectively cut their territory in half, rendering them a majority in neither Afghanistan nor Pakistan. The border also cut straight through Kafir territory, leaving the Black Kafirs under the laissez-faire British government of India, and the Red Kafirs under the vicious rule of Abdur Rahman.

The ink on the agreement barely dry, the Iron Emir – who, as we know, was a devout Sunni – made preparations for his grand assault on the pagan Kafirs. In 1895–6 his men poured into hundreds of valleys from all sides, invading with superior numbers and modern British weaponry. His usual savagery was tempered only by his deference to the British. The Red Kafirs crumbled in 40 days. Seven hundred camels carried away the loot, 5,000 Kafir men were sent to Kabul for military service, and scores of carpenters were commissioned to build mosques. Kafiristan was renamed Nuristan or Place of Light, and – as is common with the recently converted – remains to this day one of Afghanistan's most conservative Muslim provinces.

Meanwhile, the Black Kafirs, living under British jurisdiction, preserved their ancient religion as before. Robertson, who visited in 1896, wrote them off as 'a most servile and degraded race', in contrast to their warlike cousins, and, 'not the true independent Kafirs of the Hindu Kush, but an idolatrous tribe of slaves', possibly echoing local prejudice.

Yet it was probably their peaceful nature that enabled them to survive for so long. Submitting to servitude under the Chitrali mehtars, Kalashas were viewed with a mixture of awe and disgust, kept at arm's length and yet consulted for their 'mystic powers of divination'.

But who were these Kafirs or Kalashas anyway? Some academics observe certain similarities between their pantheon and that of the ancient Indian Vedic gods. Others say they are an example of Indo-Aryans, an Indo-European subgroup that split into Iranian and Indian branches *c.* 2000 BCE.

Kalashas themselves say they come from Tsiyam, an unknown land. This has been variously interpreted by historians, but most amusingly by the travel writer Colonel R. C. F Schomberg in his book *Kafirs and Glaciers: Travels in Chitral* (1938), who assumed they were talking of present-day Thailand:

> The Kalash [*sic*] have a tradition that they originally came from Siam, of all extraordinary places, and were much interested when I told them that I had been there twice. They said that, years ago, a Kalash had gone there, and reported that the women were charming like their own but that the men were dogs. They were anxious to know how true this was. And I said that although perhaps the Siamese men were not the handsomest of mankind, they certainly could not be called dogs.

When *Kafirs and Glaciers* was published, the Kalashas were living under the servile 'protection' of the Chitralis, who reported to the British-controlled Chief Minister. But in the two decades following Pakistan's independence, the attitude towards the Kalashas would sour. The drinking of wine, the carving of idolatrous funerary effigies and the comparatively liberated position of women, who walked unveiled and unchaperoned, was too much for many conservative Muslims. Offended by this paganism, mullahs and *tablighis* (proselytisers) subjected Kalashas to aggressive pressure, haranguing them with threats of damnation and converting them to Islam through persuasion, trickery or force. Vast tracts of ancient forest were requisitioned by the powerful Pathan forestry companies, and Kalashas were in danger of losing both their identity and environment.

From the Seventies, however, the Kalashas' lot would improve. The Pakistani government finally took note of their potential for attracting tourism. And the Government enfranchised them under a national minority constituency of non-Muslims, affording Kalashas some level of political protection. Benazir Bhutto continued this work, building roads to the valleys in the Eighties, and the Kalashas have ever since been shielded from large-scale conversion campaigns. The real danger to Kalasha culture today comes from the slow creep of modernisation, which arrives at the Kalasha valleys largely through the prism of Islam.

In spite of everything, Kalasha culture is surprisingly robust. They continue their ancient economy, ploughing and goat-herding, with traditional observance of the dualism of purity and impurity – the central theme of the Kalasha religion and way of life. They claim to be flattered that tourists want to visit them, and are slightly bewildered by all the attention they receive.

I squeezed into the back of the minibus, my legs up to my chest and my backpack on top of me. I longed to be small and possess the Zen-like patience of the wizened man next to me who sat cross-legged on his sack of rice.

We chugged into the countryside, slowly making our way north. This vast and unimaginatively named North West Frontier Province (NWFP) is one of Pakistan's remotest regions, spreading from the baking lowlands of Baluchistan up to the foothills of the Himalayas. Once a region of petty despotism, these lands were ruled by local princes, nawabs and mehtars who kept legendary harems and hunting dogs. Even the British only exerted the barest control over the region.

Today the NWFP is one of the most troubled of Pakistan's

provinces and territories. Its border is a source of constant spats with the United States, tired from hunting down Taliban cadres that have slipped through the porous border with Pakistan.

After some hours, we stopped to refuel. A small restaurant exuded the inviting smells of chapattis and curry. The driver wagged his finger at me and said, 'No eat,' but I was too hungry not to try my luck. I dived into the restaurant, found a vegetable curry and I was still wiping my mouth as I ran back to the bus, only making it by shoving my foot in front of the closing door. My elderly neighbour was not so lucky. I saw him through the back window running behind us, waving his arms. I tried to alert the driver, but he spoke no English.

'Stop the bus!' I shouted. No one responded or seemed to care.

Feeling angry on the old man's behalf, and linguistically helpless, I forced open the window next to me and let in the cool breeze. The sky began to roughen and spit, and the wind tousled the fern-clad hillsides. Street children tucked their cricket bats under their arms and headed indoors.

The following day, I continued my journey up to Chitral, where the scenery changed dramatically with the end of the monsoon belt. We'd passed the tropics and were now entering the realm of the Hindu Kush, the air suddenly dry and bracing. The forest gradually disappeared. At the foot of a slope beside the road was a broad basin where a slow-moving river hugged islands of silt, which shepherds crossed in cream *pakul* hats and pashminas. At the approach of the bus, a whole line of ginger-bottomed goats disappeared off the cliff's edge, as if leaping into nowhere. Far in the distance was the misty peak called Tirich Mir, where fairies were thought to live.

This was the beginning of a region more rarified than anything in the lowlands. The Hindu Kush, and the Himalayas further north, were lands of primeval forests, streams of snowmelt and wheeling hawks. At higher altitudes lived the majestic markhor, a shaggy antelope with two long twisted horns, said to belong to the fairies, and the solitary broad-pawed snow leopard.

Cut off from the great trading routes of Kabul and Wakhan,

travel had always been arduous here. Flash floods would destroy roads and snap bridges within hours. Avalanches would obscure paths, and snow falls block the passes for the winter. It was no wonder that the wheel only arrived here in the last century. I began to understand now how a people could remain so long a mystery.

A man in the seat in front, who had a long face and an enthusiastic smile, asked me in old-fashioned English, 'Where do you hail from?'

I told him England, suppressing a laugh.

His eyes shone with a nervous excitement. 'A Britisher!'

'Yes.'

'Britisher!' he said again.

I was always relieved at the reaction to being British in Pakistan. So often it was positive, excited, even awestruck. In Afghanistan the reaction could be ambivalent, confused ('Is England the same as America?') or plain hostile.

'The last Britisher who stay with me was on April the fifth, nineteen eighty-five,' he said, grinning manically. 'Come, let us have tea.'

We stopped at a small roadside hut thick with steam and woodsmoke. Rain started to fall in thick, cold globules. We made a dash for the safety of its interior, where we sat on charpoys – string tea beds – and ate dhal on low, heavy tables. From the hearth came the rich, aromatic scent of cedar, crackling as the rain thudded outside.

'You shouldn't listen to the BBC,' he said. 'No al-Qaeda here. They've have all gone to Iraq.'

But just as the bus pushed off again I noticed a roadside placard that read, in English and Urdu: WE DESIRE DEATH MORE ARDENTLY THAN LIFE.

The first sign of our arrival at Chitral was a slope littered with square houses, as if a giant toy box had been up ended. It was a small, pleasant town, a shambling string of roads and open-fronted shops, and the fast-flowing, mud-coloured Mastuj river.

Bales of fabric formed piles in almost every shop, spun into *patous* and jerkins in chocolate, terracotta and cream. Chitral was a true child of the Hindu Kush, with its wooden architecture, bracing air and white-topped peaks. But there was a prim gentility here, the traces of a long-forgotten world: a polo club, well-tended English lawns and the barracks of the Chitral Scouts, a border unit set up in 1903, where levies stood in patent leather shoes and high, checked socks.

Chitral had long reposed in undisturbed peace, but, with the Russian invasion of Afghanistan in 1979, it became a boom town of refugees and aid agencies. The 20,000-strong population today was a mix of Pashtuns, Gujurs, Bashgalis from Nuristan, but the most numerous were the Khos, who spoke Khowar, the main language. Like Nuristanis, the Khos are recent converts, turning to Islam only three centuries ago. They have become renowned for their conservative outlook. Women rarely showed their faces, even in the long, veil-like dupatta, and they refer to the Kalashas grimly as infidels and pagans.

As soon as I was ready, I set out to find out what I could about the Kalasha people. I began with one of the local NGOs, the most influential of which was the Aga Khan Rural Support Program, which had worked in the region since 1983.

Following directions, I passed the bulbous onion domes of the Great Mosque and came to a collection of whitewashed buildings, fronted by an English lawn. Hydrangeas grew in neat flower beds, with a very un-English Tirich Mir towering more than 7,000 metres high in the background.

Navid was an energetic young Chitrali of about 30, who was sitting quietly at his desk. He showed not the slightest agitation at being disturbed, and welcomed me in with tea and faultless English.

Of the three Kalasha valleys, he explained – Bumboret, Rumbur and Birir – the first was most in danger of 'invasion'. In recent years it had become a magnet for tourists, local and foreign, raising fears of inundation. I sat with Navid for at least an hour, sipping tea as he outlined the various issues faced by the Kalashas today.

'The big hotels totally ruined Bumboret,' he said.

'Too many foreigners like me?' I ventured.

'Well, actually the problem is more with the locals.' He paused, tapping his fingertips together. 'You see, Pakistanis don't understand the Kalashas, don't get religious diversity. You know what "kafir" means?'

'Unbeliever.'

'That's right. Infidels. People who have no god. But the Kalashas do have a god. Several, in fact. Here's an example. The Kalashas don't write, they have no book. So everything they know is passed on by word of mouth. The locals think if they have no holy book, then the Kalashas must have no religion. So they go in there, swagger about, blunder into peoples' houses, make improper comments.'

'They can't respect them. Is that it?'

'Naturally,' he said. 'They watch them dancing in festivals, drinking wine and they think to themselves, "Who are these people? They must be immoral." And so they are fascinated, and disgusted. It is really a problem.'

'Is that why the mullahs tried so hard to convert Kalashas in the Fifties and Sixties?'

'That's it. But, this is by no means all Pakistanis of course, just the less educated ones. In fact, some great development work is done locally. You know CAMAT?'

'Tell me.'

'It's an NGO, the Chitral Association for Mountain Area Tourism, headed by a guy called Maqsood ul-Mulk. You know him?'

I didn't.

'The mullahs used to get very angry about Jashni, the Kalasha spring festival, where there were a lot of girls dancing. The mullahs tried to ban it, but Maqsood revived it. And you know the irony? He's a cousin of the last mehtar – last in a long line of enslavers of the Kalasha people. And look at the mehtars now.' Navid spoke with earnestness, a true belief in the importance of his work.

'Yes,' he said with a sigh. 'They are always on their guard, the Kalashas.'

'But how much is Kalasha religion really under threat?' I asked. 'How can they stop the conversions?'

Navid thought for a minute. 'I did a social survey in Bumboret not long ago and I found that the Kalashas were demanding separate schools. You see, children would go to state schools and the teachers would make them to say the Kalima . . .'

'"There is no god but Allah and Muhammad is Allah's Messenger"?'

'Well done. And when you've said the Kalima there's no way back. Each conversion is claimed as a triumph for Islam.' He leaned forward in his chair.

I was impressed that Navid, a Muslim himself, could speak with such equanimity about the Kalasha religion.

'So how many are left now?' I asked.

'There are about 6,000 ethnic Kalasha.'

'How many have converted?'

'Just over half. When a Kalasha woman converts she will cut off her long braids. Some Muslims think that if you get hold of a Kalasha girl's braid you automatically go to heaven.'

'That's like the Kafirs cutting off the ears of their enemies.'

He spat out a short laugh. 'Yes it is, isn't it?'

On the way back, I found a tea shop, where I sat down with a slice of 'toast' – bread fried on a griddle – and a cup of very white tea. A cauldron boiled furiously on a trivet. Men crouched on slippers exchanging gossip in Khowar, their heels as flattened and shiny as the soles.

I picked up a copy of the *Chitral Times*. 'ANOTHER KALASHA CLAIMED FOR ISLAM,' read a headline.

My lift to Bumboret was in a pickup truck. It shifted off outside Chitral to pick up more passengers. Men with red beards and kohl-painted eyes clambered in with sacks of rice and tins of ghee. When the back of the truck was bursting with cargo, other hitchers swinging from the sides, we began our 30 km journey to the Kalasha valleys.

The sky was white with wispy clouds and the air smelt of moss and wet leaves. Heading out of town, we passed streams and weed-hugged, drystone walling. Groves of chenar trees were in full leaf and slatey scree slopes soon tumbled on both sides of the road. Just as the view opened up, so did the clouds, causing a riot in the back of the truck. A canvas tarpaulin was unrolled over our heads and we were sunk in a hot, breathy darkness.

After an hour, through the eyelets in the tarpaulin, I could see the greenery begin to fall away. The road became slatey, like a Welsh hill-track. The giant slate slopes, previously loose, now hardened into a chessboard of shards that hung over the road like graphite. Only after the town of Ayun, where the land dried out and the river turned the colour of tea, and the shale turned a shade of terracotta, did the moist greenery return. The rain stopped at last and I helped pull off the tarpaulin as we reached the mouth of Bumboret, the largest and most populous of the Kalasha valleys.

Bumboret was deliciously green, its small alluvial fields growing in a patchwork close to the valley walls, moist and mint against the pale mountainside. High in the pastures cedar and pine forests bristled like needles in the distance.

By this time most of the travellers had already leapt out, dragging their rice and tea to their villages. My only other travelling companions were two adolescent Kalasha girls in the front seat, the first I'd seen in the flesh. Their costume was so outré, so different from anything I'd seen. The girls were beautiful, with long plaits, dark and glossy against their light skin. On their heads they wore thick bands of black wool, known as a *susutr*, woven with hundreds of cowrie shells. A long strip of material, beaded and belled, ran down the length of their backs next to lianas of plaited black hair. I could understand very easily why tourists – local or foreign – were fascinated by them.

The jeep stopped. One of the girls got out near her house and I watched her climb over a drystone wall. She looked back at the jeep, waved to her friend, and smiled at me playfully. I smiled back. It was a strange sensation. I think it was the first eye contact I'd made with the opposite sex since leaving Tajikistan a month before.

I walked up the path, taking in the good air, the willow and mulberry trees, and the fields of sugar cane and maize. Beyond the sound of gushing water I could hear something like pan pipes. I wanted to agree with all the travel writers, confirm that it was idyllic, Arcadian, bucolic, and fall into the trap of all the orientalising travellers seduced by these charming valleys, but I held myself in check.

The only people in view were women. They sat in the fields in full traditional dress and multiple necklaces, gathering maize stalks. Work was rigidly demarcated between the sexes. While they toiled in the fields, gathering the crops and harvesting wheat, the men were hard at work, too, spending the spring and summer in the high pastures with their goats or working in Chitral and Peshawar. The herders were due to return any day now.

After a few hundred metres I found the arterial road, and a line of hotels built by foreign contractors. I saw instantly what Navid meant. They looked completely out of place with their clipped lawns and had touristy names like the Hotel Shalimar. There were few tourists, though. Since 9/11 Pakistan was off most people's holiday list. One hotel tout, a Punjabi, stood by his painted fence. He called me over.

'Welcome to Bumboret,' he said. 'So, you gonna have a walk around? Drink a little Kalasha wine?' he tilted an imaginary glass to his mouth.

'Don't know.'

He pointed to the other side of the street where two girls in their embroided skirts were sitting on a drystone wall under the shade of a spreading chenar tree.

'Cute, aren't they?'

It was odd. I'd never heard anyone in Afghanistan or Pakistan comment on a girl's beauty.

'The two girls, don't you see them?'

'Yes, I see them,' I said, but somehow I couldn't join in.

I wanted to visit all three Kalasha valleys, and I needed a guide. I was told that the best place to find one was at the hotel run by the Pakistan Tourism Development Corporation, the Hilton of the Kalashadesh, as the three valleys were collectively known.

Akram, a short, stocky Kalasha youth of about 20, appeared in the lobby within minutes of my enquiries. He was square-jawed and suspicious, as if I'd summoned him for a telling-off. It turned out he was a student on vacation for the summer. He was working as a guide to improve his English.

'What is required of me?' he asked formally, as we sat in the lobby over tea.

'Very little. I just want to walk around the valleys, understand a bit more about your people and culture.'

He nodded. 'So we just walk around? That all?' It seemed too easy.

'Yes, for a week or so.'

He stroked his jaw. 'Great,' he said.

We walked together up the hill, ready to plan our trip. A drizzle was falling, like a cloud of sea spray.

'Come, let's find shelter.' He took me by the arm to seek refuge in a tea house, a stone and wood building, where we sat beside a giant sack of walnuts, freshly picked from the mountainside.

'It shouldn't be raining today,' he said. 'I hope it doesn't last. Prun festival is coming up.' He stuck his hand out of the awning's shelter like a divining rod. It started to thunder. 'Fairies playing polo,' he said, and laughed.

'No, I'm serious,' he said. 'Anyway, that's the belief.'

The rain pattered hard and we made ourselves comfortable. He handed me a nut and cracked one for himself.

'You know, we have a tradition that when the weather is bad and the rain never seems to stop, the women all gather to leave. The women say, "The weather is too bad, we are going back to Tsiyam." They march a little way down the hill and the men plead with them to come back.'

Tsiyam was the homeland of Kalasha myth.

'Once, many years ago, the women didn't listen to the men's pleas and they got to Tsiyam, where they married dogs. That's why they always come back. I think it's because they don't want to marry dogs.'

'I see. And where exactly is Tsiyam?' I asked, curious as to what he'd say.

'Nobody knows, but it was Nanga Dehar who led our people from there.'

'Nanga Dehar the shaman?'

'You've heard about him?' he asked.

'I've read a bit.'

I knew Nanga Dehar would come up sooner or later. I'd read about him as the greatest shaman in Kalasha history, a *mishari moch* – a man that mixes with fairies. He was the shaman-prophet of the last independent king of the Kalasha, Bula Singh, and was more or less the founder of the modern Kalasha religion. He instructed his people how to worship, how to sacrifice and established the distinction between the pure and the impure.

According to tradition, Nanga Dehar lived twelve to fourteen generations beyond the living elders (between four and six centuries ago) when Bula Singh controlled Chitral. But when a new Muslim power centre arose – the Muslim Rais – and Bula Singh was defeated, Nanga Dehar was visited by the gods and told to lead his people from Tsiyam to Rumbur (one of the three Kalasha valleys) where he was to transfer all of the altars to the gods.

Nanga Dehar climbed up to the ridge that now separates Afghanistan from Pakistan and shot two arrows, one red and one black. Where the black arrow fell he ordained a *dewa dur* to be built, a House of God. This would be a pure – *onjesta* – place only entered by men. Where the red arrow fell, lower down in the valley, he would build a *bashali* – a menses house, where women would give birth and menstruate. This was the most impure – *pragata* – part of the valley. In this way the *onjesta/pragata* division was established. In the following years, this duality has become more refined. It can be so complex, in fact, that many Kalasha men aren't sure where they should or shouldn't step. And it's the women who strengthen and reinforce this distinction. Broadly speaking, though, what is *onjesta* includes men and men's work, goats, and the high pastures, while the *pragata* includes women (especially during menstruation), outsiders, evil spirits and Muslims.

We sat for a while drinking tea and talking. The rain stopped and the sky cleared to blue, sending a pure breeze into the cedar-smelling interior. It was time to make a move up the valley. The Kalashadesh did not have the stark beauty of Afghanistan or the dramatic sweep of the steppe. This landscape was soft, Alpine in feel, a refreshing combination of summer heat and mountain crispness.

The more I spoke to Akram, the more I realised that the valleys were littered with sacred spots, springs, trees, vines and rocks connected with the life and miracles of Nanga Dehar and the gods. The best plan would be to visit some of these landmarks, learning what I could along the way. I'd also get to see some of the most beautiful countryside of my journey.

'We could visit Sarik Jao, further up,' said Akram, thinking aloud. 'This was where Nanga Dehar died. Kazi Mas should be up there now. He lives next door, and he can tell us more.'

The *kazi*, he explained, was a latter-day Kalasha historian, an expert on the rites and taboos that the shamans used to know. Ironically, *kazi* is also the title of a Muslim judge.

'When we go to Rumbur,' Akram continued, 'we can talk to Kazi Khoshnavaz. He is also famous for his knowledge. He knows thousands of stories. There is the spring of Mingonutz and the sacred vine. Let's go to Sarik Jao first, it's only a short walk away.'

The sky now turned a deep, almost arctic blue, clear behind the high, white mountains. We set off up the valley to the sound of tinkling water, past the chalets of Shindur and over the bridge to Durwatak. As we walked, Akram told me the Kalasha names for some of the trees and berries: *bonj* for the chenar tree, and also the *bonmut* and *sarazmut* trees from upper Chitral.

Each time a woman passed, Akram would take her hand and kiss it, saying '*Shpata vai*' ('Greetings, sister'). She would do the same and reply, '*Shpata baba*' ('Greetings, brother'). It was a formalised rite, but not without affection.

Kalasha houses were perfect in their own way. Square structures made of stone and wood, they were built without nails and they perched on impossible slopes, tracing the contours of the hills. The lower storeys were used as stables. Maize cobs dried on the roofs. Kalasha women busied themselves on cantilevered verandas, sweeping dust while dressed in their elaborate clothing, or sat on stools sorting the good walnuts from the bad.

At Batrik we passed a different kind of structure, a Jestak Han, a hypostyle hall where ritual dancing took place at festivals and funerals. Intricately carved with wedges and interlocking swirls, its columns were topped with sculpted goats' heads. I was reminded of the beguiling knots of a Celtic brooch or the animal head capitals at Persepolis, the ancient ceremonial Persian capital. It was obvious to me now why Kafir craftsmen were dispatched *en masse* to Abdur Rahman's court.

We walked up a winding path that led up an earth and scree slope, towards a narrow grove where two chenar trees grew. Finally, we caught sight of a veranda, some distance away, where an old man sat on a stool, surrounded by goatskin hangings. He was polishing his shoes with a spit, squeak, spit, squeak, that resounded over the valley like the call of an unfamiliar bird.

'That's Kazi Mas,' said Akram, 'and this is Sarik Jao, where Nanga Dehar died.' On the spot was a sacred tree called a *bizu*, which had small, tough branches like a hawthorn. Akram walked around it, treading carefully on its spreading roots. He picked up one of its berries, which had fallen between the roots, and sucked it.

'It's hundreds of years old, this tree, but its berries are always good. Kazi Mas will tell us more.'

We scrambled down the slope towards the *kazi*'s veranda, where Akram greeted the elder properly. Kazi Mas's face was scraped by age and sun into rows of walnut wrinkles, and his eyeballs were set in a web of red capillaries. He turned in my direction for a second, then said something in a high-pitched rasp.

'The *kazi* asks,' said Akram, 'if you know that this is where the last great king of the Kalasha lived.'

I said I didn't. We three sat on stools and looked out over the hillside with the sacred tree in view.

The old man looked at me, suspiciously. He chattered some more with Akram, who after a while turned to me to translate.

'Kazi Mas asks if you know that Sarik Jao is a very holy place?' he said.

I nodded.

'Sarik Jao is a magical place,' said Akram, translating. 'When the *bizu* tree grew it had power over the whole valley. Even now it is very holy.' So *onjesta* was the tree, he said, that the village was not fit for human habitation. Only the most *onjesta* of animals, the goat, could be stalled here, and some very *onjesta* men. Women, who were *pragata*, were strictly barred.

'Kazi Mas asks if you have heard of Nanga Dehar,' said Akram.

I said I had, and there was a change in the *kazi*. He looked encouraged.

'He wants to tell you a story,' said Akram. I listened attentively.

'One day Nanga Dehar went to Birir. When he got there he met two men. Suddenly, an angel shot him with an arrow. No one knows why. He was very pure, but these things are not for us to know. As he lay there, dying, he suddenly saw the destinies of his two travelling companions. To one, the shaman said, "Never catch a flying axe or you will die," and to the other he said, "Do not take off your shoes or you will die of a snake bite." They took him here to Sarik Jao and laid him down, but Nanga Dehar survived for a while longer. He lay in pain for five months until finally the arrow head came out of his body. "Now I will die," he said, and did so.

'Soon after, a tree called *bizu* came out of the ground. It was a special tree. It had two stems: one pointed up and one pointed down. If one stem became ill or diseased, one side of the valley suffered. If the same happened to the other stem, the opposite side of the valley suffered. One day one of the stems was ill and a man cut it off. He went *cunjer* – mad. The surviving "good" stem grew and grew, and this is the tree it became.' He nodded towards the *bizu*, 'the most *onjesta* in the Kalashadesh.'

I asked the *kazi*, through Akram, whether anyone dreams like that these days, or predicts people's futures. He spoke for a long while, and I hoped Akram could remember it all. Finally Akram explained.

'Shamans these days can't dream like Nanga Dehar. And none can perform miracles. Kazi Mas says that Kalasha villagers sometimes go to Muslim *ziarats* now, the shrines of Muslim holy men. They trust them more than *dehars*.'

I remembered Navid's words: Kalashas have no scripture. Belief and ritual is passed by word of mouth from generations of *dehars* (shamans), who received instructions from gods and spirits in trances and dreams.

Kalashas believed that *dehars* really could diagnose problems and predict the future through direct communication with the supernatural. They declared land to be *onjesta* or *pragata*, and ordered purification with the blood of a goat and smoke from a spray of juniper – a very *onjesta* tree. Together with the *kazis* they were the guardians of Kalasha culture.

One of their reputed powers was to locate and extract evil implanted by a bad fairy. One story was told to the French travel writer Jean-Yves Loude by a Kalasha shepherd who had complained of aches and fatigue. The shepherd had invited Khan Dehar to his house, whereupon the *dehar* fell into a trance and waved his axe around, growling wildly. He then dropped his axe and sank his teeth into the shepherd's shoulder, sucking out a bone as long as a nail, then spitting it out without a trace of blood. The *dehar* picked up the axe again, spun round and let it fly towards a beam. And there, where it fell, lay an evil spell – planted by a malicious fairy – that had been the cause of the shepherd's trouble. The charm was extracted and burnt, and Khan Dehar received a he-goat, an axe and an iron tripod in reward.

Shamanism – the process of visiting other worlds in a trance, speaking with unearthly entities and the spirits of dead ancestors

– was not something I'd come across in my Central Asian journey. It was still an important part of life for many Siberian and Inner Asian peoples. In the Hindu Kush, shamanism had once been extremely widespread. But today, apart from the tiny pockets of Muslim shamans in Hunza and Gilgit, outside the Kalashadesh shamanism has been completely wiped out. Even in these valleys it looked on the verge of extinction.

'I don't know why there are so few left,' Akram said, chewing on a berry. 'It may be because the Kalashadesh is not so pure any more, not as holy as it once was. This is what Kazi Mas says.'

It was thought that with each conversion to Islam, the valleys became increasingly impure. There was barely a Kalasha family now without at least one member that had converted to Islam.

The *kazi* grew tired. He looked up at me and nodded. We bade him goodbye, and he turned back to cleaning his shoe, which he spat on and rubbed, and the squeaking followed us all the way down to the path.

Akram spoke again. 'Kazi Mas also said that Nanga Dehar prophesied that one day the whole of the Kalashadesh would convert to Islam.'

The Gambak Pass was a saddle-shaped mountain ridge separating Bumboret from the next valley, Birir. This was the valley of grapes, where the largest and sweetest grew. According to tradition, it was also the site of the first God-given vine, and where the Kalasha festival dedicated to the vine crop was celebrated.

Prun marked the beginning of the grape and grain harvests. Mothers made flower caps for their daughters and would sometimes dress up as shepherds to match their husbands, who were descending from the high pastures.

Akram was small and solidly built, spending most of the day hiking up and down the steep Kalasha slopes. He seemed to think we could cross the Gambak Pass in a day. I wasn't so sure.

But we took supplies, a small pack filled with chapattis and walnuts. We picked some shiny apples from a neighbour's orchard and set off. Following a path where wild almond and walnut trees grew, we soon reached a slatey scree slope that became progressively steeper. In parts, the gradient stiffened into a near wall of magenta rock, where giant scabs of sedimentary rock stood, as shiny as gunmetal, blinding in the sun's glare.

I clambered breathlessly, slipping down the vertical grain of the rock, my trousers torn by the red thickets. Akram leapt forward like a Himalayan goat, though he was carrying two packs.

The goal was the higher reaches, clothed in a rich band of pine trees that stood defiantly up above a steep slope, bristling like brushes. Akram always waited patiently, standing high up, almost out of view. And when I'd finally caught up he would leap ahead again with the soft clack of a dislodged stone.

Hours later we rested on the steep slope, looking down on the Lilliputian valley below, chewing chapattis in silence as the menthol air dried the sweat from our bodies.

Suddenly, there came a tinkling sound and the clatter of falling pebbles. A flock of twist-horned goats was shambling down the slope. Behind them strode a shepherd with a fleecy beard and puttees on his shins. He sang in a rich baritone, '*Ai ai ai ai!*'. The goats ran on. '*Ai ai!*' sang the shepherd again, thumping his crook on the rock. The goats halted obediently, with a tumble of falling pebbles, and peered round at their master like guilty children. The shepherd drew near, a lithe figure, swinging a sack of pine nuts, and greeted Akram with the customary, '*Shpata baba.*' He offered us some walnut bread, but said little. After months in the *onjesta* pastures he was used only to silence and the company of goats. He also seemed to speak to the animals in a language they understood. '*Ai*' meant, 'stop', the shepherd explained, '*ah*' meant, 'be careful', '*kich*' meant '*go*', and '*kulu*', meant 'come'. 'There was a time when men could understand *their* language,' he said.

The long-haired flock waited, packed together, in anticipation of their next command. The shepherd rose, swung his sack on his shoulder and boomed, '*Kich!*' Off they jingled, their pastor bounding after them.

As we pushed on higher, the sky became a deeper blue, the air even fresher. We entered a forest of huge cedars. The earth was carpeted with brown needles and cones, sticky with sap. Logs rotted into the texture of sponge cake, topped with variegated fungi. These forests were centuries old, Akram explained. If they were cut down, as was constantly threatened, they would take thousands of years to grow back.

The view at the top of the pass was more intense than I could have imagined – the distant peaks speckled with juniper and pine, and behind them pitched the glacial horizon of the Hindu Kush. Akram squeezed my shoulder in congratulation.

After a rest, we launched ourselves over the other side to the smallest of the three valleys, and half-slid, half-walked down the sea of shale between high red cliffs.

By sunset, calves twitching, we entered into lush, narrow Birir. We walked through tinkling water channels and crossed groves of persimmon and peach, stopping to pick sugar cane. With what little strength remained, we hopped through the village of Guru, the houses built on stilts like matchsticks, with beautiful railed verandas, and landed at last at a small guest-house balcony, where we were greeted with a large, hot goat curry.

Later, we sat in contemplation on our wicker seats. The valley was now in darkness and Akram was reading a tattered French grammar by the lamplight.

'Do you know French?' He looked up.

'A bit,' I said, being only half-competent.

'Can you teach me some? There is a French tourist in the hotel next to my house. She is very beautiful, and so maybe if I learn some of her language I can be her guide.' A mischievous grin spread across his face.

'OK,' I laughed, and took his book. I showed him how to pronounce French greetings. He looked at me with disgust. I pronounced '*Merci*' and he repeated '*Mekhhsi*' in astonishment. 'It's like Arabic. It is a *very* strange language.' He tossed the book aside.

Akram was restless, and went over to the balcony.

'Look at this,' he said. I glanced up from my book.

Far in the dimness, wood torches swayed and flickered, and we could make out the sound of soft chanting.

'That's it, that's it!' he howled, and leapt in the air. 'Prun *has* come! I thought it was tomorrow. *Merkhsi commont allee voo, commont allee vooo!*'

True enough, a phalanx of robed women was proceeding out of the darkness like a funereal chorus in a Greek tragedy. Their faces and skeins were lit up by the swaying torches and they were wearing their ceremonial headdresses, the *kupas* – the tall, flat-topped head-dress, placed on top of the *susutr*, decorated with hundreds of cowrie shells, beads, and pompoms. With every step of the procession the hundreds of stitched bells jingled as one. '*Cher mala pio, volishai rolimai, guan,*' they seemed to be singing.

'That is the Song of the Virile Shepherd,' explained Akram.

We went down into the road to join them. The procession left the track and all was shrouded in black in the wake of the naked flames. We followed the glint of shells and glass beads and the bright yellow embroidery of their hems, the dark fabric blending into the night.

We crossed gullies and scrambled up hillocks. At each house, the door would open and faces would be lit up in the garish orange light. A small burst of chatter was followed by fistfuls of grapes, huge bunches of sweet, pear-shaped grapes with a thick bloom and a taste of quince. Everyone would join in, mothers with all their daughters, singing the same refrain, '*Cher mala pio, volishai rolimai, guan.*' We continued the march over narrow paths, and their headdresses bobbed in their light of the torches. Their skeins swished and snapped as we marched through the thickets.

The procession ended in a house built on stilts at one of the furthest corners of the valley where the first of the dancing began. A crew of *pakul*-hatted musicians sat in the corner with a tight skin drum and a jerrycan. A penny whistle struck up a tune. The tempo increased and a master of ceremonies picked dancers from a throng of shy adolescents. Two at a time they took to the floor, amid shrieks and clapping. The jerry can puttered, two strikes to a beat, until the smiling drummer was in a trance of his own, his face glistening and beaming like a child. The dancers flung their skirts around, their arms splayed, bunching and spreading their hands into star shapes. They twirled in a circle, stepped side to side, clapped and clicked, while their long dark plaits, weighted with coloured pompoms, swing to a rhythm of their own.

I prodded Akram, but he wasn't paying attention. He was watching one of the dancing girls. She was about 15, wheeling around with a glassy determination. Her orange neck beads were as fine as fabric, and pulsed to the rhythm of her body. Her skin was unblemished and her eyebrows finely arched. Her gaze flitted, for a split second, towards him.

The piping seemed endless, the drumming hypnotic.

'In the old days,' said Akram, eventually, 'when the shepherds came down from the mountain they could pick any girl they wanted. According to custom the girl couldn't refuse.'

'And now?'

'Not any more,' he sighed. 'The *dehars* stopped it. Or I would have been a shepherd.'

He said, a while later, 'Do you know the story of how the grape came?' Akram explained how many years ago the first vine came to Birir in spring. 'All the girls were dancing round Nanga Dehar. He had a big knife and struck the earth. The earth parted and the *dehar* jumped inside. A little while later he came out of the mountain with a huge boom, a vine sprig in his hand. He said to the girls, "This is the gift of the gods to the Kalasha people." He threw it onto the hillside and there the vine grew.'

'What happened to it? Is the vine still there, like the tree at Sarik Jao?'

'No,' he said, very matter of factly, 'there is a mosque over it now.'

It was morning in Birir. I emerged on to the veranda after a bracing bucket shower. When I was ready, Akram took me to meet someone who was said to be a Kalasha 'expert'.

We walked by a fast-flowing stream along bright green alluvial meadows to a short slope, topped by a classic stone-and-wood structure.

Maureen Lines – or 'Aya' (Mother) to her friends – was a force of nature, renowned for her commitment to the protection of the valley's fragile environment. Following a life of wandering, she'd somehow ended up in the Kalashadesh in 1980. Falling in love with the place, she returned six years later to Birir to live and work. Fluent in Kalasha and Pashto, she ran two NGOs – the Hindu Kush Conservation Association and the Kalash Environmental Protection Society – and was forever lobbying UNESCO to declare the valleys a world heritage site.

But her work was not always well-received. Her campaigns led to accusations that she cared only for the Kalasha, not the Muslim community, and a smear campaign by mullahs led to her expulsion by the district administration. But since gaining her Pakistani passport a few years ago, she has continued her work, whatever the personal risk.

Akram led me up the slope to a two-roomed house. A mother was feeding her baby on a bare charpoy. A boy sat on a stool whittling a stick. In a wicker chair sat a stout woman with a mop of silver hair. Her dress was defiantly Western – a black waistcoat and trousers – and her right hand gripped a cane.

'Where *is* that man?' she hissed. 'If he's not here in the next ten minutes there's no way we'll get to Peshawar on time.'

Our shadows announced our arrival. She registered Akram's Kalasha face, but looked at me with mild fatigue that said: 'Not another journalist.'

Akram introduced me, and asked if I could talk to her.

'All right,' she said, 'but my driver's coming any minute now.' She issued a curt command to the boy on the stool who jumped to fetch some tea.

'I just wanted to ask a few questions about Birir,' I said, gingerly. 'Do you mind if I take notes?'

'Mind?' Her mouth twitched into a half-smile. 'No, I don't mind.'

Maureen ran a dispensary, she explained, arching her neck round the door every so often to check on her lift. She also organised sanitation projects and helped build latrines. For a woman pushing 70 she showed no sign of flagging. Only a painful leg and back slowed her down a little.

'Some have commented that your work concentrates on the Kalasha more than the Muslim community,' I said.

'Well that's rubbish!' she spat. 'My NGOs exist to benefit everybody. Muslims are the majority here in Birir.' Her hand gripped the knob of her cane tightly.

'Din Mohammad, where's our tea?'

'What about the pressure to convert to Islam?'

Her demeanour softened.

'It's a big issue, but don't get hung up on conversion. It's all part of a much bigger problem.'

'Which is?'

'Globalisation. People want things now. Material objects, VCRs, money, land. To get those things they have to leave the valleys and go to the outside world. When I first came in the Eighties they didn't *use* money, they bartered things. You see ...' her hands formed a cup, '... the outside world to the Kalasha *is* Islam. Globalisation comes to these valleys through that lens, do you see?' She waited while I wrote.

'What are you doing here, out of interest?'

I told her about my journey and she regarded me with a little more sympathy.

'Sometimes Kalashas leave the valleys in search of money or better prospects or diplomas. When they reach the outside world they find people who don't tolerate unbelievers. Here Muslims and Kalashas live generally well together, but it's not always so outside. There are two or three cases from Birir. They were bribed with cash to convert, sent to Peshawar and "re-educated". Next thing, they ended up fighting in Kashmir or Iraq, without having a clue what they're doing. One time I put pressure on the authorities to transfer a Kalasha man from a Kabul jail to a Peshawar jail. He was sent to Peshawar and was later released, I'm glad to say.'

The milky tea arrived. I handed one to Akram, who was sitting quietly to one side.

'But listen . . .' – she was so commanding I had no choice – 'right now the Kalasha birth rate outstrips the conversion rate. Don't let the journalists tell you otherwise. Kalasha culture isn't dying, it's robust – though it may not always be so. But the important thing for all these people – Nuristanis, Kalashas, Chitralis – is education. They need to know that the only way to get on is to respect other cultures.'

A honk sounded from down below.

'My ride,' she sighed. 'Good to meet you, Daniel, and I'm extremely interested in your journey.'

We shook hands and she limped down the slope to a waiting driver, who was no doubt in line for a drubbing.

That afternoon it was time for us to see the third and final valley, Rumbur, lying to the north of Bumboret. There was no pass to climb, at least not one that I could manage The only way was by jeep. It was said that Kalasha culture was strongest here and Kalasha-Muslim antagonism was at a minimum. It was also here that Nanga Dehar first guided his people from Tsiyam.

Rumbur was narrow, but seemed wild and rugged, its peaks higher. We pitched up to a charming hotel that served excellent walnut bread and had a small library of books left over from travellers: guidebooks, Japanese novels, even Robertson's *The Kafirs of the Hindu-Kush*.

Akram and I sat down to a bean curry and an acidic, home-made wine. In Rumbur he had promised me an introduction to Kazi Khoshnavaz, one of the most famous *kazis*.

'He has a very small head,' Akram had warned me repeatedly, ever since the Gambak Pass. 'But he knows *everything*.'

We made our way to the *kazi*'s house along the main valley track, flanked by shrubs of violet and gold. Akram showed me the *beoow* tree, with silvery eucalyptus-shaped leaves, and we stopped next to a bush with edible berries. He sucked one and handed another to me.

'Try this.'

I put it into my mouth. It was dry and bitter. It had little hairs that drew the moisture out of the mouth, and tasted disgusting. He grinned as I scraped the remains off my tongue. Further down the road, we found the house we were looking for.

Kazi Khoshnavaz was sitting on the steps outside his home in a pale blue *khalat*. His head was indeed very small – shrunken, even. His skin was dark and leathery, and his eyes were set deep in his skull.

Akram greeted him respectfully and asked if we might consult him. His eyes were expressionless and, like Kazi Mas, he slurred and mumbled his words.

'There are 4,000 stories connected with Nanga Dehar,' he said. 'They might drive you mad.'

'Mad? How?' I was already hooked.

'Once there was a professor, English like you.' He poked me with a bony finger. 'He wanted to find out all the stories too. I told him I knew 4,000 stories, but he wouldn't go away. He stayed with me over a year. Every day I recited the stories and every day he wrote them all down until at the end of 14 months he counted them up. He only had 700. 'How many are there left?' he asked. I told him I had 3,300 more. And he went mad.'

I listened to Akram's translation with growing interest.

'May we take a chance?'

The *kazi* wriggled his fingers. 'Rupee,' he said.

'Don't worry,' said Akram under his breath. 'He even charges *us* for stories.'

The old kazi led us into a one-roomed cedar-and-stone house. Women bustled over an open fire, which curled up to a corbelled smoke-hole. A family sat round the fire on walnut stools or rested on goat-hair charpoys. An hour-glass mortar as tall as a person stood by the door. The area behind the fire was empty and untrodden. It was sacred to Jestak, the goddess of the family, and was adorned with juniper. We were seated on stools and handed *tasili*, buttery corn pancakes.

Akram asked him to give me a story that would help me understand shamanism. I must say I felt slightly uncomfortable.

Here was one of the most learned *kazis* in the Kalashadesh, who charged cash to tell stories. Surely I was part of the problem.

The *kazi*'s eyes looked up to the ceiling, apparently deep in thought. I wondered if he'd thought twice about driving another Englishman mad. But after a few minutes he began to speak. Why Khoshnavaz picked this story I don't know, but as we sat listening to him by the crackling fire, the family one by one stopped their tasks and sat down to listen too. They looked at us with warm smiles, handing us more and more *tasili*, mildly assuaging my discomfort about paying for the story.

'Once there was a wedding between the daughter of Chakon and the son of Samir. The bride was called Nikel and the groom was called Shamint, of the Bumbdeinak tribe. Nikel's dowry was a flock of goats and four charpoys. Chakon, the bride's father, went out one day to hunt. He saw a deer and aimed his arrow at it, but the deer said to him, "Don't shoot. You already have many deer." Nevertheless, he let fly his arrow and the man fell unconscious. When he came to, he found his leg was injured. He took a stick and walked slowly back to his village, unsure what had happened.

'The marriage preparations for his daughter had started and everyone was filled with excitement. Suddenly Nanga Dehar arrived at the house of Chakon in the form of a blackbird. He flew through the skylight and began to sing a tale of woe. Nanga Dehar sang to Chakon, "You were away for seven full years. You were in Palaishaimena with the angels. You danced in Atalishay with a diamond bed. You are welcome here, Chakon, son of Bazik, but your diamond dancing house is shaking and falling." Chakon's wife, who was vexed by the song tried to catch the blackbird. "This is a bad story," she said. "Why are you singing it?" Her husband jumped to stop her. "No!" he said. "Don't kill him. He knows all about me. It is Nanga Dehar!" The blackbird flew up out of the skylight and the old couple awaited the doom that they knew would befall their house.

'Meanwhile, Nikel, who was getting ready to marry, was walking in the valley. Suddenly, a boulder that had come loose on the slopes fell down and struck her on the head, killing her instantly. The guests who had come for the wedding were now mourners at her funeral. Chakon fell ill. Sacrifices were offered and entreaties uttered, to no avail. Nanga Dehar came again to Chakon and said to his father, who was standing by his bedside, "Your son must die." And so it came to pass.'

The *kazi* stopped speaking, Akram stopped translating and I was left in silence. I thought it was a wonderful story, confusing certainly, but full of mystery and the inscrutable power of the gods.

'Kazi Khoshnavaz says,' explained Akram, 'that Nanga Dehar was passing a message from God that their time had come. Whatever Nanga Dehar said always comes to pass.'

The *kazi* sat trussed in his *khalat*, watching us with knowing, glinting eyes.

I still wondered if there were any *dehars* left in the Kalashadesh, however old or infirm. I was sure that there must be at least one shaman left, and I was too curious not to ask. The hanging cauldron seethed in the silence, and the family still sat around us, entranced. Finally the *kazi* spoke again.

'Kazi Khoshnavaz says there is one man who has the power,' said Akram. 'But it is too late. He has already converted to Islam.'

Even if it was too late, I still wanted to meet him. The Kazi explained carefully where we could find the man.

We met the *dehar* in secret. He was afraid. No one was to know he was still a practising shaman. We found him on a gently sloping field out of sight of his house, crouched in between two fields, neither in one nor the other. He had a substantial white beard that tufted in a curve like a spade from his chin, the rough texture of goat-hair. The lines on his tanned brow and eyes were deep and careworn.

'I'm sorry I cannot show you into my house,' he said. 'My daughter-in-law is not veiled and you may not come in.'

We promised him we'd keep his identity secret. He told us a heart-rending story of a broken life. Since adolescence he had practised as a shaman, until one day he needed to go to Chitral for a minor operation. His relatives, who had all already converted to Islam, took him to the hospital and arranged everything. When he awoke from sedation he found his son leaning over his bed. He said, 'You are a Muslim now, and never deny it.'

'I was distressed,' said the old man. 'I've been a *dehar* since childhood. My father was a *dehar* and my grandfather too. I was needed at festival times and consulted for my powers. I can never be a Muslim, but it breaks my heart that my entire family has converted. I am not a believer and I know I never will be a Muslim in my heart.'

Conversion to Islam is an irreversible step, and any attempt to reconvert to being a Kalasha – which is as much a religious as an ethnic denominator – was impossible. He would run the very real risk of being murdered.

'But I still have the dreams,' he said, anguished. 'I consult, still, but everything must be secret. House visits are no longer possible, of course, and all my work must be conducted through messengers.'

He told me about a man who had a pain in his back. The sufferer went to Peshawar to see a doctor, but none could ease his pain.

'You see, he had touched an impure woman,' said the *dehar*, 'and the *pragata* had spread round his body. I knew how to heal it. The angels had told me in a dream. They said the man must sacrifice a goat and take especial care to avoid women who were nearing their menstruation. I delivered the message to him and soon afterwards the man was cured.'

The *dehar* looked round him, watching his house through the trees.

'Are we OK?' I asked. He nodded.

'My power is no longer the same,' he continued. 'Since my conversion to Islam I dream less. I can't fall into a trance so easily. The angels are angry with me. They are snatching my dreams away. My people have made me *pragata*.' The *dehar*'s eyes darted. He wiped his brow on his wrist. But he needed to get back before his family came looking for him, and he hobbled quickly back to his house.

We wandered back to the guest house, and I felt a growing sense of unease, thinking over the confidences that had been entrusted to me that day. Akram said little and went to bed early. A pale moon had risen and I sat alone on our veranda, watching a soft, silvery light creep over the fields.

The following day was my last in the valley. Akram waited with me until the lift was ready.

'I hope I was of service,' he said. I laughed. He was a more knowledgable guide than I could have ever hoped for, and he had become a better friend than I could have expected. I gave him his fee, which he didn't count, and we shook hands warmly.

I sat at the back of the Chitral-to-Peshawar minibus, my legs once more pressed to my chest, my luggage lashed to the roof. I had only just recovered from the 47 nauseating switchbacks when we arrived at the Lowarai Pass. The road had been swept away by a mud-stream that issued like a titanic effluent from the mountain peaks.

Darkness had fallen. The sky was a brawl of storm clouds that showered in sweeping volleys. A river ahead was tumbling over the road, cascading from the hillside, carrying boulders and running over anything in its path. The men waded across, while our minibus slowly eased over on unsteady wheels, until it was safely across. Fourteen men in soaking cotton salwars climbed aboard again.

I made it the following day to Peshawar. My pack was soaked, a pocket had burst open and my medicine pack had been washed away by the terrible weather and jolting journey. But I didn't need my medical kit any more. I was going home.

There was one thing I still wanted to do. When I was in Chitral I'd learned of a curious character, a relic of a forgotten England. Major Geoffrey Langlands was well known in this part of Pakistan as the only British resident in Chitral, and the oldest British teacher in the world.

Having come to India as a commando in the British Indian Army in 1944, Langlands was one of the few who chose to stay in Pakistan after partition. He'd been teaching continuously for the past 50 years and now, at about 90, was Head of the Sayurj School in Chitral, a secular private school where he still taught maths.

I'd already tried to track him down in Chitral where his deputy head received me with undue deference. He told me the Major was in Peshawar. I asked if I could get in touch with him.

'Oh yes, sir,' he said, beaming.

'Do you have his number?'

'Yes sir, I do, sir, yes,' he said, his teeth glinting with every word. 'Will you have tea, sir?'

'Thank you, no.'

'Oh thank you, sir. Goodbye.' He took my hand in both of his, clasped it together and bowed, still smiling.

Equipped with the major's number I dialled from the hotel telephone in Peshawar. A clipped and authoritative voice answered, the type I hadn't heard in a long while. I introduced myself and said I was intrigued to meet him. The old man seemed delighted.

I changed into my cleanest shalwar kameez, bought a box of macaroons and rickshawed over to a suburb of electric gates and guard boxes. I rang at the house of the late General Habibullah and was shown into a beautiful drawing room, with a very old school book collection: *Recollections of Dönitz* and *The Life of Lord Nelson* in matt cloth-covered hardbacks.

The Major sat on the edge of a floral sofa, immaculate in a blue blazer with gold buttons, listening to the World Service on a Roberts short-wave radio.

'My dear boy,' he exclaimed, as a trolley arrived, laden with madeleines and eclairs. My macaroons suddenly looked cheap and greasy.

In spite of his shrivelled frame, Langlands had the kind of tone that would put anyone on their best behaviour. He had a charming way of laying stress on unusual words, which he would boom out unexpectedly, as if addressing a classroom. His eyes sparkled and he had a quivering smile that hung, almost childlike, for minutes at a time. For two hours I listened to stories from his life over tea. I was certainly not the first to pay a visit. Several journalists had sought an article out of this living relic of the Raj and I guessed that some of the Major's stories were well-honed.

Major Geoffrey Langlands's teaching career had begun in a small Croydon prep school in 1936. Having served as a commando in the Dieppe Raid in 1942, he came to British India two years later. He stayed on after independence in 1947 and taught for a quarter of a century at Aitchison College, the 'Eton of Pakistan', where cricketers, statesmen and future generals underwent the rigours of the Major's trigonometry lessons.

Awarded an MBE in 1983 for services to teaching, he prided himself on his incorruptibility.

'No one has ever tried to bribe me to send his son to my school, because they know it won't WORK,' he said.

After repeated threats against foreigners, following the US-led coalition that toppled the Taliban in 2001 all foreign residents were expelled from the North-West Frontier Province, including Langlands.

'Of course, I wasn't going to leave,' he said. 'When they realised I was serious they sent me a 24-hour guard who sat on my veranda. But when I found him asleep on a charpoy it quickly transpired that I was protecting HIM!' He shook with laughter.

Now the Major would rise each day at 5 a.m. with a bowl of oats before a full day's teaching at the Sayurj, which he had founded in 1989. He never bothered to learn Khowar, but spoke passable Urdu, in which he communicated with his aged cook, Mohammad Ali.

Then Langlands explained how he was kidnapped in the Tribal Areas. It was one of his favourite stories.

'When this was reported to the Afghan army officers,' he said, 'they hardly believed it. "But even WE can't go there," they told me.' He gave a snort.

'In 1979 the malik of one of the Waziri tribes wanted to win the elections, so they thought that if they kidnapped me – you see, at the time I was close to many influential political figures – then they might have a chance. Of course, it was absolute ROT.' He cackled with mirth. 'This was near enough no-man's-land, and the landscape wasn't too pretty, I can tell you. So they took me up to their fort and lodged me in their guest's quarters, on a charpoy. Well I protested that this was no way to treat a hostage and I demanded better conditions. So they went off and spoke with one another and decided to take me into the house. That was very interesting. There was a lot of squabbling going on between the malik and his wives, who were making no secret of the fact that this kidnapping was a FRIGHTFULLY bad idea.

'So at 4 a.m. next morning they took me to a hut a little way down the hill, where I discovered two other hostages. They were Afghans who had been silly enough to pass through Waziri territory and had been staying at the malik's pleasure for four and a half MONTHS. They made me promise to take them with me when I was released. For six days I was given mutton, great pieces of meat, all day every day. It was three or four times more than the other two, and I couldn't finish it. Never had so much meat in my life. That got the other two angry. Well, at last the Government got their act together and negotiated my release. With all that publicity the two Afghan hostages came, too, I'm glad to say.

'It was some time later that a meeting was organised with the malik, as he wanted to APOLOGISE. He said, "You must realise we kidnap people all the time, but never have we APOLOGISED. Now a rival tribesman is at your school and he is bound by our code to take vengeance on us. What are you going to do?" So I thought for a while and said to him, "While a father can be held responsible for his son's mistakes, a son cannot for his father's".'

Langlands paused for my reaction, clearly proud of his diplomatic coup.

'After a bit of confabulation they seemed to accept this. And so quite EXCEPTIONALLY . . . the issue was brought to an end.'

I asked him if he'd ever been afraid.

'My dear boy, I thought CONSTANTLY that I would be killed.

But, you see, I didn't mind. I'd led a very good and full life up to that point.'

He was certainly a great raconteur. My tea had turned cold. I asked him if he'd ever considered writing all these experiences down.

'A lot of people ask me that, but the reason I've never done it is because I've never had the LEISURE,' he said. 'You see, I'm always terribly BUSY.'

For a man who had devoted so many years to a country not his own I asked if he would ever consider opting for Pakistani nationality, as Maureen Lines had done.

He answered without a moment's hesitation.

'I was born and I shall die an Englishman.'

'Then have you never considered going home?' I asked.

'First, I can't afford it, and second, they'd never let me be a teacher at my age.' He finished with a chortle and a final sip of tea.

I wandered out into the street, shielding my eyes from the bright sunset. The guards nodded to me from their boxes as I walked slowly out of the prim, swept streets of the late General Habibullah, back to the scrum of the town. It was evening. Rickshaws began to click and zip in the evening bustle, and the bazaars were illuminated by dozens of hanging bulbs. I found a small curry house, where rows of men sat cross-legged with tea and cigarettes. I sat in a far corner on a green upholstered sofa. I brought out my notebook, already thick with the jottings of half-remembered thoughts, other peoples' recollections, notes to self. When the rickshaws on the street and the frying onions and the unfamiliar speech formed a continuum of sound, and I hardly even knew where I was any more, I felt at last a clarity of thought. I surrendered to it, afraid it would leave me, and began to write.

Bibliography

Abazov, Rafis, *Historical Dictionary of Turkmenistan*, London, 2005.

Abbot Hill Art Gallery, *The Turcomans of Iran*, Kendal, 1971.

Abdullaev, Kamoludin, *Historical Dictionary of Tajikistan*, London, 2002.

Adamec, Ludwig, *Historical Dictionary of Afghanistan*, Oxford, 2003.

Akademiia Nauk SSSR, Institut Etnografii, *Trudy Khorezmskoi arkheologovo-etnograficheskoi ekspeditsii,* Moscow, 1952.

Alaudin, *Kalash: The Paradise Lost*, Lahore, 1992.

Allworth, Edward, *The Modern Uzbeks from the Fourteenth Century to the Present: A Cultural History*, Stanford, 1990.

Andreev, Mikhail Stepanovich, *Po Tadzhikistanu: Kratkyi otchet o rabotakh etnograficheskoi ekspeditsii v Tadzhikistane v 1925 godu*, Tashkent, 1927; *Materialy po etnografii Yagnoba, (zapiski 1927-1928 gg)*, Dushanbe, 1970.

Applebaum, Anne, *Gulag: A History of the Soviet Camps*, London, 2003.

Arends, Shirley Fischer, *The Central Dakota Germans: Their History, Language and Culture*, Washington, D.C., 1989.

Azarpay, Guitty, *Sogdian Painting: The Pictorial Epic in Oriental Art*, London, 1981.

Bachmann, Berta, *Memories of Kazakhstan: A Report on the Life Experiences of a German Woman in Russia*, Lincoln, NE, 1983.

Bailey, Frederick Marshman, *Mission to Tashkent*, London, 1946.

Bashir, Elena, Ud-Din, Israr (eds.), *Proceedings of the second international Hindu Kush cultural conference*, Karachi, 1996.

Benyaminov, Meyer, *Bukharian Jews*, New York, 1992.

Bisell, Tom, *Chasing the Sea: being a narrative of a journey through Uzbekistan, including descriptions of life therein, culminating with an arrival at the Aral Sea, the world's worst man made environmental catastrophe, in one volume*, New York, 2003.

Bohr, Annette, *Uzbekistan: Politics and Foreign Policy*, London, 1998.

Bradley, Catherine, *Kazakhstan*, Brookfield, CT, 1992.

Bremmer, Ian and Taras, Ray (eds.), *New States, New Politics: Building the Post-Soviet Nations*, Cambridge, 1997.

Brumfeld, William Craft, *A History of Russian Architecture*, Cambridge, 1993.

Buber, Margarete, *Under Two Dictators*, London, 1950.

Burnes, Alexander, *Travels into Bokhara*, London, 1834.

Byron, Robert, *The Road to Oxiana*, London, 1937.

Capisani, Giampaolo, *The Handbook of Central Asia: A Comprehensive Survey of the New Republics*, London, 2000.

Conseil Régional de Basse-Normandie, *Les Survivants des Sables Rouges: Art Russe du Musée de Noukous, Ouzbékistan, 1920-1940*, Caen, 1998.

Cummings, Sally (ed.), *Power and Change in Central Asia*, London, 2001.

Curzon, George Nathaniel, *Russia in Central Asia in 1889 and the Anglo-Russian Question*, London, 1889.

De Gaury, Gerald and Winstone, H.V.F. (eds.), *The Spirit of the East*, London, 1979.

Deshen, Shlomo and Zemmer, Walter (eds.), *Jews Among Muslims: Communities in the Pre-colonial Middle East*, New York, 1996.

Dupree, Nancy Hatch, *The Road to Balkh*, Kabul, 1967; *The Valley of Bamiyan*, Kabul, 1962, 2002.

Edelberg, Lennart, *Nuristani Buildings*, Aarhus, 1984.

Embree, Ainslie (ed.), *Encyclopedia of Asian History* (4 volumes), New York, 1988.

Ferguson, Robert, *The Devil and the Disappearing Sea: A True Story About the Aral Sea Catastrophe*, Vancouver, 2003.

Ferrier, Joseph Pierre, *Caravan journeys and other wanderings, in Persia, Afghanistan, Turkistan and Beloochistan*, London, 1856.

Foltz, Richard, *Religions of the Silk Road*, Basingstoke, 1999.

Fox, Robin Lane, *Alexander the Great*, London, 1973.

Frye, E.N., *Tajikistan*, 1994.

Gross, Jo-Ann, *Muslims in Central Asia: Expressions of Identity and Change*, Durham, NC, 1992.

Harpviken, Kristian Berg, *Political Mobilisation among the Hazara of Afghanistan, 1978-1992*, Oslo, 1995.

Hodgson, Marshall, *The Venture of Islam: Conscience and History in a World Civilisation*, Chicago, 1974.

Hopkirk, Kathleen, *Central Asia: A Traveller's Companion*, London, 1993.

Hopkirk, Peter, *The Great Game*, London, 1990.

Holt, P.M., Lambton, Ann, Lewis, Bernard, (eds.), *The Cambridge History of Islam*, 1978.

Irons, William George, *The Yomut Turkmen: A Study of Social Organization among a Central Asian Turkic-speaking Population*, Ann Arbor, MI, 1975.

Iskhakov, M.M., Nikitenko, G. N., Dzhumaev, A.B. (eds.), *Evrei v Srednei Azii: voprosy istorii i kul'tury*, Tashkent, 2004.

Jettmar, Karl, *The Religions of the Hindu Kush,* Warminster, 1986.

Kipling, Rudyard, *The Man who would be King*, Allahabad, 1888.

Klimburg-Salter, Deborah, *The Kingdom of Bamiyan: Buddhist Art and Culture in the Hindu Kush*, Naples, 1989.

Knobloch, Edgar, *Monuments of Central Asia*, London, 2001.

Koch, Fred, *The Volga Germans in Russia and the Americas, from 1763 to the present*, London, PA, 1977.

Kondaurov, A.N., *Patriarchal'naia domashniaia obshchina i obshchinnye doma u yagnobtsev*, Moscow, 1940.

Kurilo, Ol'ga Vadimovna, Liuterane v Rossii, XVI–XX vv, Moscow, 1996.

Landau, Jacob, *Politics of Language in the Ex-Soviet Muslim States: Azerbaijan, Uzbekistan, Kazakhstan, Kyrgyzstan, Turkmenistan,*

Tajikistan, London, 2001.
Leslie, Donald, *Jews and Judaism in Traditional China: A Comprehensive Bibliography*, Sankt Augustin, 1998.
Leslie, Donald and Dehergne, Joseph (eds.), *Juifs de Chine: À Travers la Correspondance Inédite des Jésuites du Dix-Huitième Siècle*, Rome, Paris, 1980.
Lines, Maureen, *The Kalasha People of North-Western Pakistan*, Peshawar, 1996.
Lipsky, Vladimir Ippolitovich, *Gornaia Bukhara: Rezul'taty trekhletnikh puteshestvii v Sredniuiu Aziiu*, St. Petersburg, 1902.
Litvinsky, Boris Anatolievich and Ranov, Vadim Aleksandrovich, *Istoriia Tadzhikskovo naroda*, Dushanbe, 1998.
Locher, Lieselotte, *Jewish and German Emigration from the Former Soviet Union in the 1990s*, Berlin, 2002.
Lockhart, Laurence, Avery, Peter, Hambly, Gavin, Melville, Charles, (eds.), *The Cambridge History of Iran*, volumes 1-7, Cambridge, 1968-91.
Loewenthal, Rudolf, *The Jews of Bukhara*, Washington, D.C., 1961.
Loy, Thomas, *Jaghnob 1970: Erinnerungen an eine Zwangsumsiedlung in der Tadschikischen SSR*, Wiesbaden, 2005.
Luknitsky, Pavel Nikolaevich, *A Trip to Tajikistan*, Moscow, 1953.
Maclean, Fitzroy Hew, *Eastern Approaches*, London, 1949.
Maggi, Wynne, *Our Women are Free: gender and ethnicity in the Hindukush*, Anne Arbor, MI, 2001.
Maillart, Ella, *Turkestan Solo*, London, 1934.
Manz, Beatrice (ed.), *Central Asia in Historical Perspective*, Boulder, CO, 1994.
Maraini, Fosco, *Where Four Worlds Meet: Hindu Kush 1959*, London, 1964 (translated from the Italian *Paropàmiso*.)
Masson, Charles, *Legends of the Afghan Countries. In verse. With various pieces, original and translated*, London, 1848.
Mir Munshi, Sultan Mohammad Khan (ed.), *The Life of Abdur Rahman, Amir of Afghanistan*, London, 1900.
Mirzozoda, Saifuddin, *Iaghnoby Zivok*, Dushanbe, 1998.
Mousavi, Sayed Askar, *The Hazaras of Afghanistan: An Historical,*

Cultural, Economic and Political Study, London, 1998.
Nurgaliev, R.N., *Karagandinskaia oblast': entsiklopediia*, Alma-Ata, 1986.
Nurmukhamedov, M. K. (ed), *Razvitie zhanra poemy v karakalpakskoi sovetskoi literature*, Tashkent, 1976.
Olcott, Martha Brill, *The Kazakhs*, Stanford, 1995; *Kazakhstan: Unfulfilled Promise*, Washington, D.C., 2002.
Olufsen, Axel Frits Henrik, *Old and New Architecture in Khiva, Bokhara and Turkestan*, in *The Second Danish Pamir-Expedition*, Copenhagen, 1904.
Palin, Michael, *Himalaya*, London, 2004.
Palmer, Hurly Pring, *Joseph Wolff: His Romantic Life and Travels*, London, 1935.
Pao, Basil, *Inside Himalaya*, London, 2004.
Peshchereva, Elena Mikhailovna, *Iagnobskie etnograficheskie materialy*, Dushanbe, 1976.
Petrosova, Elizaveta Artemovna, *Karakalpakskii tanets: metodicheskoe posobie*, Tashkent, 1976.
Pohl, J. Otto, *Ethnic Cleansing in the USSR, 1937 – 1949*, London, 1949.
Poliakov, Sergei Petrovich, *Everyday Islam: Religion and Tradition in Rural Central Asia*, Armonk, NY, 1992.
Polo, Marco, *The Most Noble and Famous Travels of Marco Polo, together with the travels of Nicolò de'Conti*, London, 1937 (ed. N.M. Penzer).
Pope, Arthur Upham, *Persian Architecture*, London, 1965.
Pugachenkova, Gallina Anatolievna, *Iskusstvo Turkmenistana: Ocherk s drevneishikh vremen do 1917 goda*, Moscow, 1967.
Rashid, Ahmed, *The Resurgence of Central Asia: Islam or Nationalism?*, London, 1994; *Taliban*, London, 2002.
Reichl, Karl, *Turkic Oral Epic Poetry: Traditions, Forms, Poetic Structure*, London, 1992.
Reznichenko, Grigori, *The Aral Sea Tragedy*, Moscow, 1992.
Robertson, George Scott, *The Kafirs of the Hindu Kush*, London, 1896; *Chitral: The Story of a Minor Siege*, London, 1898.
Roden, Claudia, *The Book of Jewish Food: An Odyssey from Samarkand and Vilna to the present day*, London, 1997.

Ro'i, Yaacov, *Islam in the Soviet Union: from the Second World War to Gorbachev*, London, 2000.
Rowland, Benjamin, *The Art of Central Asia*, New York, 1974.
Ruthven, Malise, *Islam in the World*, London, 2000.
Schomberg, Reginald Charles Francis, *Kafirs and Glaciers: Travels in Chitral*, London, 1938.
Sheehy, Ann, *The Crimean Tatars, Volga Germans and Meskhetians: Soviet treatment of some national minorities*, London, 1980.
Shterenshis, Michael, *Tamerlane and the Jews*, London, 2002.
Sidky, H., *The Rise and Fall of the Graeco-Bactrian Kingdom*, Jaipur, 1999.
Smirnitskaya, S.V. and Barotov M.A., *Nemetskie govory severnovo Tadzhikistana*, St Petersburg, 1997.
Sokolovna, Valentina Stepanovna, *Ocherki po fonetike iranskikh iazykov*, Moscow, 1953.
Speake, Jennifer (ed.), *Literature of Travel and Exploration: An Encyclopaedia*, London, 2003.
Swinson, Arthur, *North-West Frontier: People and Events, 1839–1947*, London, 1967.
Talbot Rice, David, *Islamic Art*, London, 1965.
Talbot Rice, Tamara, *Ancient Arts of Central Asia*, London, 1965.
Thrower, James, *The Religious History of Central Asia from the Earliest Times to the Present Day*, New York, 2004.
Thubron, Colin, *The Lost Heart of Asia*, London, 1994.
Újfalvy [de Mezö-Kövesd], Charles de, *Les Aryens au nord at au sud de l'Hindou-Kouch*, Paris, 1896.
Vambery, Arminius (also Vámbéry, Ármin), *Travels in Central Asia*, London, 1864; *Scenes from the East: Through the Eyes of a European Traveller in the 1860s*, London, 1876.
Vitkovich, Viktor, *A Tour of Soviet Uzbekistan*, Moscow, 1944.
Von Meyendorff, Georg, *A Journey from Orenburg to Bokhara in the year 1820, translated by Capt. E.F. Chapman*, Calcutta, 1870.
Waley, Arthur David, *The Real Tripitaka, and other pieces*, London, 1952.
Whitfield, Susan, *Life along the Silk Road*, London, 1999; *The Silk Road: Trade, Travel, War and Faith*, London, 2004.

Williams, Hattie Plum, *A Social Study of the Russian German*, Lincoln, NE, 1916.

Wolff, Joseph, *Researches and Missionary Labours among the Jews, Mohammedans and other Sects*, London, 1835; *Narrative of a Mission to Bokhara, in the years 1843–1845, to ascertain the Fate of Colonel Stoddart and Captain Conolly*, London, 1845.

Wood, John, *A Personal Narrative of a Journey to the Source of the River Oxus, by the Route of the Indus, Kabul and Badakhshan, performed in the years 1836, 1837, and 1838*, London, 1841.

Wynn, Anthony, *Persia in the Great Game*, London, 2003.

Yakovenko, Y.I. (ed.), *Istoriia i kul'tura nemtsev Kazakhstana v regional'nom aspekte*, Pavlodar, 2004.

Yalcin, Resul, *The Rebirth of Uzbekistan: Politics, Economy and Society in the Post-Soviet Era*, Reading, 2002.

Zhdanko, T.A. (ed.), *Materialy i issledovaniia po etnografii Karakalpakov*, Moscow, 1958.

Articles and Essays

Bashiri, Iraj, *The Yaghnobis*, 1997 (electronic only).

Bosworth, A.B., 'Alexander and the Iranians', *Journal of Hellenic Studies*, 100, 1980.

Bushkov, Valentin, 'Population migrations in Tajikistan past and present', *Population movement in the modern world*, 3, 2000.

Ferdinand, Klaus, 'Preliminary notes on Hazara culture. Danish scientific mission to Afghanistan 1953–5', *Det kongelige Danske videnskabernes selskab. historisk-filosofisk meddelelser*, 5, 1959.

Fierman, William, 'Glasnost' in practice', *Central Asian Survey*, 2, 1989.

Gawęcki, Marek, 'The Hazara farmers of central Afghanistan: some historical and contemporary problems', *Ethnologia Polona*, 6, 1980.

Hisao, Komatsu, Chika, Obiya, Schoeberlerin, John, 'Migration in Central Asia: its history and current problems', *Population movement in the modern world*, 3, 2000.

Jettmar, Karl (ed.), *Cultures of the Hindu Kush: selected papers from the Hindu-Kush Cultural Conference held at Moesgård 1970*, Wiesbaden, 1974.

Klimburg, Max, 'The arts and societies of the Kafirs of the Hindu Kush', *Asian Affairs*, 3, 2004.

Leach, Hugh, 'From Bavaria to Bokhara to Isle Brewers: the

extra-ordinary life and times of Dr the Revd Joseph Wolff', *Asian Affairs*, 3, 2007.

Lipovsky, Igor, 'The Central Asian cotton epic', *Central Asian Survey*, 4, 1995; 'The deterioration of the ecological situation in Central Asia: causes and consequences', *Europe Asia Studies*, 7, 1995.

Loude, Jean-Yves, 'The Kalasha shamans' practices of exorcism' in Bashir, Elena, Ud-Din, Israr (eds.), *Proceedings of the second international Hindu Kush cultural conference*, Karachi, 1996.

Parkes, Peter, 'Enclaved knowledge: indigent and indignant representations of environmental management and development among the Kalasha of Pakistan' in Bicker, Alan, Ellen, Roy, Parkes, Peter (eds.), *Indigenous environmental knowledge and its transformations*, Amsterdam, 2000.

Pohl, J. Otto, 'The deportation and destruction of the German minority in the USSR', a paper presented at Columbia University, 2001.

Rumer, Boris, 'Central Asia's cotton economy and its costs', in Fierman, William (ed.), *Soviet Central Asia: The Failed Transformation*, Boulder, CO, 1991.

Thesiger, Wilfred, 'The Hazaras of central Afghanistan', *The Geographic Journal*, 3, 1955.

Zand, Michael, 'Bukhara VII: Bukharan Jews', in *Encyclopaedia Iranica*, Volume 4, London, New York, 1990.

Index